PROPERTY OF
MICHAEL D. MOBERLY

UNDERSTANDING HERBERT HOOVER

Understanding Herbert Hoover: Ten Perspectives

Edited with an Introduction by
LEE NASH

Hoover Institution Press
Stanford University, Stanford, California

The Hoover Institution on War, Revolution and Peace, founded at Stanford University in 1919 by the late President Herbert Hoover, is an interdisciplinary research center for advanced study on domestic and international affairs in the twentieth century. The views expressed in its publications are entirely those of the authors and do not necessarily reflect the views of the staff, officers, or Board of Overseers of the Hoover Institution.

Hoover Press Publication   354

Copyright 1987 by the Board of Trustees of the
 Leland Stanford Junior University

All rights reserved. No part of this publication may be reproduced, stored in a retrieval system, or transmitted in any form or by any means, electronic, mechanical, photocopying, recording, or otherwise, without written permission of the publisher.

First printing, 1987

Manufactured in the United States of America

91 90 89 88 87   9 8 7 6 5 4 3 2 1

Library of Congress Cataloging in Publication Data
Understanding Herbert Hoover.

  (Hoover Press publication ; 354)
  Includes index.
  1. Hoover, Herbert, 1874–1964. 2. Presidents—United States—Biography. I. Nash, Lee.
E802.U53   1987   973.91′6′0924 [B]   87-21379
ISBN 0-8179-8541-7

Design by Elizabeth F. Gehman

Contents

Contributors	vii
Introduction	xi
1 Herbert Hoover: The Popular Image of an Unpopular President — *Joan Hoff-Wilson*	1
2 The Social Philosophy of Herbert Hoover *George H. Nash*	25
3 Herbert Hoover and the Conservation of Human and Natural Resources — *Mark O. Hatfield*	43
4 The Quaker Faith of Herbert Hoover *David Burner*	53
5 Neo-Institutional History and the Understanding of Herbert Hoover — *Ellis W. Hawley*	65
6 Herbert Hoover and the Two Great Food Crusades of the 1940s — *Susan Estabrook Kennedy*	85
7 Herbert Hoover and the Great Debates over Foreign Policy, 1940–1941 and 1950–1951 — *Gary Dean Best*	107
8 Hoover and FDR: Reminiscent Reflections *Frank Freidel*	125
9 Hiram Johnson Looks at Herbert Hoover *Robert E. Burke*	141
10 Herbert Hoover's Indian Reformers Under Attack: The Failures of Administrative Reform *William G. Robbins*	165
Index	191

Contributors

Gary Dean Best: Professor of History, University of Hawaii, Hilo. Has taught at Sophi University, Japan. Ph.D., University of Hawaii; Fulbright Scholar. Author of *The Politics of American Individualism* (Westport, Conn., 1975) and *Herbert Hoover: The Postpresidential Years, 1933–1964,* 2 volumes (Stanford, Calif., 1983).

Robert E. Burke: Professor of History, University of Washington. Has taught at the University of Hawaii. Ph.D., University of California, Berkeley. Author of *Olson's New Deal for California* (Berkeley, 1953); editor of *The Diary Letters of Hiram Johnson,* 7 volumes (New York, 1984).

David Burner: Professor of History, State University of New York, Stony Brook. Has taught at Oakland University, Colby College, Hunter College, and College of the City of New York. Ph.D., Columbia University; Guggenheim Fellow, Carnegie Teaching Fellow. Author of *The Politics of Provincialism: The Democratic Party in Transition, 1918–1932* (New York, 1968) and *Herbert Hoover: A Public Life* (New York, 1978).

Frank Freidel: Bullitt Professor of History, Emeritus, University of Washington; Charles Warren Professor of American History, Harvard University. Has taught at Shurtleff College, the University of Maryland, Pennsylvania State College, Vassar College, University of Illinois, Stanford University, and Harvard University. Ph.D., University of Wisconsin; Guggenheim Fellow. Author of *Franklin D. Roosevelt,* 4 volumes thus far (Boston, 1952, 1954, 1956, 1973) and *Over There* (Boston,

1964); Co-editor, *Harvard Guide to American History* (Cambridge, Mass., 1974).

Mark O. Hatfield: U.S. Senator from Oregon since 1966. Formerly Oregon Governor, Secretary of State, State Senator, and State Representative. Taught and served as Dean of Men at Willamette University. M.A., Stanford University, thesis title "Herbert Hoover and Labor: 1899–1929." Author of *Not Quite so Simple* (New York, 1968); *Conflict and Conscience* (Waco, Tex., 1971); and *Between a Rock and a Hard Place* (Waco, Tex., 1976).

Ellis W. Hawley: Professor of History, University of Iowa. Has taught at North Texas State University and Ohio State University. Ph.D., University of Wisconsin. Author of *The New Deal and the Problem of Monopoly* (Princeton, N.J., 1966) and *The Great War and the Search for a Modern Order: A History of the American People and Their Institutions, 1917–1933* (New York, 1979); editor of *Herbert Hoover as Secretary of Commerce: Studies in New Era Thought and Practice* (Iowa City, 1981).

Joan Hoff-Wilson: Professor of History, Indiana University; Executive Secretary, Organization of American Historians. Has taught at California State University, Sacramento; and Arizona State University. Ph.D., University of California, Berkeley; Guggenheim Fellow. Author of *American Business and Foreign Policy, 1920–1933* (Lexington, Ky., 1971); *Ideology and Economics: United States Relations with the Soviet Union, 1918–1933* (Columbia, Mo., 1974); and *Herbert Clark Hoover: Forgotten Progressive* (Boston, 1975).

Susan Estabrook Kennedy: Professor of History, Virginia Commonwealth University. Has taught at Hunter College and Temple University. Ph.D., Columbia University; Guggenheim Fellow. Author of *The Banking Crisis of 1933* (Lexington, Ky., 1973) and *If All We Did Was to Weep at Home: A History of White Working-Class Women in America* (Bloomington, Ind., 1979).

George H. Nash: Research Fellow, Hoover Presidential Library. Ph.D., Harvard University. Author of *The Conservative Intellectual*

Movement in America Since 1945 (New York, 1976) and *The Life of Herbert Hoover: The Engineer, 1874–1914* (New York, 1983).

William G. Robbins: Associate Professor of History, Oregon State University. Has taught at Oregon College of Education. Ph.D., University of Oregon. Author of *Lumberjacks and Legislators: The Political Economy of the Lumber Industry, 1890–1941* (College Station, Tex., 1982).

Introduction

This book emerges from the biennial Herbert Hoover symposia begun at George Fox College in Newberg, Oregon in 1977. That October a group of Hoover scholars helped the College dedicate the Herbert Hoover Academic Building, and every two years since then another group has come to share their research.

In 1885 eleven-year-old Bert Hoover, orphaned in Iowa the year before, moved to Newberg to live with his uncle and aunt, Dr. Henry John and Laura Ellen Minthorn. Dr. Minthorn had recently opened Pacific Academy, and Bert enrolled on arrival. He studied under dedicated Quaker mentors and helped pay his way by tending furnace, sweeping floors, and cleaning blackboards. "As a young student there for three years," President Hoover said in later life, "I received whatever set I may have had toward good purposes in life."

The success of the academy encouraged sponsors to found Pacific College in 1891; the academy closed some time later, and the successor school was renamed George Fox College in 1949. Nevertheless, that early connection with a person who became one of this century's world leaders seemed adequate justification for establishing a recurring scholarly conference on the site.

Half of the essays herein are handy distillations of central interpretations of Hoover's career by major scholars. The others are significant topical soundings that also contribute to an understanding of Hoover's major interests and commitments.

The 1977 meeting featured a differing duo of these general interpretations. Joan Hoff-Wilson harvested favorite insights into the image and essence of Herbert Hoover from research behind her distinguished book in the Little, Brown and Company's Library of American Biography series, and George Nash shared an interpretive essay on Hoover's overall "social philosophy," which was written toward the beginning of his work on a multivolume biography. Also present in 1977, to give the keynote address for the day, was U.S. senator Mark Hatfield, George Fox College trustee who wrote his Stanford M.A. thesis on Hoover. The Hatfield talk blended Hoover's concerns for people and for nature into a multifaceted "conservation" theme.

The second Hoover symposium, in April 1980, again brought two scholars to the campus who approach the thirty-first president's career from contrasting standpoints. From humanistic, psychological perspectives David Burner analyzed the contributions of Hoover's Quaker background to his values, style, and career. From the platform of neo-institutional history and selected sociological outlooks, Ellis Hawley revealed the shape and significance of Hoover's creative new vision for America and its institutions. Following their presentations, Burner and Hawley entered a stimulating public dialogue—nearly a debate—on their divergent viewpoints, and William Robbins critiqued the two papers at the lunch hour talk. For this collection Robbins submitted an essay on Hoover's American Indian policy that incorporates the alternative assumptions from which he approaches the subject.

At Hoover Symposium III, held in February 1982, two scholars who have done extensive research on Hoover's postpresidential years presented complementary papers. Susan Estabrook Kennedy related the poignant and finally triumphant story of Hoover's efforts during and after World War II to repeat his famine-relief services of the first world war. Gary Dean Best insightfully discussed Hoover's contributions to the two decisive public debates—in the summer and fall of 1941 and the fall of 1950—on the extent to which America should become involved in international peacekeeping. With the illness of scheduled luncheon speaker Robert Burke, his University of Washington colleague Frank Freidel consented to speak informally at lunch on the relationship between the subject of his multivolume biography, Franklin Delano Roosevelt, and Herbert Hoover. An admirer of both men, Freidel pointed out the tragic losses to a nation that can result from a bitter political falling-out. His informal remarks drew much upon his own personal contacts with Hoover and with the Roosevelt family, and the audience was fascinated. Professor Freidel has generously consented for his remarks to be published very much as delivered. Robert Burke's intended address, an engrossing selection of Hoover-related references from the acerbic, intelligent, judgmental personal correspondence of California senator Hiram Johnson, is also included here.

I offer grateful acknowledgement to David Packard and to U.S. senator Mark Hatfield, who together made our Hoover symposia, and thus these essays, possible.

Lee Nash
George Fox College

UNDERSTANDING HERBERT HOOVER

1

Herbert Hoover:
The Popular Image of an Unpopular President

Joan Hoff-Wilson

The centennial of Herbert Clark Hoover's birth took place in 1974 with the usual number of commemorative and academic events. They occurred exactly ten years after his death in 1964 at the age of 90. The largest of these gatherings was planned on his birthday, August 10, at his birthplace in West Branch, Iowa. However, it was overshadowed in press accounts and in the public mind by the resignation of President Nixon on the previous day. Organizers of this major Hoover centennial celebration included the Hoover Presidential Library, the National Endowment for the Arts, the National Park Service, and the National Archives and Records Service. The president himself had been scheduled to appear as the honored guest of the occasion. Needless to say, Nixon was a "no show," and Secretary of the Interior Rogers C. B. Morton gave the main address instead.[1]

Thus, history once again robbed Hoover of the chance to be honored without qualification and without untoward and unprecedented events intervening—such as the worst depression of the country's history or the first resignation of a president of the United States. Certainly since the crash of 1929 the most commonly held image of him has been at best that of a chubby Calvin Coolidge,[2] and at worst that of an uncaring, political reactionary in the time of economic crisis. Both images are inaccurate, as so many popular (or in this case, unpopular) images are. Moreover, they are in direct contradiction to the considerable popularity that he enjoyed as a national figure between 1914 and 1929.

The contrast between Hoover's prepresidential popularity and his extreme unpopularity as president remained a unique and distinct feature of his political career until a rash of presidents, beginning with Lyndon Johnson, suffered similarly extreme shifts in public ratings.

Joan Hoff-Wilson's paper was previously published in slightly altered form under the title "Herbert Hoover Reassessed," in [Arthur S. Link, ed.], *Herbert Hoover Reassessed: Essays Commemorating the Fiftieth Anniversary of the Inauguration of Our Thirty-First President* (Washington, D.C., 1981), pp. 103–19.

Since the late 1960s, Johnson, Richard Nixon, Gerald Ford, Jimmy Carter, and even Ronald Reagan at the end of 1986 all experienced what Hoover had known because of the impact of the Great Depression on his reputation. Thus, the most recent residents in the White House have learned, like Hoover did, that the magnitude of certain events—such as the Depression of 1929, the Vietnam War, Watergate, Nixon's pardon, and hostage questions—can quickly nullify previous popularity and hamper even the most articulate president's ability to effectively communicate. Hence, the meaning of the title of this essay, "The Popular Image of an Unpopular President," can now be applied to others, although Hoover alone bore its stigma for 34 years until he died in 1964.

In all honesty it must be admitted that, even before the Great Depression, Hoover's supporters had expressed some reservations about his popular public image. The most common one was summed up in the title of a magazine article in 1928 that pointedly asked: "Is Hoover Human?" This question apparently occurred to many Americans in the course of his long public career, which began in 1914 and continued unabated until the last year of his life in 1964. Despite all the efforts of his loyal friends and sympathizers to convey an image of Hoover as a selfless humanitarian in time of war, peace, and depression, the picture has remained unconvincing and one-dimensional, with little life or human warmth.

A large part of this "public amnesia" with respect to both the personality and public achievements of the thirty-first president of the United States is obviously due to the negative impression he created during the depression years and to the ignominy Democrats continued to heap on him after he left office in 1933. However, the "inhuman" or cold-blooded Hoover had been common in the public mind even before economic disaster struck his administration in 1929 and before Democratic hatchet men like Charles Michelson began to work his image over with modern, mass media smear tactics.[3] In time, of course, even those who had suffered most from the depression gradually began to suspect that Hoover's partisan enemies protested too vehemently and too long against an aging, but nonetheless devoted, public servant. Yet his lifeless image persisted.

I do not believe that Hoover's cold, impersonal image in the minds of most people today, and at the height of his public career, can be blamed exclusively on the writings of such liberal, democratic historians as Arthur Schlesinger, Jr., who wanted to enhance the reputation of FDR and the New Deal at the expense of Hoover and of most politicians and conditions of the 1920s. On the contrary, his negative image stems in large measure from the fact that his various publicity staffs inadvertently oversold him between 1914 and 1928 while they promoted the important projects with which he was associated during those years.

First they oversold him as an incomparable engineer or "human symbol of efficiency," then as the unemotional savior of starving Europeans, later in the 1920s as the "super businessman" and great salesman, and finally as an "omniscient economist." All of these "sell jobs" evolved into the superman image of "some great impersonal force" capable of solving any and all problems the country might encounter under his presidential leadership. During the 1928 campaign the publicity staff realized the necessity of planting articles in newspapers and magazines about his personableness. He is "charming to intimates and children, and demonstrates a shyness appealing to women," proclaimed one headline.[4] These attempts to reveal the "real" human or natural Hoover became all the more frantic and unconvincingly evident after the Great Depression began. But what had not caught the public imagination during years of prosperity had little chance of succeeding in time of economic crisis and anxiety.

Part of this failure in public relations can be attributed to the jealous way Hoover and his wife, Lou Henry, guarded their private lives from public view after their marriage in 1899. Even the opening in 1985 of 550 boxes of Lou Henry Hoover's papers shed little additional light on the personal side of his life. The most intimate piece of primary material by Hoover (as opposed to secondhand statements about him) concerning his private life before 1914 remains a "love letter" he wrote to a young Quaker girl named Daisy Trueblood at the age of thirteen or fourteen. He and his brother, Theodore, were apparently competing for her affections in 1887 and 1888. It read:

> Friend Daisy,
> (and I hope you are more than my friend, although I do not dare to head it [the letter] that way yet.) You do not know the extent to which I am enthralled, and I am sure that no girl should be allowed such mastery over any person's heart, unless there are such feelings in her own heart. I could not have helped paying my attentions to you, if I had

tried and I am sure I did not try very hard. I do not think you care. Do you?
Answer this please,

Bert[5]

In contrast to this very private glimpse of Hoover as a "love-sick" youth, his official papers reveal voluminous facts and figures from 1914 about Herbert Hoover, the public man. He appears from these documentary sources to be the almost perfect example of the ideal statesman, a figure of "matchless integrity" and boundless energy devoted to the selfless service of his country. Such a commendable image carried with it an enormous liability, as Hoover came to realize only too well. "It is impossible for people to believe someone would try to save the country," he wearily told a close friend in 1939, "without being motivated by politics or vindictiveness."[6]

Another factor contributing to this failure in public relations was Hoover's own personality. Here, apparently, was the perfect public man whose official image masked an inordinately shy, self-effacing private individual who was a lamentably poor speaker and who harbored strong asocial and apolitical feelings. I do not mean to imply that Hoover was an unsuccessful politician before 1929 because he was apolitical. I am using this term because he refused to practice or endorse traditional electoral or power politics and insisted on a noncoercive role for government whenever possible. But his disdain for traditional, particularly congressional politics was more than balanced by his successful application of nontraditional, administrative policies and tactics. Unlike his apolitical approach, however, his asocial nature was a distinct liability for which Hoover developed no compensating tactics.[7]

His public image, for which there is an abundance of factual evidence, remains, therefore, flat and uncomfortably unbelievable—an internationally known statesman and humanitarian frozen into a cold exterior by his own personality. As one contemporary biographer summed it up: "Herbert Hoover can do things more intensely personal with a more helpless and hopeless impersonality than almost anybody else."[8] How could there be a successful American politician who refused to backslap, fraternize with local supporters, kiss babies, or engage in any of the expected social and political amenities of the Roaring Twenties? "Truly amazing," exclaimed his supporters; "truly suspicious," grumbled his opponents. In fact there is something both appealing and pathetic in the image of President Hoover struggling painfully through endless state dinners scarcely talking to anyone while press releases about him reported that his favorite song was "Hail! Hail! The Gang's All Here!"

Thus, his oversold public image and lack of charisma, combined with the secrecy surrounding his family life and his own retiring, asocial nature, have led most of his biographers—both hostile and friendly—to conclude that Hoover's career represented a paradox, an enigma, something disturbingly enticing and undecipherable. New research, which began with the opening of the Herbert Hoover Presidential Library in 1966, is finally breaking down this myth about the unfathomable, mystifying Hoover. His public career is being studied in a depth that was never possible before, and psychohistorical methods are shedding more light on his reticent personality. Although his private existence continues to elude historians, Hoover's known personality traits can now be related to his public career, rather than made to appear in contradiction to it. Furthermore, his contributions to U.S. domestic and foreign policies are currently undergoing such drastic reevaluation by revisionist historians that he is emerging as a major twentieth-century figure. This positive reconsideration comes as a surprise, no doubt, to his friends, relatives, and hagiologists, who cherish the ideal memory of a man who could do no wrong. It must also come as a surprise to those few unforgiving enemies who managed to outlive him.

Few enemies, or friends for that matter, did outlive the 90-year-old Hoover. It is fitting that the life of this man whose first public image was that of the "Great Engineer" spanned every major technological innovation from the invention of the electric light bulb to travel in outer space. Perhaps it would be useful to point out some of the little-known "firsts" about his long and varied life experiences. For example, he was in the first class to graduate from Stanford University; the highest paid and richest engineer of his time; the first man to personally direct relief efforts on an international scale; the first to make the secretary of commerce a major cabinet position; the first Washington official to systematically employ public-relations techniques and national conferences on a massive administrative scale; the first image transmitted on closed circuit television in 1927; the first Quaker president;[9] the first president born west of the Mississippi; the first president whose inaugural was carried by three media—radio, talking motion pictures, and shortwave;

the first president to install a telephone and intercom system in the White House; and finally, the first president to use federal power in the time of depression.

His "lasts" are not usually recorded, but at least some of them should be. Hoover is, to date, the last of the Horatio Alger presidents of the United States (the private careers of Truman, Nixon, Ford, Carter, and Reagan were not as meteoric nor as financially rewarding as Hoover's before they turned to politics). Hoover's rags-to-riches life began when he left Stanford University in May 1895 with a little less than $50 in his pocket and an A.B. in geology. At that time the country was in the midst of a severe national depression, but by 1914 he was a millionaire engineer at the age of 40.[10]

With the possible exception of Carter, in many ways Hoover can also be considered the last Progressive president, combining many of the best ideas of both Theodore Roosevelt and Woodrow Wilson. But unlike them he made the mistake of becoming a depression president and so is seldom thought of as a reformer. Thus far he remains the last president to be in office during a major depression; whether this dubious historical honor will last remains to be seen.

Although it is beyond the scope of this paper, I am also convinced on the basis of my own research and that of other revisionist historians that Hoover was the first and possibly the last president in this century to bring to the White House "a comprehensive scientific, organizational approach for dealing with the political economy of the United States" and an equally "comprehensive, noncoercive approach to foreign policy."[11] Although his domestic and foreign policies have been seriously re-evaluated by a wide array of historians since the 1950s, it will take the rest of this century for his enhanced reputation to be integrated into textbooks for appreciation at any mass level because it has not yet penetrated very deeply into the ranks of establishment historians.

Before the 1960s, when largely left-of-center revisionist historians led by William Appleman Williams and a few members of the radical right tried to cast him in a more positive light, Hoover had been accorded more vindictive and vicious treatment than all presidents except those who have traditionally been deemed absolute failures by historians: namely, John Tyler, Zachary Taylor, Millard Fillmore, Franklin Pierce, James Buchanan, Andrew Johnson, Ulysses S. Grant, Warren G. Harding, and Calvin Coolidge. Until 1982, when historians added the Nixon and Carter administrations to this list of failures, all the "failed" presidencies could be found clustered between 1840 and 1870 (the notable exception being Lincoln) and in the 1920s between World War I and the Great Depression.

Since Hoover has never been categorized as a failure by historians (instead he has been accorded average status), one wonders why concerted efforts by revisionist historians for the past twenty years to rehabilitate his economic and foreign policy views have not succeeded. Polls of U.S. specialists, for example, indicate that Hoover's success rating as president has remained essentially the same over the last 40 years. He was ranked twentieth in 1948, nineteenth in 1962, eighteenth in 1968, and twenty-first in 1981–1982. Nonetheless, this last poll indicated a growing recognition of certain similarities between the much more popular Woodrow Wilson and Hoover, largely in terms of their "inflexible idealism" even though their political ideologies were considered to be quite different. Indeed, much of the revisionist work on Hoover since 1970 has documented many similarities in the political ideologies of these two presidents and other positive facts about Hoover's presidential record, about which historians polled earlier knew little, if anything. The 1981–1982 poll also shows that Hoover, Andrew Jackson, Lyndon Johnson, and Richard Nixon are ranked as the four most controversial presidents in U.S. history. The authors conclude that "any future survey [of] the relative positions of Nixon, Lyndon Johnson, Hoover, and Jackson are more likely to change than those of [any] other presidents."[12]

Consequently, there is still a good deal of talk today in academic circles about a "new" Hoover, largely because the "old" one has been so misinterpreted or ignored; this was partly because of the long delay following his presidency and the official opening of his papers. Moreover, "disparate political groups ranging from the far right to the far left think they are rediscovering him." The simple fact is that his progressive philosophy contained ideas whose time has finally arrived. Americans had to experience the Great Depression, the New Deal, the Cold War, the Vietnam War, Watergate, and the Iran/*contra* controversy before they could begin to contemplate a value change in domestic and foreign policies along the cooperative, decentralized anti-interventionist lines Hoover suggested in the 1920s.[13]

Rather than belabor this particular point, I want to review briefly the major positive and negative images Hoover projected from 1914 to 1964. Some of them, such as that of the Great Engineer and the Great

Humanitarian, are obviously derived from his professional and public activities before and during World War I. In particular, his relief work first in Belgium and then in Europe and Russia, along with his position as food administrator in the Wilson administration, made him the best-known postwar public figure in the United States next to President Wilson himself. As a result, he was sought after as a presidential candidate by progressive reformers in both political parties in 1920.[14]

The images his publicity staff cultivated of him in the course of the 1920s were largely combinations of the original reputations he had earned as an engineer and humanitarian. Thus, for the first half of the decade as secretary of commerce, Hoover appeared at the lowest common denominator of public opinion to personify the efficient engineer turned super-businessman or great salesman. At the same time, more discerning public opinion groups, such as economists and engineers, recognized him as an advocate of some of the most advanced ideas on scientific social planning and of economic theories for controlling business cycles.[15] His humanitarian reputation was also considerably enhanced during the 1927 Mississippi flood, when he completely overshadowed President Coolidge as director of flood-relief measures. His relief recommendations included an unsuccessful attempt to break up large southern plantations by subdividing them into family-sized farms that could be bought on reasonable credit terms by tenant farmers and sharecroppers.[16]

Hoover's increasing popularity in the 1920s did not rest on his work in the Mississippi valley alone. In retrospect, however, given the cold, impersonal exterior that Hoover projected in all of his activities, it is somewhat difficult to believe he was as popular as the mass media reported. This is especially true when Hoover is placed next to notables of the jazz age such as Paul Whiteman, Louis Armstrong, Charles Lindbergh, Amelia Earhart, F. Scott Fitzgerald, Ernest Hemingway, Mary Pickford, Rudolf Valentino, Gloria Swanson, Clara Bow, Douglas Fairbanks, Mae West, Aimee Semple McPherson, Paul Robeson, Will Rogers, Rudy Vallee, Charlie Chaplin, Al Capone, and Izzy and Moe—(the two best-known prohibition agents). That Hoover should capture the political limelight in such a bizarre and colorful period seems unusual. In fact, however, the new era was a curiously lackluster political decade, and by any criteria Hoover was obviously the most active, the most vocal, and hence, perhaps by default, the most popular political leader. Americans were, after all, weary of the crusading, charismatic leaders that the war had produced at home and abroad. With Herbert Hoover they had an apolitical man who represented the best of the 1920s—a blend of the modern and the traditional.

Even so, Hoover was personally uneasy about his own peculiar brand of popularity by the time he became a presidential candidate in 1928. For example, after delivering his nomination acceptance address on August 11, 1928, he turned to a friend near him and said: "I wonder if this speech will help me to live down my reputation as an engineer." He was apparently apprehensive that this positive public image had been exaggerated out of all proportion by the time the presidential campaign officially began. Later, as president-elect, he was more explicitly pessimistic about his greatly inflated reputation. "My friends have made the American people think me as sort of superman, able to cope successfully with the most difficult and complicated problems," he confided to Willis J. Abbot, editor of the *Christian Science Monitor.* "They expect the impossible of me and should there arise in the land conditions with which the political machinery is unable to cope, I will be the one to suffer." It was as though Hoover's administrative machinery for publicizing his activities had acquired an independent existence over the years that was beyond his control by 1928. He feared a negative reaction, a backlash of resentment against him even before the depression occurred. In 1932, during the worst economic crisis the country had ever experienced, he was all the more convinced that he had "been absurdly oversold." As he told Senator George Moses of New Hampshire, "No man can live up to it."[17]

In retrospect, Hoover's concern about his inflated image as a superhuman engineer, economist, businessman, and humanitarian who could solve all problems was certainly warranted. He had spent a good portion of his adult life trying to convince the general public, the business community, and individual engineers that they all should be socially responsible.[18] Ultimately, however, he did not successfully convey his most complex ideas about reorganizing the U.S. economy along the lines of "cooperative individualism" any more than he did his foreign policy views about "independent internationalism."[19]

This meant that on the eve of the Great Depression he had not succeeded in effecting any basic value change among Americans in general, corporation leaders, or most engineers. In view of this failure, Hoover's most remembered and most negative public image—that of the Great Depression president—was as inevitable as it was accidental.

With characteristic stubbornness he did not quietly accept this single horrendous portrayal of himself as the man who was both responsible for and did nothing about the worst depression in the nation's history. If anything Hoover compounded the situation by becoming one of the most vociferous (and in my opinion one of the most prophetic) critics of the New Deal and of U.S. foreign policy both before and after World War II.[20] It is true that after FDR's death in 1945 Hoover's reputation improved slightly, because both Truman and Eisenhower sought his advice and employed him as an efficiency expert to improve the organization of the executive branch of government. In addition, reports can still be heard from time to time about the work of so-called Little Hoover commissions at state level, and, for brief periods before and after World War II, he re-emerged in his humanitarian role as director of European relief projects.[21]

By and large, however, Hoover's public image remained more negative than positive to the end of his long life because of his consistent opposition to both the New Deal and bipartisan Cold War tactics. Portrayed for years by historians as a laissez-faire conservative and isolationist, it is ironic that Hoover is now emerging as the darling of the New Left (or the New Right, depending on your point of view). Since this image of Hoover is currently the least understood or accepted among the general public and the academic community, I would like to elaborate upon it.

First, his criticism of the New Deal never waned after 1933, much to the chagrin of most members of his own party who, by the election of President Eisenhower, had accepted most of FDR's antidepression measures. Thus, Hoover's unwavering stand against the New Deal placed him not only outside the mainstream of American politics for the remainder of his life, but also outside the majority within his own party; he became a member of what has come to be called the Old Right.[22] Yet like his criticism of U.S. foreign policy before and after World War II, his attacks on the New Deal sound modern; that is, they sound much like the criticisms of domestic and foreign policy that became so common in the last half of the 1960s and that continued into the 1970s.

Both publicly and privately Hoover struck out at those Democrats and Republicans whom he deemed "totalitarian liberals": those politicians devoted to an excessive use of state power, especially in terms of massive government expenditures but also in terms of increased presidential power over foreign affairs because of the secrecy and deception that often accompanied such power. Moreover, he accused the New Dealers in general and FDR in particular of authorizing interventionist diplomatic and military actions without public or congressional knowledge and of using government propaganda to arouse emotions and deceive the American people. Finally, he lashed out at Congress for abdicating its constitutional authority over both domestic and foreign affairs, saying that this could only lead to an undermining of the Bill of Rights and of participatory democracy.[23]

Because this country has been through the traumas of Vietnam and Watergate, many Americans have almost become inured to statements about the dangers of an "imperial presidency" or of a "Gestapo frame of mind" in governmental circles. Consequently, similar statements made by Hoover and other so-called reactionary critics of both the New Deal and the Cold War do not now sound like the crazy aberrations they were made out to be in the 1930s, 1940s, and 1950s. It is all too easy to forget in either the agony or euphoria produced by the end of the Vietnam War (followed by the fall of South Vietnam and most of Indochina to the communists, the resignation of Nixon, runaway deficits, and exposure of Reagan's hostages-for-arms deal), that not too long ago the reputations and in some cases the careers of several generations of sincere men and women who openly opposed the welfare state and the Cold War mentality could be tarnished by liberal internationalists. Ironically, such supporters of what is usually called the New Deal consensus on foreign and domestic policy used the same tactic against conservative nonconformists like Hoover that Joseph McCarthy did against alleged communist sympathizers—namely, guilt by association.[24]

On the one hand, Hoover and others like him were conveniently labeled foreign policy isolationists, which automatically made them guilty of being friends either of Hitler before 1941 or of Stalin after 1945. On the other hand, they were also written off as domestic conservatives who were out of touch with the need for an ever-expanding economy (and national deficit) accompanied by an increasingly anonymous and autonomous governmental bureaucracy. What is curious about this use of guilt by association by liberal New Dealers before and after World War II is that they never recognized they were practicing a form of reverse McCarthyism. Their blindness with respect to the righteousness and rightness of their own domestic and foreign policies is best illustrated, I think, when the Cold Warriors of the Truman administration actually accused Hoover of being "a tool of the Kremlin" because of his strong opposition to the ideological nature of the Korean War and because his anticommunism was too moderate by their postwar standards.[25]

Hoover was not alone in his struggle against mainstream U.S. domestic and foreign policies. In fact, he was associated with such leading liberal and conservative politicians, journalists, businessmen, and historians as Charles A. Beard, Oswald Garrison Villard, Senator Robert A. Taft, I. F. Stone, James Paul Warburg, Charles C. Tansill, Walter Lippman, Harry Elmer Barnes, Senator Claude Pepper, Henry A. Wallace, Senator Glen H. Taylor, John T. Flynn, Senator Gerald P. Nye, Charles A. Lindbergh, and Lawrence Dennis. I do not mean to imply that these men always agreed with each other, but their reputations, like Hoover's, are now undergoing a gradual rehabilitation in the hands of revisionist historians in the United States—most of whom did not experience the Great Depression, the New Deal, or even the origins of the Cold War as adults. This is not to say that all aspects of the activities and ideas of these New Deal and Cold War critics are equally laudable in retrospect. It is simply a case of their best and most prophetic thoughts and suggestions on foreign and domestic policy now being singled out for reconsideration.[26]

What I have found most surprising in my own attempt to rehabilitate some of Hoover's best domestic and foreign policy ideas is the extent to which he was associated with revisionist historians like Charles Beard and Harry Elmer Barnes. There now exists conclusive documentary proof that he not only provided them with information from his own private files but, in the case of Barnes, actively encouraged him and sought funding for his research through the wealthy Portland, Oregon lumberman, John W. Blodgett, Jr., the Joseph Pew family of Philadelphia, and Jesse Jones, the former Reconstruction Finance Corporation chairman. Similarly, Hoover supported the projects of revisionist historian Charles Tansill.[27] Beard did not have private financial needs and so in his case Hoover simply provided him with access to restricted documents, including several confidential position papers that he wrote to Secretary of War Henry Stimson and President Truman in May 1945 for ending the war with Japan, which would not have necessitated the use of the atomic bomb, and for avoiding a Cold War in Europe with the Soviet Union.[28]

This final image of Hoover, therefore, is not that of an obsolete progressive reformer, or a neo-Wilsonian, or even a moderate advocate of New Dealism, multilateralism, and globalism, let alone a precursor of Nixonomics as some historians would have us believe.[29] Rather he offered basic alternatives to Americans in the fields of both foreign and domestic policy that were not particularly well articulated or appreciated during his lifetime.

Hoover was not alone in anticipating the negative, internal results of modern total warfare. These were commonly held fears among many old-time Progressives of both parties, the Republican Old Right, those concerned primarily with domestic reform, and knowledgeable isolationists and pacifists in the late 1930s. World War II did effectively end New Deal reform, just as World War I had killed progressivism as a national movement and the Indochina war was to end Lyndon Johnson's attempt to create the Great Society. Most important, from Hoover's point of view, was the abandonment of noncoerciveness as a mainstay of U.S. foreign policy in direct proportion to the acceptance of unlimited U.S. intervention in world affairs. Stimsonianism rather than Hooverism became the most pervasive of all the diplomatic legacies of World War II; the defense of a U.S. political, economic, and military empire abroad was its major raison d'être. Such an empire—based on rigid ideological motivation and military tactics—meant to Hoover the extinction of both international and domestic cooperative communities. He had always defined such communities as self-regulating entities. If self-serving groups of political, business, and military bureaucrats were to manage the governing process, then the people would no longer be in control of the country or its foreign policy. The Indochina war and the Watergate scandal have amply demonstrated his worst fears of a society and economy run from the top down by a coercive system of expertise and by what has been called an "arrogant elite guard of political adolescents."[30]

The real tragedy of World War II for Hoover lay ultimately, therefore, in its impact on his domestic dreams: U.S. self-sufficiency, cooperative individualism, associationalism, and a decentralized economy. The Great Depression and the New Deal had already retarded serious consideration of the merits of public versus private power, of the importance of cooperative versus elitist individual action in a modern, technological nation, and of the impact on the democratic process of employing the immense power of a managerial, corporate state in an unlimited fashion at home and abroad. Moreover, the material benefits associated with the New Deal and World War II further delayed consideration of these basic questions; only recently have domestic and foreign-policy problems been increasingly attributed to a bureaucratic, elitist, community-destroying federal power that borders, some say, on U.S. fascism.

Like many Marxist and non-Marxist anti-establishment historians, Hoover had been asking these significant and enduring questions about the domestic and foreign affairs of the United States since the 1920s. It is no wonder that he criticized the negative implications of such an arrogant, interventionist approach to reform and foreign policy before they were anything but the vaguest fears to most critics of the New Deal.

It is true that Hoover placed too much confidence in the ability of his own informal corporatism both to employ expertise in the public interest without succumbing to selfish elitism and to establish a proper balance among industry, agriculture, and labor. He also had too much faith in the willingness of capitalists to produce efficiently and maintain enough competition to ensure that profits would pass on to the workers in the form of lower prices and higher wages. Hoover himself realized that these ideals were unrealized and that the problem of technological unemployment, for example, was very real. While his belief in a cooperative, humane, commonsense capitalism never materialized in the 1920s, it was rooted in the sound idea that only through scientifically controlled expansion could the best of individualism and neo-guildist corporatism serve the people, the country, and the world. In other words, there were clearly defined limits to the American system that had to be honored if the United States was not to stumble onto the path of state socialism, fascism, or monopoly capitalism—all of which would destroy the material independence of people, their innovativeness, and their sense of significant political participation.

However correct his theories may appear in retrospect, there were serious defects in Hoover's methodology. Nonetheless, there is much to be said for the best of the transitional ideas that Hoover came to embody. Despite the limitations of his personal philosophy and temperament, they did allow for an alternative foreign policy after both world wars that was not based on unlimited interventionism or the military suppression of revolutions based on communist ideology, but rather on disarmament and peaceful coexistence. His views also recognized the relationship between domestic reform and international relations and called for a coordination of national and international policies. They also perceived the dangers of making individuals increasingly dependent on government bureaucracies they no longer controlled and the necessity of preserving a sense of community participation. That such ideas were not endorsed by his successors in the White House cannot be blamed on Hoover.[31]

His unpopularity and the state of mind of the American public prevented a serious reconsideration of these ideas until the 1970s and 1980s. He was, therefore, a transitional figure who failed to change people's thinking while he was alive, but his ideas are finally coming into their own.

The question remains: What more could Hoover have done as an ex-president to erase his lingering negative image and to have a greater impact on policy? With the exception of his influence over Truman's and Eisenhower's governmental reorganization plans and over famine relief immediately following World War II, Hoover's policymaking role as an ex-president was minimal, especially in the area of his greatest expertise—foreign policy. This ineffectiveness was not unique to Hoover. Even those ex-presidents who have not left office under a cloud have experienced it. The solution to this problem lies in the office of the ex-president as much as it resides with their particular personalities or policies as president, but as yet no institutionalized way has emerged for a former president to be an effective force in the formulation of domestic or foreign policy.

Perhaps Hoover should have sought elective office. In fact, he had two chances to become a senator. The first opportunity passed him by in 1945 when California governor Earl Warren appointed William Knowland to fill the unexpired portion of Hiram Johnson's term in the Senate. Hoover had quietly lobbied for the appointment. Then, in 1949 New York governor Thomas Dewey offered to appoint him to fill the vacancy created by the retirement of Senator Robert Wagner. This time, Hoover at the age of 75 refused the appointment on the grounds that the GOP needed "young blood on its fighting fronts."[32] Although 61-year-old John Foster Dulles lost his bid for election to the Senate, it certainly did not harm his rise within the ranks of the Republican party and would probably have enhanced Hoover's standing as well.[33]

Curiously, a strong-minded woman physician and social reformer, Alice Hamilton, had put her finger on Hoover's future dilemma as an ineffective ex-president even before he left office in January 1933 after she dined at the White House. In an unflattering account of the evening and the lame-duck president, Hamilton concluded a letter to her sister with these words:

> Hoover is pitifully nervous, his feet are not quiet for a minute, and he wore creaking patent leather pumps so that, as I sat beside him, I heard the undertone of little squeaks all the time. And Mrs. Hoover's foot swayed or tapped continually. Poor things, they have been through a purgatory. Once he said, when we were talking of the thirty hour week, "Who wants a short day, who wants to work only eight hours? What do you suppose I feel like when I think of going back to California?" That is the hard thing about our system. *He ought to pass into the Senate and fight there for the things he believes in.*[34] (emphasis added)

He probably should have done just that. It might have restored his reputation more quickly than the snail's pace improvement that has taken place since the opening of the Herbert Hoover Presidential Library in 1966.

NOTES

1. Herbert Hoover Presidential Library Association, *News* 2 (August and September 1973).

2. Ray T. Tucker, "Is Hoover Human?" *The North American Review* 226 (November 1928): 519. The concluding paragraph of this article, from which this description of Hoover comes, reads: "It may be, after all, that the Hoover whom the public sees only faintly is a fanciful, frustrated figure. It may be that he would prefer to be a people's idol—a rollicking Roosevelt, say, rather than a chubbier Coolidge."

3. Eugene Lyons, *Herbert Hoover: A Biography* (New York, 1964), p. 10; Craig Lloyd, "Aggressive Introvert: A Study of Herbert Hoover and Public Relations Management, 1912–1932" (Ph.D. diss., University of Iowa, 1970), p. 296 (subsequently published by Ohio State University Press in 1972); William A. Williams, "What This Country Needs . . . ," *New York Review* (November 5, 1970): 7 n. 1; Hoover to Lewis L. Strauss, September 10 and October 1, 1934, individual file, Herbert Hoover Post-Presidential Papers (hereafter cited as HHPPP), Herbert Hoover Presidential Library, West Branch, Iowa; Lewis L. Strauss interview, February 13, 1967, pp. 27–29, Hoover Oral History Program (hereafter cited as HOHP), Herbert Hoover Library. According to Strauss, Hoover was so angry with Michelson that he nicknamed a piece of blue and white china with a dragon on it, "Charlie."

4. *Nation's Business* 13 (November 1925): 81; John Hays Hammond, *The*

Autobiography of John Hays Hammond, vol. 2 (New York, 1935): 712; Lloyd, "Aggressive Introvert," 270–71; Will Irwin, *Herbert Hoover: A Reminiscent Biography* (New York, 1928), pp. 30, 58; Oswald Garrison Villard, *Prophets: True and False* (Freeport, N.Y., 1969; reprint of original 1928 edition), pp. 19–36; Tucker, "Is Hoover Human?" p. 513.

5. Burt Brown Barker Papers, Herbert Hoover Presidential Library, West Branch, Iowa.

6. David Hinshaw, *Herbert Hoover: American Quaker* (New York, 1950), p. xix; Hoover to Ashmun Brown, July 11, 1939, individual file, HHPPP.

7. For more details about this brand of administrative politics, see John Westrate, "The Administrative Theories and Practices of Herbert Hoover" (Ph.D. diss., University of Chicago, 1963); Peri Arnold, "Herbert Hoover and the Department of Commerce: A Study of Ideology and Policy" (Ph.D. diss., University of Chicago, 1972); Barry Karl, "Herbert Hoover and the Progressive Myth of the Presidency" (Paper delivered at the August 1974 Hoover Centennial Seminar); Jordan A. Schwarz, *The Interregnum of Despair: Hoover, Congress and the Depression* (Urbana, Ill., 1970).

8. William Hard, *Who's Hoover* (New York, 1928), p. 10.

9. I have purposely avoided discussing Hoover's image as a Quaker in this paper because I believe that the influence of his religious background has generally been exaggerated by most of his biographers. For recent examples, see David Burner, "A Quaker in the White House: Toward an Understanding of Herbert Hoover" (Paper delivered at the August 1974 Hoover Centennial Seminar; David Burner, *Herbert Hoover: A Public Life* (New York, 1979); and Morton Frisch, "Hoover's Political Philosophy" (Paper delivered at the October 1974 Hoover Centennial Seminar. Except for his conservative style of dress (which could also be attributed to his generally dour personality and indifference to fashion), as an adult Hoover retained few outward signs of his boyhood faith. Moreover, his life was simply too disrupted as a child and there were important influences on his thinking—such as his engineering career and the progressive movement—that contributed to his philosophy and actions as an adult. Probably the two most important legacies of Quakerism that he retained were abstract in nature. They were a sense of the harmony and unity of voluntary community cooperation and a predisposition toward any plans for perpetuating peace through nonviolent means. It should also be noted that one of his least publicized images was that of a Quaker. Finally, his ideas about domestic and foreign policy were too complex and so highly economic in orientation that it would be difficult to attribute any single one of them exclusively to his Quaker background. He had, in other words, become too worldly and experienced to act primarily as a Quaker once he became a public figure.

10. The best source about his financial situation before and after 1914 remains an article in *Fortune* (August 1932). All primary material of a financial nature is not open to research at the Hoover Library. Minor additional information about his finances can be found in the appendixes of both Roy V. Peel and

Thomas C. Connelly, *The 1932 Campaign: An Analysis* (New York, 1935) and Walter W. Leggett, *The Rise of Herbert Hoover* (New York, 1932). See also Burner, *Herbert Hoover: A Public Life*, pp. 21–62.

11. I have discussed both subjects extensively in *Herbert Hoover: Forgotten Progress* (Boston, 1975). I have dealt even more extensively with Hoover's economic and political foreign policies in *American Business and Foreign Policy, 1920–1933* (Lexington, 1971) and *Ideology and Economics: United States Relations with the Soviet Union, 1918–1933* (Columbia, Mo., 1974). See also Melvyn P. Leffler, *The Elusive Quest: America's Pursuit of European Stability and French Security, 1919–1933* (Chapel Hill, 1979), pp. 273–315 *passim*. The most sophisticated ideas can be found in the published and unpublished writings of Ellis W. Hawley. See, for example, Ellis W. Hawley, *The Great War and the Search for a Modern Order: A History of the American People and Their Institutions, 1917–1933* (New York, 1979), pp. 100–229 *passim*.

12. See Gary M. Maranell, "The Evaluation of Presidents: An Extension of the Schlesinger Poll," *Journal of American History* 57 (June 1970): 104–13 and Robert K. Murray and Tim H. Blessing, "The Presidential Performance Study: A Progress Report," *Journal of American History* 70 (December 1983): 535–55.

13. Much of this paragraph is quoted and adapted from Hoff-Wilson, *Herbert Hoover: Forgotten Progressive*, p. 269.

14. This is not meant to imply that there was little criticism of Hoover's work as food administrator or as director of foreign relief. In neither position did he act as objectively as his memoirs would lead one to believe. There is now abundant evidence that he favored certain business interests over others and that he sometimes used food relief as a way to maintain high agricultural prices in the United States and as a weapon against communist forces abroad. Feminists, for example, criticized him for portraying women as the major wasters of food in the United States, while others have noted his economic and ideological biases. See Anne Henrietta Martin, "Will Women Vote for Mr. Hoover?" (1920 draft copy, box no. 1, Martin Collection, Bancroft Library, University of California, Berkeley); Gary Dean Best, "Food Relief in Price Support: Hoover and American Pork," *Agricultural History* 44 (October 1970); William R. Johnson, "Herbert Hoover and the Regulation of Grain Futures," *Mid-America* 51 (July 1969): 155–74; George W. Hopkins, "The Politics of Food: United States and Soviet Hungary, March–August 1919," *Mid-America* 55 (October 1973): 245–70; Benjamin M. Weissman, "The American Relief Administration in Russia, 1921–1923: A Case Study in the Interaction Between Opposing Political Systems" (Ph.D. diss., Columbia University, 1968), pp. 36–37, 51–56, 75–76, 107–9, 138–39, 180–81, 208–9, 263–64, 341–49, 354 (subsequently published by Stanford University Press in 1974); Murray Rothbard, "Hoover's *Memoirs* and His 1919 European Work" (Paper delivered at the October 1974 Hoover Centennial Seminar. Despite such criticism of his relief and food activities, Hoover remained a promising presidential candidate in 1919–1920. See Hoff-Wilson, *Herbert Hoover: Forgotten Progressive*, pp. 47–53, 73–78 and

Gary Dean Best, "The Hoover-For-President Boom of 1920," *Mid-America* 53 (October 1971), 227–44.

15. J. Joseph Huthmacher and Warren I. Susman, eds., *Herbert Hoover and the Crisis of American Capitalism* (Cambridge, Mass., 1973); Ellis W. Hawley, "Herbert Hoover and the Economic Planners, 1931–1932" (Paper delivered at the Southern Historical Association Convention in November 1968; Ellis W. Hawley, "Herbert Hoover and Economic Stabilization, 1921–1922" (Paper delivered at the April 1974 Hoover Centennial Seminar; Ellis W. Hawley, "Herbert Hoover, the Commerce Secretariat, and the Vision of an 'Associative State,' 1921–1928," *Journal of American History* 61 (June 1974): 116–40; Ellis W. Hawley, "Herbert Hoover and American Corporatism, 1929–1933," in Martin L. Fausold and George T. Mazuzan, eds., *The Hoover Presidency: A Reappraisal* (Albany, 1974); Carolyn Grin, "The Unemployment Conference of 1921: An Experiment in Cooperative National Planning," *Mid-America* 55 (April 1973): 83–107.

16. Bruce Alan Lohof, "Hoover and the Mississippi Flood of 1927: A Case Study of the Political Thought of Herbert Hoover" (Ph.D. diss., Syracuse University, 1968), pp. 210–13.

17. Much of the last two paragraphs are quoted and adapted from Hoff-Wilson, *Herbert Hoover: Forgotten Progressive*, pp. 117, 128.

18. Kent Schofield, "Herbert Hoover and the Engineers in the 1920s" (Paper delivered at the American Historical Association [AHA] Convention in December 1974); David Burner and Thomas R. West, "A Technocrat's Morality: Conservatism and Hoover the Engineer," in Stanley Elkins and Eric McKitrick, eds., *The Hofstadter Aegis: A Memorial* (New York, 1974); Burner, *Herbert Hoover: A Public Life*, pp. 63–71; Edwin T. Layton, Jr., *The Revolt of the Engineers: Social Responsibility and the American Engineering Profession* (Cleveland, 1971).

19. These were not Hoover's terms, but they are ones I have defined and used to refer to his domestic and foreign policies. See Hoff-Wilson, *American Business and Foreign Policy*, pp. xv–xvii, 240–41; Hoff-Wilson, *Herbert Hoover: Forgotten Progressive*, pp. 6–7, 26–27, 57–58, 64, 168, 175, 179; Hoff-Wilson, "A Re-evaluation of Herbert Hoover's Foreign Policy," in Fausold and Mazuzan, *The Hoover Presidency: A Reappraisal*.

20. For details about his initial criticisms of the New Deal and his views on foreign policy following World War II, see Joan Hoff-Wilson, "Herbert Hoover's Progressive Response to the New Deal" (Paper delivered at the Conference on Three Progressives from Iowa, March 1979) and Joan Hoff-Wilson, "Herbert Hoover's Plan for Ending the Second World War," *International History Review* 1 (January 1979): 84–102.

21. Charles D. Cary and Russell M. Ross, "Herbert Hoover and Executive Reorganization: An Appraisal" (Paper delivered at the October 1974 Hoover Centennial Seminar; see footnotes for other accounts of his reorganization activities); Hoover to Truman: May 30, 1945 (three memoranda on food relief and

related economic problems); April 21, 1946; December 3, 1946; January 18 and 19, February 26, March 12, 18, and 29, and April 21, 1947; February 6, 9, and 14, June 19, and July 4 and 9, 1949; Truman to Hoover: January 18, 1947; November 12, 1948; February 11 and July 14, 1949; Hoover to Eisenhower: January 13 and April 23, 1954; April 29, 1955; April 22 and December 27, 1956; February 7 and 25 and May 18, 1957; February 11, June 7 and 10, and August 8, 1958; Eisenhower to Hoover, October 15, 1956; January 3 and 8, February 4, and June 6, 1957; February 11, 1958. All of the above correspondence are in individual files, HHPPP.

22. By the end of the 1930s the Old Right was composed largely of the least conservative Republicans who were drawn together by their common opposition to the New Deal; by that time the ultraconservative big business and banking interests had retired from the battle against the New Deal after discovering they had little to fear from its moderate reforms. It was this middle or left-of-center group of Old Right Republicans that New Dealers first characterized as conservatives (because of their opposition to FDR) and later renamed as isolationists. For more information about this group see Leonard P. Liggio, "A New Look at Robert Taft" and Justus D. Doenecke, "The Strange Career of American Isolationism, 1944–54" (Both papers delivered at the AHA Convention in December 1973); Ronald Radosh, *Prophets on the Right: Profiles of Conservative Critics of American Globalism* (New York, 1975).

23. Hoover's private correspondence with John Callan O'Laughlin is probably the most valuable source for his criticisms of foreign and domestic policy from 1933 to 1949. It is housed in the Library of Congress. See also Hoff-Wilson, *Herbert Hoover: Forgotten Progressive*, pp. 208–68.

24. "Goldwater on the State of the U.S.," *San Francisco Chronicle*, October 3, 1973, p. 37; Arthur M. Schlesinger, Jr., "The Imperial Presidency," *Sacramento Bee*, sect. P, December 2, 1973, p. 1. In 1955 the Hoover Commission warned against "the growth of license and abuse of power" inherent in the super-secrecy accorded U.S. intelligence-gathering agencies. See *San Francisco Chronicle*, December 15, 1974, p. 21. For the similarity of tactics between liberals and McCarthy, see Wayne S. Cole, "A Tale of Two Isolationists—Told Three Wars Later," *Society for Historians of American Foreign Relations Newsletter* 5 (March, 1974): 11–12.

25. Justus D. Doenecke, "Harry Elmer Barnes" (Paper delivered at the Organization of American Historians Convention in April, 1972); Cole, "Tale of Two Isolationists," pp. 2–16; Hoff-Wilson, "Hoover's Plan for Ending the Second World War," pp. 92–93.

26. Justus D. Doenecke, "Harry Elmer Barnes," *Wisconsin Magazine of History* 56 (Summer 1973): 311–23; Justus D. Doenecke, "Harry Elmer Barnes: Prophet of a 'Usable' Past," *The History Teacher* 8 (February 1975): 26–76; Justus D. Doenecke, *The Literature of Isolationism: A Guide to Non-Interventionist Scholarship* (Colorado Springs, 1972); Radosh, *Prophets on the Right*; Thomas G. Paterson, *Cold War Critics: Alternatives to American Foreign Policy in the Truman Years* (Chicago, 1971).

27. John W. Blodgett, Jr. to Hoover: December 15, 1950; November 5, 1951; March 4, 1952; February 2 and May 10, 1954; Beard to Ray Lyman Wilbur, October 9, 1945; Wilbur to Hoover, October 16, 1945; Hoover to Beard, October 16, 1945; Ray Henle to Hoover, June 10, 1958; all in individual files, HHPPP. Barnes to Hoover, May 12, 1952, William R. Castle Papers, Hoover Presidential Library. Hoover to Barnes: January 12, 1946; July 17, 1947; July 19, 1950; January 12, June 12, and November 10, 1951; February 12, 1952; December 25, 1959; Barnes to Hoover: January 9, 1946; January 9, June 9, and November 8, 1951; May 12, 1952; William Neumann to Blodgett, October 16, 1947; Barnes to Blodgett, January 9, 1953; Blodgett to Barnes, June 9, 1953; all in the Henry Elmer Barnes Collection, Coe Library, University of Wyoming.

28. Mrs. Alfred (Miriam) Vagts to author, March 30, 1971. These confidential position papers are now part of the Public Statements Collection at the Hoover Library and were published for the first time in Hoff-Wilson, "Hoover's Plan for Ending the Second World War," pp. 93–102.

29. Donald R. McCoy, "Herbert Hoover and Foreign Policy, 1939–1945" (Paper delivered at the October 1974 Hoover Centennial Seminar); Alexander De Conde, "Hoover and Foreign Policy" (Paper delivered at the August 1974 Hoover Centennial Seminar); Selig Adler, "Hoover's Foreign Policy and the New Left," in Fausold and Mazuzan, *The Hoover Presidency*; Melvyn P. Leffler, "Political Isolationism: Economic Expansion or Diplomatic Realism? American Policy Toward Western Europe," in *Perspectives in American History* 7 (1974): 413–61; Michael J. Hogan, "The Private Structure of Cooperation in American Foreign Policy, 1918–1928" (Ph.D. diss., University of Iowa, 1974); Joseph Brandes, "Herbert Hoover's Anti-Monopoly Campaign at Home and Abroad" (Paper delivered at the April 1975 Hoover Centennial Seminar); Donald J. Mrozek, "Herbert Hoover and Conservative Opposition to Truman's Overseas Military Policy" (Private paper in possession of author); *New York Times*, June 25, 1975, p. 53.

30. Vice President Ford, quoted in *San Francisco Chronicle*, March 31, 1974, p. 1.

31. The last five paragraphs are quoted and adapted from Hoff-Wilson, *Herbert Hoover: Forgotten Progressive*, pp. 277–81.

32. Hoff-Wilson, *Herbert Hoover: Forgotten Progressive*, pp. 263–65; "Our Present Foreign Situation," September 4, 1954, memorandum in post-presidential subject file under foreign policy, Hoover Presidential Library, West Branch, Iowa.

33. Gary Dean Best, *Herbert Hoover: Postpresidential Years, 1933–1964* (Stanford, 1983), 1:276, 2:332–33.

34. Alice Hamilton to Edith Hamilton, January 28, 1933, Schlesinger Library, Radcliffe College, Cambridge, Mass.

2

**The Social Philosophy
of Herbert Hoover**

George H. Nash

Of the several hundred million people who have lived on the North American continent since the days of the Pilgrims, only thirty-eight have become president of the United States. What do we think of when we hear the name of one of these men, Herbert Hoover? What images arise? What aspects of his long life spring to our consciousness?

All of us, no doubt, automatically associate him with the Great Depression of the 1930s; it was Hoover's personal misfortune to preside over the nation when the Great Bull Market spluttered and collapsed in October 1929. Some of us may have recollections of an elderly man addressing Republican national conventions in 1952, 1956, or 1960—sentimental occasions when throngs of men and women cheered a seemingly quaint figure from a seemingly distant past. Some may know that Herbert Hoover was the first president born west of the Mississippi River or that he was the man who appeared in the first public demonstration of television in 1927. Some may be aware of his Quaker upbringing and of his enormous humanitarian relief work in Europe during and after World War I. Five years ago, Aleksandr Solzhenitsyn remarked that the American Relief Administration under Herbert Hoover's direction saved the lives of literally millions of Russians during the great famine of 1921 to 1923. Indeed, at the height of this massive relief effort—which was but one of many programs of the ARA after the First World War—Hoover's organization fed fifteen million Russian men, women, and children a day.

Even this summary does not encompass Hoover's interests and

George H. Nash's paper was originally published in the *Annals of Iowa* 45, no. 6 (Fall 1980): 478–96; reprinted by permission. It was one of several essays submitted by various historians to Senator Mark Hatfield of Oregon in 1979 for insertion in the *Congressional Record* to commemorate the fiftieth anniversary of President Hoover's inauguration. The general theme of the essays was "Herbert Hoover Reassessed."

achievements. As a mining engineer and multinational businessman, for example, with gigantic and far-flung enterprises from the late 1890s to World War I, he traveled around the globe five times before 1914—five times, that is, before the advent of the airplane. In all, he spent more than 2 years of his life on ships at sea. Later, in the 1920s, when he served in the cabinets of Presidents Harding and Coolidge, it was said that Hoover was secretary of commerce and under-secretary of every other department. After his four years in the White House he lived longer as an ex-president (31½ years) than any other former president in our history. Those of us who have visited Palo Alto, California and West Branch, Iowa can immediately point to two of his most visible benefactions, the Hoover Institution and the Herbert Hoover Presidential Library. When Hoover died in 1964, he had lived ninety extraordinarily productive years, including a full fifty in public service. Few American careers have been as multifaceted and remarkable as his.

What is significant for us today about the life of this man? If our parents or grandparents were asked this question, they might readily answer by quoting from a poem by Longfellow which school children of yesteryear used to learn:

> Lives of great men all remind us
> We can make our lives sublime,
> And, departing, leave behind us
> Footprints on the sands of time.

Certainly this is one reason why biographies of great men and women remain popular. We like to read about how others have coped with the adventures, challenges, and immutable realities of life.

But in the case of a figure like Herbert Hoover, our concern transcends the transient particularities of "human interest," fascinating though his life story is. For Hoover did not simply lead a career rich in accomplishment; he reflected on the circumstances which made such a career possible. Unlike most American men of affairs, who have been content to act on the public stage but not to meditate much about it, Hoover did not leave it to his biographers to extract some meaning from the kaleidoscopic events of a busy life. Instead, he developed and in his time came to personify a perception of America, a vision of America, a political and social philosophy which could explain the greatness of the country he loved—and, incidentally, the ground for his own achievements. It is in this vision and this philosophy that we can discover some of the enduring significance of Herbert Hoover.

He was born in 1874 in the little Quaker community of West Branch, Iowa, the son of the village blacksmith. Before he was seven his father had died. His mother, a recorded minister in the Society of Friends, died a little over three years later, so that in early 1884, before he was ten, young Herbert, his brother, and his sister were orphans. Hoover's brother Theodore in his autobiography wrote of the desolation that the children of Jesse and Hulda Hoover felt when their mother died: "The lady of the golden sunshine of little brown house had gone away, and there were left only three small children, adrift on the wreck of their little world."[1]

Despite these traumas, Herbert Hoover's later reminiscences of his Iowa childhood were gentle and almost idyllic. In the most famous of these recollections, first delivered in 1927, Hoover began:

> I prefer to think of Iowa as I saw it through the eyes of a ten-year-old-boy—and the eyes of all ten-year-old Iowa boys are or should be filled with the wonders of Iowa's streams and woods, of the mystery of growing crops.[2]

Hoover remembered the old swimming hole, the joys of fishing and hunting for game, the delights of his Aunt Millie's cooking, and other features of life in rural Iowa. Of his native state he declared: "The good Lord originally made it the richest stretch of agricultural land that ever blessed any one sovereign government. It was populated by the more adventurous and the more courageous, who fought their way along the ever-extending frontier."[3]

From Iowa in 1885 young Herbert Hoover was sent west to Oregon to live with the family of his uncle, Dr. Henry John Minthorn, the newly appointed superintendent of a Quaker academy (now George Fox College). Newberg, Oregon—said the 1886–1887 Catalogue of Friends' Pacific Academy—"is a temperance town, and has a moral and enterprising class of people. There are no saloons nearer than eight miles."[4] It was in such a sturdy and upright environment that Hoover grew into his teens. From Newberg in the late 1880s he traveled with his relatives to Salem, Oregon, where he became clerk and office boy for his Uncle John's Oregon Land Company, an enterprise which sold fertile soil to settlers in the Willamette Valley. One summer Hoover had a different job: weeding onions near Sherwood, Oregon, for fifty cents a day plus board.

After nearly six years in Oregon, Hoover traveled down to California in 1891 to become a member of the entering, or Pioneer, class at newly founded Stanford University. Here he soon became a campus leader, obtaining such positions as manager of the football team, president of the Geology Club, and student treasurer. After graduating in 1895, Hoover spent some time working in the mines of the Sierra Nevada until, early in 1896, he obtained a position on the staff of an eminent San Francisco mining engineer, Louis Janin. A little over a year later a London firm cabled Janin asking him to recommend an American engineer for work in its mines in Western Australia. There was one stipulation: the man should be thirty-five. Herbert Hoover was not yet twenty-three. Janin decided to take a chance and recommended Hoover anyway. But he admonished his young assistant the he had better *look* thirty-five before he reached Australia. Hoover took his advice; he grew a beard. When he reached London en route to the land "down under," his British employer marvelled at how Americans were able to preserve their youth.

Hoover's journey to London and then to Australia, via France, Italy, the Suez Canal, and India, must have been an intensely stimulating one to a young man of twenty-two. Years later, reflecting on this voyage, he remarked significantly, "History became a reality and America a contrast."[5] It was Hoover's first exposure to the world outside the United States, and in his responses to it we find one of the principal sources of his later political and social philosophy.

Of all the places on earth where men have dug for gold, Western Australia in 1897 must have been the most desolate and remote. When Hoover disembarked on the coast of Australia that year, he headed inland nearly four hundred miles to the mining towns of Coolgardie and Kalgoorlie, deep in the inhospitable outback. Hoover's descriptions of life in this rugged land were vivid. "It's a country of red dust, black flies, and white heat," he wrote from Kalgoorlie to an Oregon friend, Burt Brown Barker. "I could not portray the misery of any one of them on paper. The country is an endless desert, no water, no nothing but mines. All water must be condensed—costs $63.25 per 1000 gallons. The typhoid is rampant, there being an average of 3 deaths daily in this town (9000 people)."[6] During the Australian summer, the daytime temperature might be 110 degrees in the shade, 150 degrees in the sun. It was a land to make one think of home. Writing to his cousin in August 1897, Hoover declared: "Am on my way back to Coolgardie. Am glad to get back within the borders of civilization. Coolgardie is three yards inside of it; Perth is about a mile, and of course San Francisco is the center. Anybody who envies me my salary can just take my next trip with me, and he will then be contented to be a bank clerk at $3 a week for the rest of his life, just to live in the United States. Stanford is the best place in the world."[7]

In other letters home, Hoover commented on the customs of the aborigines and the idiosyncrasies of his fellow men in the gold fields. "I have found out many things about Englishmen," he reported to a friend. "They are very particular about such things as dignity of position, social names, etc., etc. They are very distant and friendliness approaching familiarity is greatly abhorred. . . ." He told Barker, "Yankees are not well received. They only have us because they have to. They don't know how to make their mines pay dividends. We do."[8] In view of these sentiments, it is not surprising that Hoover acquired a nickname in Western Australia. H. C. were the initials of his first and middle names. H. C. Hoover. His friends said that "H. C." stood for "Hail Columbia."

In late 1898, after a successful stint as a manager of one of the greatest mines in Australian history, Hoover left the land down under for a new and more responsible mining position in China. On the way he stopped in California, married his college sweetheart, Lou Henry, and took her with him to a new home in the Orient. Once more Herbert Hoover, not yet twenty-five, found himself living among strangers and encountering a foreign civilization. Once more the process of sifting impressions and comparing the world outside with America proceeded.

At this point we can detect one of the threads of Herbert Hoover's early life. From the cornfields of Iowa to the orchards of Oregon, to the spacious acres of Stanford University, to the rugged Sierra Nevadas, to the dusty gold fields of Australia, even to the coal mines of northern China, we discern a repeated pattern: Herbert Hoover's early days were spent on or near frontiers. It is symbolically appropriate that he was a member of the Pioneer Class at Stanford. His was largely an outdoor life, lived in environments which rewarded initiative, industry, resourcefulness, and merit. Since the day when Hoover's Swiss-German ancestor, Andreas Huber, landed in Philadelphia from the Old World in 1738, the Hoover clan had moved gradually westward until, with Herbert, the trek circled the globe. Benjamin Franklin is supposed to have said that America is a country where we ask of a man not "Who is he?" but "What can he do?". Hoover's was a society populated by people who held this attitude and who had moved away from a constricted and stratified civilization.

In late 1901 Hoover left China for England and a partnership in an eminent firm of mining engineers. Until World War I, London, the mining and financial capital of the world, was his base of operations while he traveled continually, inspecting, financing, and developing mines from Burma to Australia, from South Africa to Siberia. For some Americans with similar careers and lifestyles, the temptation might have been irresistible to become an expatriate. For Herbert Hoover, if anything the opposite was true. Throughout these years abroad, his thoughts turned often toward his native land. His home in London became a mecca for American mining men, journalists, and Stanford graduates visiting Europe. As early as 1907, Hoover expressed to the president of Stanford University his longings to retire from his profession (he was only thirty-three) and to turn to a life of service in the United States. In 1912 he became a trustee—and an exceedingly active one—of Stanford University. In the summer of 1914 he was negotiating the purchase of the *Sacramento Union* in California when war interfered. Had it not done so, Hoover might have entered public service as a newspaper proprietor.

And all the while, Hoover was observing, analyzing, and evaluating the social systems of the Old World and the New. Long voyages at sea gave him an opportunity to read about the politics, economies, and cultures of countries all over the earth. It was, he later said, "a reeducation of myself" that compensated for the utilitarian emphasis of his formal studies at Stanford.[9] On one of these ocean trips, a British lady asked him what his profession was. An engineer, he said. "Why," she exclaimed, "I thought you were a gentleman!"[10] This anecdote, which Hoover later recounted in his *Memoirs*, epitomized his distaste for the class consciousness and social rigidities of Europe. From all of this he turned. In a revealing letter written to an American friend in 1912, Hoover observed:

> The American is always an alien abroad. He never can assimilate, nor do other peoples ever accept him otherwise than as a foreigner.
>
> His own heart is in his own country, and yet there is less and less of a niche for him when he returns. One feels that one should have built

one's fortune in America, altho it might have been less imposing. Yet one would be among one's own people and the esteem one hopes to build among one's associates would not be wasted by leaving them behind to go home and build at it again.

I have got to that stage now where I am playing the game for the game's sake, as the counters don't interest me any longer. I am disgusted with myself when I think how much better off you people are who stuck by your own country and place. When you walk down the street you meet a hundred men who have a genuine pleasure in greeting you. I am an alien who gets a grin once in nine months.[11]

Two years later, the conflagration of World War I enveloped Europe and changed the course of Herbert Hoover's life. While giant European armies bogged down in the trenches, Herbert Hoover, working without pay, directed the Commission for Relief in Belgium, a neutral organization which procured and distributed food to the civilian population of Belgium, caught between the German army of occupation and the British naval blockade. It was a noble undertaking which ultimately brought food to ten million people a day and which catapulted Hoover to worldwide fame as a humanitarian. One of the noteworthy themes of Hoover's correspondence as chairman of the CRB was that this largely American volunteer organization reflected American ideals. It was a source of pride to him that while Europeans fought and slaughtered one another, an American-led relief effort was saving the lives of noncombatants.

What was the effect of this experience upon Herbert Hoover? The more I study his three years in Europe from 1914 to 1917, as head of the Belgian Relief, the more surprising it seems that he ever endured the ordeal. For behind the uplifting routine of providing daily food to needy Belgians lay a depressing world of conspiracy, national rivalry, and festering intrigue. As early as December 1914, less than two months after he had assumed leadership of the CRB, Hoover observed with some incredulity:

> The amount of small jealousy that exists around amongst the Belgians themselves and amongst Relief Committees and professional charity workers throughout the world, and the malice which they can all of them display at times is beyond belief. Were it not for the haunting picture in one's mind of all the long line of people standing outside the relief stations in Belgium, I would have thrown over the position long since.[12]

From the day of its inception the CRB had to cope with critics in the various belligerent governments who were convinced that this unprecedented humanitarian work was enhancing the military strength of one side or the other. Scarcely a month went by which did not witness some challenge to the continued existence of the CRB. Stories were circulated impugning Hoover's integrity; in England in 1916 an investigation of his leadership of the CRB was begun. Even some of the Belgian officials with whom Hoover worked conspired at one point to whittle down American influence, and there is reason to suspect that jealous Belgians spread rumors about allegedly dishonest conduct by Hoover while he was a mining engineer. Many times, weary from incessant conflicts with one belligerent power or another, Hoover contemplated and even threatened resignation. During one crisis in January 1916, he wrote to his friend Hugh Gibson that "the Commission is getting hammered from all sides. . . . I am free to confess that this business had gone on too long . . . and I find staring me in my dreams a large poster entitled, 'Go back to the lead mines,' in which occupation one obtains a modicum of human gratitude and a large liberty from hammers of all sizes. . . ."[13] Hoover, of course, did not quit, but from his disillusioning encounter with the emotions of war and the ancient antagonisms of Europe, he derived a lesson. On February 2, 1917 (one day after Germany resumed unrestricted submarine warfare), he told a friend:

> If we have got to go into this war, I am extremely anxious that we should not go into it in alliance with anybody. . . . I dread the horrible entanglement of this country with all of the objectives of certain of the allies. . . . [14]

A few weeks later, the United States entered the war, and Hoover sailed back to America to direct our wartime Food Administration. But within two years he returned once more, this time to feed Europe while President Wilson and the Allies strove to draft a peace treaty at Versailles. From November 1918 to September 1919, Herbert Hoover crisscrossed Europe as director-general of the American Relief Administration, organizing the supply of food for starving millions and facilitating the emergence of stable economies. The year 1919 was one of the most turbulent in our century; it was also one of the pinnacles of Herbert Hoover's life. Food had helped to win the war. Now, he believed, it must win the peace. The grim alternative was chaos, famine, a new generation of embittered Europeans, and the possibility of Communist revolution over much of the continent. Thanks in considerable measure to the herculean efforts of Hoover and his staff, perhaps one-third of the population of postwar Europe, including Russia, was saved from famine and death.

But if Hoover could take comfort from his outstanding humanitarian accomplishment in postwar Europe, there was much that he saw which profoundly alarmed him and helped to determine his future political and social thought. Although Hoover at this point was hardly naive, he was stunned and sickened by what he experienced in 1919. I do not think he ever got over it. For months an angry and frustrated Hoover pleaded and argued with the Allies to lift the blockade on the defeated enemy and to allow the currents of peaceful exchange to flow. Only after a long struggle did he attain this objective. Every day Hoover witnessed the profusion of national rivalry, jealousy, greed, myopia, and desire for revenge. Writing to John Maynard Keynes in June 1919, Hoover said, "I am completing my work in a few weeks and I shall leave Europe with a heavier heart than even in the worst days of the war."[15]

When Hoover finally returned to the United States in late 1919, he vigorously supported the Treaty of Versailles—not because he was an innocent idealist, nor because he considered the treaty perfect (he did not), but primarily because he deemed a settlement essential to a worldwide recovery from war. Hoover was not an irreconcilable like Senator Hiram Johnson of California. And yet, as he later observed in his *Memoirs*, he did leave Europe with "one absolute conviction": that while America could win wars, "it could not make lasting peace." To Hoover it now seemed that "irreconcilable conflicts" in ideals and experience separated the Old World from the New. "The two worlds were indeed strangers to each other," he declared.[16] The New World, he came to believe, was remote from the imperialism, fanatic ideologies, racial antipathies, dictatorships, power politics, and class stratifications of Europe. As he expressed it in his *Memoirs*, "the forces which lay behind the rejection of American ideas at Paris [in 1929] were far deeper than the intrigues of diplomacy or the foibles of European statesmen. Here was the collision of civilizations that had grown three hundred years apart."[17]

In 1921 Herbert Hoover became secretary of commerce of the United States; in 1928 he was elected president. Of the thirty-eight men who have occupied the Oval Office, Herbert Hoover undoubtedly enjoyed more extensive acquaintance with foreign peoples and their social systems than any of his predecessors or successors. In another respect, he was unusual: he attempted to distill from his unique experiences a coherent understanding of the American experiment that he cherished. Few of our presidents have ventured self-consciously into the realm of political philosophy. Herbert Hoover did.

His first systematic effort in this field appeared in 1922: a little book entitled *American Individualism*.[18] This work represents the crystallization of the attitudes and perceptions which I have been describing in this essay. According to Hoover, the revolutionary upheavals of World War I and its aftermath had produced a world in ferment. In this cauldron several ideologies (he called them "social philosophies") were competing for the minds of men, among them Communism, Socialism, and Syndicalism. To Hoover, who had seen the vicious results that emanate from a blending of "bestial instincts" with idealistic humanitarian jargon, the need for a definition of the American system was urgent. He called this system "American Individualism."

By this term he definitely did not mean unfettered, old-fashioned laissez-faire, as he explicitly emphasized in the book. Hoover was anxious that individual initiative always be stimulated and rewarded, but it must, he said, be "tempered" by "that firm and fixed ideal of American individualism—*an equality of opportunity.*"[19] Equality of opportunity, "the demand for a fair chance as the basis of American life," in Hoover's words, was "our most precious social ideal."[20] Hoover insisted that equal opportunity and a "fair chance" for individuals to develop their abilities were "the sole source of progress" and the principal impulse behind American civilization for three centuries. The American pioneer, he asserted, exemplified this spirit.

Hoover did not believe that equality of opportunity was automatically self-sustaining in a modern, technological economy. A certain measure of governmental regulation and guidance, some governmental legislation (such as anti-trust laws), were necessary, he felt, to prevent economic autocracy, *in*equality of opportunity, and the throttling of individual initiative. (Just two years before, in 1920, Hoover had labeled himself an "independent progressive.")[21] To Hoover it was imperative that *"we keep the social solution free from frozen strata of classes."*[22]

But the nature and extent of this governmental involvement must be carefully defined and, above all, kept consistent with the broad American traditions of voluntary cooperation, local self-government, and individual initiative. While not unmindful of the faults of unchecked capitalism, Hoover was an uncompromising foe of socialism and the totalitarian state.

Hoover's apotheosis of the United States as a land dedicated to the ideals of equal opportunity and freedom to carve one's own destiny won the assent of another distinguished American in 1923. Professor Frederick Jackson Turner, exponent of the famous "frontier thesis," was enthusiastic about Hoover's "meaty little book." "It contains," said Turner, "the New and Old Testament of the American gospel and I wish it a wide circulation."[23] Perhaps it is not coincidental that when Turner's book, *The Frontier in American History*, was published in 1920, he had given a copy to Hoover, who read it (according to his secretary) "with very great interest."[24]

Twelve years after the publication of *American Individualism*, the world had drastically altered. By then Herbert Hoover was an ex-president, and something called the New Deal was abroad in the land. Once again Hoover took up his pen, this time to write *The Challenge of Liberty*, a powerful critique of statist ideologies and a reaffirmation of the unique social philosophy of America, "one of the last few strongholds of human freedom."[25] Political theorists who examine this book might term it an expression of modified classical liberalism. But whatever the label, it articulated a philosophy forged in the aftermath of World War I which Hoover expounded, often with eloquence, for the rest of his life. Speaking before a Boys' Club in 1940, for example, he interpreted his version of the American Dream:

> By a classless America our forefathers meant far more than a sociological expression. There were to be no stratifications in life that handicapped the rise of any boy from the bottom to the top. The human particles should move freely in the social solution. . . . This idea of a fluid classless society was unique in the world. It was the point at which our social structure departed from all others.[26]

And always he drew the contrast between the America he loved and the Old World with its pestilent ideologies. Listen to his words at his birthplace in Iowa in 1948:

I have seen the squalor of Asia, the frozen class barriers of Europe. And I was not a tourist. I was associated in their working lives and problems. I had to deal with their social systems and their governments. And outstanding everywhere to these great masses of people there was a hallowed word—*America.* To them, it was the hope of the world.

My every frequent homecoming has been a reaffirmation of the glory of America. Each time my soul was washed by the relief from grinding poverty of other nations, by the greater kindliness and frankness which comes from the acceptance of equality and a belief in wide-open opportunity to all who want a chance. It is more than that. It is a land of self-respect born alone of free men and women.[27]

How, though, could social fluidity and quality of opportunity be preserved? For Hoover there were many answers. One, perhaps the most crucial, was our educational system; another was governmental action to curb domination of the economy by clusters of economic power. Another (and this may seem surprising) was inheritance taxes; Hoover contended that "the sons of the successful [should] not by any mere right of birth or favor continue to occupy their fathers' places of power against the rise of a new generation in process of coming up from the bottom."[28] Still another mechanism in Hoover's eyes was the Boys' Club movement; in it, he claimed, "there is a restoration of equal opportunity with all the other boys."[29] Indeed, many of Herbert Hoover's governmental policies and charitable activities over the years, including his long concern with child welfare, acquire a kind of thematic unity if we perceive them as attempts to promote equality of opportunity for all Americans, especially the young.

It was part of Herbert Hoover's ordeal in his later, postpresidential years that the political philosophy he developed, the vision of America that he expressed, came to seem abstract and anachronistic for many Americans. It was all right for Hoover to extol the social system that had produced *him,* many people seem to think, but were his paeans to America's traditional values relevant to the steelworkers of Pittsburgh, the tenant farmers of Mississippi, or the Okies of the Dust Bowl? Were American abundance and prosperity simply accidents of history, the products of a continent of free land? Wasn't the frontier gone now? Wasn't America's pioneer past over, and with it the supposedly outmoded Turnerian (and Hooverian) values of individualism, neighborly cooperation, and private initiative?

Herbert Hoover responded forcefully to such criticisms. It was not the mere availability of abundant land and natural resources that had blessed America, he insisted. It was a social system, animated by ideals. The "most potent force in society," he wrote, "is its ideals."[30] To Hoover the principles of American Individualism were not anemic platitudes, to be uttered, perhaps, on the Fourth of July. Nor had America become a closed, stagnant society, and Hoover hoped that it never would. New frontiers of science, invention, and human welfare were just beginning to open exciting vistas of opportunity. Hoover warned against the contrary opinion (again fashionable today):

> When we concede that progress is ended we concede that hope and new opportunity have departed. That is the concept of a static nation. It is necessarily the philosophy of decadence. No society can become static, it must go forward or back. . . . No society will function without confidence in its future opportunities.[31]

Today some may believe that Hoover's viewpoint is at last irretrievably outmoded, that he was, at most, a transitional figure to a world which has forever abandoned his values and his vision. Certainly it is true that America and the very nature of its government have altered since the days, a half century ago, when Hoover was president. When Hoover left the White House in 1933, the federal government's budget was less than five billion dollars. Today it is a hundred times higher. Since 1900 public spending in the United States has increased more than 239 times. Every year the federal deficit alone is several times greater than the entire federal budget during Hoover's years as chief executive.

And yet I suggest that there is today an increasing resonance to Herbert Hoover's philosophy, more than a decade after his death. In the current worldwide debate over "human rights" we hear echoes of Hoover's belief in the uniqueness of the American experiment and the superiority of a social system invigorated by the ideal of human freedom. Furthermore, the challenges we confront raise philosophical questions to which Hoover's answers deserve our attention.

Consider, for instance, the increasingly pervasive, and legally countenanced, use of quotas in the hiring of men and women for jobs in business, universities, and government. In our commendable desire to eliminate past discrimination, are we not perhaps invoking an antithetic creed, which measures us by the crude and irrelevant categories of race, gender, and ethnic origin? Herbert Hoover's philosophy has much to say on this point.

Or consider the much-discussed "energy crisis." If Herbert Hoover were living today, I suspect that as a lifelong champion of efficiency and the elimination of waste he would vigorously encourage efforts toward conservation of our resources. But he would also stress that a far more precious resource than oil must not be allowed to atrophy. This is our *social* energy. And the source of this liberating social energy is not an overweening, coercive, stultifying, bureaucratic government but free men and women, uncommon men and women, competing and cooperating voluntarily in an open, fluid society. It is a proper function of government, I think he would say, to stimulate initiative and to foster its harmonious use, not to *supplant* private initiative or *monopolize* social energy.

Finally, I have emphasized in this essay the roots of Herbert Hoover's philosophy in the contrast he perceived between the Old World and the New. In evaluating his American Individualism, we would do well to ponder anew the ghastly practical consequences of some of the alternative social philosophies which have motivated men and women in this often bloody century. Consider the tens of millions who have perished in the Gulag Archipelago. Consider the death camps at Auschwitz. Consider, today, the agony of the Vietnamese boat people.

Free societies, such as the one we today enjoy, are a rarity in human history, and they are not self-sustaining. To survive they require a cogent understanding of their fundamental, undergirding values and their antitheses. This Herbert Hoover realized. He spent much of his life attempting to apply these values to teach us what he learned. If you examine the record of what he did and what he said, you will find that he speaks to us still.

NOTES

1. Theodore J. Hoover, "Memoranda: Being a Statement by an Engineer," typewritten manuscript, 1939, p. 35, Herbert Hoover Presidential Library, West Branch, Iowa.

2. Herbert Hoover, "Boyhood in Iowa," *Palimpsest* 43 (August 1962): 337.

3. Ibid., p. 344.

4. *Catalogue of Friends' Pacific Academy, 1886–1887*, George Fox College, Newberg, Oregon, p. 13.

5. Herbert Hoover, *Memoirs*, vol. I, *Years of Adventure, 1874–1920* (New York, 1951), p. 30.

6. Hoover to Barker, October 25, 1897, Pre-Commerce Papers, Herbert Hoover Papers, Herbert Hoover Presidential Library, West Branch, Iowa (hereafter cited as HHP).

7. Hoover to Harriette Miles, August 5, 1897, Pre-Commercc Papers, HHP.

8. Hoover to Barker, October 25, 1897, Pre-Commerce Papers, HHP.

9. Herbert Hoover, undated biographical statement, quoted in Craig Lloyd, *Aggressive Introvert: Herbert Hoover and Public Relations Management, 1912–1932* (Columbus, Ohio, 1972), p. 15.

10. Hoover, *Years of Adventure*, p. 132.

11. Hoover to George J. Bancroft, 1912, Pre-Commerce Papers, HHP.

12. Hoover to Josephine Bates, December 10, 1914, Commission for Relief in Belgium Papers, Hoover Institution, Stanford, California (hereafter cited as CRBP).

13. Hoover to Gibson, January 25, 1916, CRBP.

14. Hoover to William C. Edgar, February 2, 1917, CRBP.

15. Hoover to Keynes, June 7, 1919, Lord Keynes Papers, The Marshall Library, Cambridge, England.

16. Hoover, *Years of Adventure*, p. 473.

17. Ibid., p. 479.

18. Herbert Hoover, *American Individualism* (New York, 1922).

19. Ibid., p. 8f.

20. Herbert Hoover, Commencement Address at William Penn College, Oskaloosa, Iowa, June 12, 1925, *Penn College Bulletin*, n.s. 19 (July 1925).

21. Hoover to Ralph Arnold, March 8, 1920, Pre-Commerce Papers, HHP.

22. Hoover, *American Individualism*, p. 9.

23. Turner to Richard S. Emmet (one of Hoover's secretaries), January 18, 1923, Commerce Papers, HHP.

24. Emmet to Turner, January 27, 1923, Commerce Papers, HHP.

25. Herbert Hoover, *The Challenge to Liberty* (New York, 1934), p. 48.

26. Herbert Hoover, *Further Addresses upon the American Road, 1938–1940* (New York, 1940), p. 221.

27. Herbert Hoover, *Addresses upon the American Road, 1945–1948* (New York, 1949), p. 77.

28. Hoover, *American Individualism*, p. 20.

29. Hoover, *Further Addresses*, p. 222.

30. Hoover, *American Individualism*, p. 16.

31. Hoover, *Challenge to Liberty*, p. 148.

3

Herbert Hoover and the Conservation of Human and Natural Resources

Mark O. Hatfield

If our meeting had been in Wood-Mar Hall today, you would have passed by a plaque placed in the main hallway in 1930 in honor of Herbert Hoover. On the plaque are listed those qualities and achievements that justify the pride of this community and this college in President Hoover. The plaque characterizes him as a "distinguished engineer," "eminent statesman" and "promoter of peace," among other things.

Not mentioned on that particular plaque was one of the interests that ran throughout Hoover's life: conservation. It is that theme I have chosen to emphasize this morning as we begin this day of seminars and dedications. No theme has greater currency and importance to us today than conservation. In looking at Hoover's commitment to conservation, we are reminded that few historical figures are as contemporary to our time or were as futuristic for their time.

You are to be commended for inviting to the campus today some of the finest scholars who have studied the life of Herbert Hoover. As Professor Joan Hoff-Wilson explains, the new studies and interpretations of Hoover allow us to speak without apology of the president who spent three years of his life here in Newberg. One of the things that gives excitement to the study of history is the constant uncovering of new evidence, which makes possible new interpretations and revisions of our understanding of the past.

One of the most profound influences on young Herbert Hoover was the extensive use of the Bible in his home and his schooling. In one of my readings of his memoirs I came upon a footnote that confirmed what I had come to feel about Hoover's attitude toward the Scriptures. In describing his work in Europe after World War I, he speaks of the disastrous spread of typhus, especially in Russia. He identified pestilence as the "Fourth Horseman of the Apocalypse," which is described in Revelations 6. In the footnote to this point, Hoover proceeded to give a thoughtful and detailed exegesis of this passage, indicating that there were actually five horsemen: war, famine, pestilence, death, and revolution.[1]

In Hoover's collection of letters from American children, entitled *On Growing Up*, there is one letter that asked for his favorite quote. He replied simply, "My favorite quote is the Sermon on the Mount."[2] A similar thought is found in his book, *The Problems of Lasting Peace*. "And always the greatest of all contributions to the building of moral and spiritual foundations of peace began with the Sermon on the Mount. Those teachings of Christ have thundered down over these 1900 years."[3]

Given these indications of a lifelong respect for the Scriptures, it is not stretching a point to find in the Bible the origins of his concerns on conservation. These convictions sprang not from religious dogma or doctrine but from an acting out and living of his faith. With respect to natural resources, the Scriptures begin with a profound respect for that which was worthy of the Creator's effort. Whereas the created order is provided for the joy and fulfillment of humankind, man was given "dominion" over it.[4] The New Testament counterpart to the word "dominion" might well be "stewardship." The concept is one of wise and farsighted use, not reckless plundering, which has characterized so much of our use of the created order.

The companion concept of conservation of natural resources is the protection of human resources, and Hoover found an abundant basis for this in the Sermon on the Mount. A person reared in the Quaker faith could not fail to be aware of the Beatitudes, especially, "Blessed are the peacemakers."[5] Other great teachings in this passage are relevant to Hoover's later career, especially: "Love your enemies and pray for those who persecute you. For if you forgive others the wrongs they have done, your heavenly Father will also forgive you."[6]

There was much in Hoover's early experiences that reinforced the biblical training he had received. With respect to natural resources, his time in rural Iowa and in Oregon during its pioneer stages instilled in him a deep love of nature. As he opens the first volume of his memoirs, "I prefer to think of Iowa as I saw it through the eyes of a ten-year-old boy. Those were eyes filled with the wonders of Iowa's streams and woods, of the mystery of growing crops."[7] In his book of essays, *Fishing for Fun*, he wrote, "Oregon lives in my mind for its gleaming wheat fields, its abundant fruit, its luxuriant forest vegetation, and the fish in the mountain streams. To step into its forests with their tangles of berry bushes, their ferns, their masses of wild flowers, stirs up odors peculiar to Oregon."[8]

There is a danger of allowing the pendulum to go too far in any historical revision. It is not necessary to romanticize Hoover or to make him into a saint or hero; his achievements speak for themselves when the layers of prejudice and misinterpretation are stripped away.

Hoover's interest in conservation can be divided into two major categories: natural resources and human resources. The primary focus of Hoover's early career was on natural resources, as he applied his academic training to the field of mining. I might be addressing you as students of Herbert Hoover College if in 1891 he had decided to enroll at Pacific College instead of Stanford.[9] Among Stanford's attractions to Hoover was a Department of Geology and Mining, free tuition, and a Quaker professor. The latter provided reassurance to the Minthorns, who would have preferred that he attend Pacific or Earlham.

Hoover's summer employment heightened his appreciation of the natural resources in the country. The first summer he mapped the zinc and coal-bearing outcrops in the Ozarks of Arkansas. This region provided him with his first exposure to poverty and malnourishment and, incidentally, to unfriendly moonshiners.

Hoover was engaged in the mining business for nine years and had abundant opportunities to become aware of the finiteness and preciousness of the world's mineral resources. One of his first significant jobs was with a British firm operating gold mines in the deserts of Western Australia. When the mines could not be developed for lack of water, he devised a filtering process to allow water to be recycled in the mines. When he established his own firm in 1908, its major activity became that of rescuing mines that had been mismanaged and unproductive. For example, he was called in to help salvage a badly managed series of mines in the Ural Mountains of Russia. By changing the smelting process and restructuring the operation of the mines, he was able to provide a profit to the owners and income to thousands of peasants.

During the debate on strip-mining legislation in 1976–1977, I thought that this country could benefit from Hoover's technical skill and his philosophy on resources. What he understood was that resources are limited, but that through careful management and stewardship the supplies can be prolonged far beyond the usual pattern of plunder.

As secretary of commerce and as president, Hoover continued to place a great deal of emphasis on conservation of natural resources. He appointed as his secretary of the interior a person not known as a conservationist but as an educator and physician—the president of Stanford, Ray Lyman Wilbur. The two of them became an excellent team as they grappled with problems of water resources, the suitable handling of oil reserves, and the proper stewardship of the national forests and land.

These issues are quite important today, of course, but not many Americans in the early 1930s sensed their urgency. Shortly after Hoover took office, he canceled the leases on thousands of acres of federal oil reserves. He said, rather prophetically, "The time will come when the nation will need this oil much more than it is needed now." As a member of the Federal Oil Conservation Board he was able to draw upon his knowledge as an engineer to warn of the dangers of over-drilling. Pumping from the oil pools too rapidly, he warned, would reduce the total production of the wells and waste the natural gas from the same reserves.

Hoover's custom was to take the long-term view, as in the case of public grazing lands, where he saw that overgrazing would destroy their usefulness in a matter of years. One solution was his appointment of the Commission on the Conservation and Administration of the Public Domain.

Some of you have grown up in southern Idaho, where massive federal reclamation projects under the Newlands Act of 1902 made possible the farming without which Boise Valley would still be barren. You will be interested to know that Hoover took major steps to provide stronger leadership and more adequate funding for completing these projects in the 1930s. He told a press conference in 1929 that this construction program was more important than the building of the Panama Canal.

Flood control and waterway projects were high priorities to Hoover. Hoover Dam was a result of the Colorado River project he started, and the Grand Coulee Dam was begun at his initiative as well as waterway projects in the central valley of California, Mississippi River, Great Lakes, St. Lawrence, and Muscle Shoals. We have mistakenly assumed that the potential for hydroelectric power has been exhausted. The Army Corps of Engineers concluded in the mid-1970s that the potential for expanding existing capacity and building new facilities would make available 207 billion kilowatt hours of electricity. This is equivalent to 343 million barrels of oil per year, or 13 percent of U.S. oil imports in 1976.

Any of you who have read some of Hoover's books and essays know that he was a devoted, almost a fanatical fisherman. He fished in many parts of the country and in so doing became aware of the problem of water pollution before most people even knew the meaning of the word. As early as 1921 he warned about the industrial pollution of the coastal waters. He was instrumental in the passage of the Oil Pollution Act of 1924 and had a part in an international conference on oil production in 1926.

In his *Remedy for Disappearing Game Fishes*, published in 1930, he discussed pollution extensively. He proposed a survey of all major streams that would lead to their categorization. Those not yet polluted would be fully protected, as has since been attempted with the Wild and Scenic Rivers program. Streams already polluted would receive lesser protection but appropriate remedies for their purification.

Those people who have struggled to make the Willamette River habitable to fish and suitable for recreation came to appreciate Hoover's comprehension of the problem and vision for its solution. Just after World War II, all the industries and municipalities along the river were dumping raw sewage into these waters. By 1959 secondary sewage treatment facilities had been developed all along the river, and now the hatcheries and other facilities have been greatly expanded to increase both sport and commercial fisheries.

Another phase of Hoover's career focused on the conservation of human resources. David Starr Jordan, the first president of Stanford, said that Hoover was the only great hero to emerge from World War I— and it seems to me that this was not an exaggeration. His heroism was in binding up the wounds of the suffering, that calling and ministry in which Quakers have excelled. Another great Quaker and one of the finest people ever to live in Newberg, Levi Pennington, called Hoover's relief efforts "the greatest life-saving enterprise the world had ever known."[10]

Hoover was deeply saddened by the coming of World War I. He did not personally subscribe to pacifism in the sense of refusing to fight in any war; his views were similar to those of his uncle, Dr. Minthorn, who liked to say, "Turn your other cheek once, but if he smites it, then punch him."[11] Nevertheless, he knew that the United States had become a part of the world community and had little hope of being only a spectator to another European war.

Hoover was drawn into the wartime relief work almost accidentally, but he soon plunged in with all his energy and organizational skill. One of his friends, the U.S. consul general, prevailed on him to help the hundreds of American tourists caught in London who were unable to cash their travelers checks and obtain passage home. Hoover enlisted fellow engineers, commandeered a hotel, and began lining up ships for the return trip; Mrs. Hoover organized tours of London for those awaiting passage. In six weeks time the American Relief Committee processed 120,000 Americans, all without a government subsidy.

In the course of getting Americans out of Belgium, Hoover and others in London became aware of the desperate need of food in that German-occupied country. Without attempting to recount the details of the massive relief effort he headed throughout the war, it is important to see its significance as a remarkable life-saving effort. If Hoover had occasion to reflect on his early training in the Bible, he might have compared his mission to that of Joseph in famine-stricken Egypt. What was thought to be a project to span a few months stretched out to four years and involved five million tons of food worth a billion dollars. The British and French governments wanted above all to maintain a tight blockade and intensify the pressures on the occupied forces, but the concern of Hoover and the Commission for Relief in Belgium was saving the lives of the ten million Belgian and French people. Even from a pragmatic perspective, Hoover pointed out that a future peace could not be built on the stunted bodies and deformed minds of the next generation.

Some of Hoover's values with respect to human resources can be seen in his handling of the position of food administrator after the United States entered the war. His assignment was to shift consumption patterns in this country and increase total production to meet the needs of Europe. Realistically it was an impossible task, since the 1916 and 1917 crops had been reduced by drought and there was no surplus to export. However, here we see a combination of Hoover's views on conservation of natural and human resources. Using price stabilization and long-term guarantees as a stimulant for production, the output of the farms jumped dramatically. Exports of crops and livestock more than doubled in three years.

Another aspect of conservation was eliminating waste and reducing consumption by Americans. Based on his relief work in Europe, Hoover sensed that it would be ineffective and costly to attempt rationing. Instead he appealed to the sensitivities of the American people to join in reducing waste and increasing production. I have in my office a copy of a pledge people took to do their part in reaching the goal of twenty million additional tons of food during the war. The goal was reached and then some. Yet again Hoover had to deal with those who dragged their feet and believed that a food blockade would hasten German surrender. Hoover argued that the soldiers and munition workers would always be fed—it would be the women and children who would suffer.

A chapter in Hoover's relief efforts, involving Russia, underscored the need for both compassion and forgiveness. He had seen Russia firsthand during the tsarist period and readily admitted that Bolshevism had arisen in response to genuine grievances, but he rejected the Bolshevik economic philosophy and the tendency toward bloodshed as a means to an end. Nevertheless, as World War I ended but fighting continued within Russia, reports came of hundreds of thousands of people starving. At first the Allies offered help on the condition that hostilities cease, but not surprisingly Lenin rejected that provision entirely. As you will recall, 1919 was the first wave of anti-Communist hysteria in the United States, a hysteria perhaps more intense than in the McCarthy era. At such a time, you can imagine the unpopularity of providing relief to people coming under Bolshevik control. Yet because of the millions of lives in jeopardy, Hoover plunged ahead with food shipments, skirting the sticky ideological disagreements. As a result, some 768,000 tons of food, clothing, and medicine were shipped from the United States to Russia.

These themes of conservation can be found in other stages of Hoover's career. The newer interpretations of Hoover's handling of the domestic economic crisis have illustrated that he was genuinely concerned to relieve suffering. He was the first president to take such substantial steps to intervene in the economic cycle. His actions differed from those of his successor, of course, not through indifference but because of his strong views on appropriate methods. He warned of "bureaucratic tyranny," an equally undesirable alternative to the extremes of fascism, socialism, and syndicalism. His work with governmental reorganization over many years, especially with the Hoover Commission, was based on the goal of conserving governmental resources and individual effort.

Again, let us resist the impulse to share the negative views of Hoover that have prevailed over several decades. A cue can be taken from those whose wisdom, versatility, and longevity were on a par with Hoover. The obvious person who comes to mind here in Newberg is Levi Pennington, who developed a close relationship with Hoover over the years. Among Pennington's remarks at a memorial service for Herbert Hoover here in Newberg was this statement, and with it I close:

> In his personal conduct, in his family life, in his business transactions, in his international affairs, [and] in his handling of all the billions of relief from America to the ends of the earth, he maintained the high ideals that had been taught him by his village blacksmith father and his Quaker teacher-preacher mother, and later by his uncle and aunt with whom he lived during his boyhood and youth in Newberg and in Salem, and by the teachers in Friends Pacific Academy, where he was a student from its very beginning and where, according to his own testimony, he received the training that led him decades later to his vast fields of human service. The Decalogue was vital law to him, as was its summary by the greatest of all his teachers, 'Thou shalt love the Lord thy God with all thy heart—thou shalt love thy neighbor as thyself.'[12]

NOTES

1. *The Memoirs of Herbert Hoover, vol. 1: Years of Adventure, 1874–1920* (New York, 1951), pp. 324–25.

2. Herbert Hoover, *On Growing Up: Letters to American Boys and Girls Including "The Uncommon Man" and Other Selections* (New York, 1962), p. 28.

3. Herbert Hoover and Hugh Gibson, *The Problems of Lasting Peace* (Garden City, N.J., 1942).

4. Genesis 1:26.

5. Matthew 5:9.

6. Matthew 5:44, 6:14.

7. Hoover, *Years of Adventure*, p. 1.

8. *Fishing for Fun—And to Wash Your Soul* (New York, 1963), pp. 37–38.

9. Pacific College opened its doors in 1891 in Newberg, Oregon, on the site of Friends Pacific Academy, which Bert Hoover had attended in 1885–1888. Pacific College changed its name in 1949 to George Fox College.

10. Levi T. Pennington, *Rambling Recollections of Ninety Happy Years* (Portland, 1967), p. 117.

11. Hoover, *Years of Adventure*, p. 12.

12. Pennington, *Rambling Recollections*, p. 118.

4

The Quaker Faith of Herbert Hoover

David Burner

Herbert Hoover was a singularly well defined public figure; he was always doing something visible or controversial: mining a continent's ore, telling financiers how to be responsible, feeding war victims, arguing the case for progressivism, or arguing the case for conservatism. Yet for all that, his personality eludes scholarship; his words, so positive and combative, fail somehow to reveal what private anger or pride or belief motivated his public self. Particularly unclear is the effect on him of the faith of his childhood, the demanding faith of the Quakers. Historians of Hoover and his times have virtually ignored the question, and with reason, since Hoover's reticence makes it highly speculative.

Hoover worked with impersonal materials: with coal and silver, hydraulic pumps, stock prices, administrative structures, and governmental statistics. Many of his best-known efforts were in humanitarian relief, but even there the style was matter-of-fact and austere. Hoover seldom spoke compassionately or in tones of moral anger; in the task of ordering resources for relief he was the brusque and efficient organizer who had also built industrial empires. This is not a convincing representative of a pietistic sect, and perhaps there was little conscious and explicit Quakerism in Hoover's mature work. Yet there were the traits of character that so resemble those of a Friend: Hoover's high seriousness; his dislike of a politician's gestures and rhetoric; and the occasional absence in him, as among earlier Quaker generations, of conventional forms in speech and behavior. His lifelong goals were Quakerly: peace, relief for war victims, the spread of education. Like other Friends, he believed with simplicity in the effectiveness of rational discourse and planning. Like them, he combined all this with a diligent pursuit of worldly success. That he remained a professing Quaker could reflect any degree of conscious adherence to the traditional tenets of the Friends. But the similarities in style, practice, and belief between Hoover and other Quakers invites speculation on the possibilities of applying the Quaker vision to the world, as Hoover's prominence gave him the opportunity to do.

Americans have been accustomed to hearing their presidents speak favorably of religion, particularly of Christianity. The nation has not, of course, expected presidents to turn the other cheek, renounce the armed forces, give all they have to the poor, and urge their fellow citizens to do likewise; but after two millennia of Christians who have not done these things, they are no longer prerequisites of popular Christianity anyway. What is expected of chief executives in their profession of faith is that they encourage spiritual values, sometimes attend church, and announce periodically that the greatness of the United States is founded on religion. The most recent suggestion of an offering that the world's richest nation can make for the religion of the poor is a daily minute's enforced silence, or enforced prayer, in the public schools.

Suppose, however, that occupancy of the White House should fall to someone whose faith involves not merely public piety but a conduct that is demanding and at odds with American ways and institutions. Among the varieties of American churches and sects there are some, from Hasidic Judaism to the Amish, that do set such requirements. The most familiar is the Society of Friends.

Even a Quaker politician can take on conventional behavior and morality. Woodrow Wilson's attorney general, A. Mitchell Palmer, did nothing to shock the religious sensibilities of average Christians as he would have done if, as a Friend, he had declared himself a pacifist and resigned as his country moved toward war. Instead, he acted as a normal Christian American would have wanted when he rounded up legally defenseless radical aliens and instructed the Labor Department to throw them out of the country. Richard Nixon, one of the century's other best-known Americans with a Quaker background, did work for détente even in the midst of another major war, and he criticized the recent stridency of cold war rhetoric. Still, that does not distinguish him from the many other Americans whose belief in the necessities of military power is tempered by sensible caution.

The Quaker community does not demand pacifism of its members. Yet is it usual to look to Friends to discipline themselves more rigorously than the generality of Christians to the spirit and conduct of peace, and so a Quaker who rejects pacifism but claims adherence to the faith should be obliged to be special in other ways that are in conformity with it. Herbert Hoover was one statesman who could at least haltingly meet the test.

Hoover's childhood had been thoroughly, densely Quaker. West Branch, Iowa, was a Quaker town. Herbert's mother Hulda became a minister in that Society which stressed the ministry of the laity as opposed to that of ordained or otherwise appointed shepherds. His great uncle John Y. Hoover was an evangelist, a calling that was acceptable to a midwestern Quakerism that had not become so domesticated to worldly norms as the Eastern branch of the Society. Antebellum Quakers in Iowa, including Herbert's future guardian Lawrie Tatum, had conducted fugitive slaves on the underground railroad, and after the war the West Branch *Local Record* told of Friends who were providing southern negroes with information on places to migrate in the North. West Branch Quakers, including Herbert's uncle Henry John Minthorn, engaged in educational work among the Indians, and John Y. Hoover made it an early part of his ministry to visit prisons. Young Herbert was enrolled in the Band of Hope, an organization for young Quakers that promoted temperance. In 1885 he was sent to Oregon to be under Minthorn's protection. Herbert Hoover's upbringing, then, must have been as sure in its peculiarity as that of Amish children in some Pennsylvania villages and as certain in its reformist morality and its nonviolence as a more typical childhood is in subscribing to mainstream American convictions.[1]

Hoover did not remain within the spiritual shelter of Quaker communities and institutions. After attending college at Stanford and receiving a degree in geology, he spent much of his early engineering and business career abroad, some of it in the Australian backcountry and in China. It was not a Friend in any sense of the word who, once in Australia, ruthlessly fired striking miners and cut wages. Yet by the time of his presidency, Hoover was attending Quaker meetings. Meanwhile he had made a virtual career out of political progressivism, humanitarianism, and the championing of enlightened business practices. All three activities are exactly fitting to a Quaker conscience and temper; they also fit exactly the consciences of innumerable men and women of other creeds. What precise Quaker convictions, if any, informed Hoover's work? How could that faith embrace the career of a businessman who commanded vast economic power and accumulated great personal wealth, and a president who commanded his nation's military forces and its domestic instruments of compulsion?

The unique place that the Quaker sect holds within Christianity has to do with its peculiarly direct associating of the two entities that Christians have kept before themselves, the spirit and the world. Catholic theologies and institutions have sought to define elaborate mediations between the two; religious orders have withdrawn from the world; other Christians have given themselves to mundane things, consciously falling short of a Christian absolute and hoping for forgiveness. But Quakers, except perhaps for the early generation of enthusiasts, have acted as though the world and its affairs were the true dwelling of the spirit. Many Christians, and many of other faiths, have combined in their lives intensive worldly work with rigorous belief, conduct, and worship. But Quakers are among the most diligent and singleminded of Christians in attending to the worldly affairs of commerce and secular reform, and they are distinctive among the worldly for attempting to discipline conduct to piety and peace. It is, of course, the Quaker witness to nonresistance that ultimately attests to belief in a world remade as a spiritual commonwealth. To seek pacifism as a social policy is to set yourself against the very grain of human nature.

The simpler course for Friends has been to occupy themselves with subduing that portion of the world that is encompassed by their community of faith—that is, to practice private discipline and engage in peaceableness and sharing among themselves, hoping that their communion may grow in numbers and be an example to the world outside. But suppose a Quaker should get the opportunity to adapt some part of that larger world to the standards of his faith. Such has been the case when Friends have organized a project of relief, or controlled a business of some scale and run it humanely, or engaged in government with some notion of service or principle; Herbert Hoover did all three of these things.

Imagine that a Quaker statesman brings about a peace treaty between two nations. Is this merely an exterior peace, an absence of war, or does that fact mean that the two countries have been brought closer to the inner peace of Friends? Or imagine that a Quaker politician wins a scheme of social insurance: are the contributing taxpayers merely that—taxpayers—or have they come to belong in some way to a community of sharing? A Quaker of an earlier and more fervent time might have insisted that the distinction between spiritual redemption and a more worldly good is absolute, and that a society might very possibly be at peace, prosperous, and economically just and yet be in darkness. But Quakerism has perhaps another way of approaching the matter. Assuming that the means of the world's redemption are already present within it, that truth is immediately available to all men and women and demands only an attentiveness to its inner promptings, Friends might have no difficulty in enlisting for their purposes even the most superficial social accommodations—anything that will make possible the beginnings of discussion among strangers, or provide some primitive shape or image of justice or of a society at peace. Quakerism will enlist these things because Quakers must relieve suffering, and because they may be themselves in some sense tracings of the spiritual order.

Quakers have a reputation for business practices founded on shrewdness, care, and honesty. This is consonant with the Quaker ethos, for if business can be a field of competition, it is also an occasion for reasoned compromise, agreement, and collective decision. Business, moreover, brings order of one kind or another by arranging merchandise, getting goods to their destination, and seeing that funds are mated with enterprise; it could appeal to a mind that wishes to entice out of the world the order that is implicit there. Finally, for all its temptation to ruthlessness, business has a history of associating itself with works of charity.

Hoover's ancestors had won prosperity from the sale of lands. His father was a blacksmith and seller of agricultural machinery. The parents left their three children the substantial sum of over five thousand dollars. Hoover had early business experience in a real estate office in Oregon and then as student treasurer and manager of a laundry trade at Stanford. His field of concentration at Stanford was not business but geology, and his early work was in mining engineering. His commitment to mining was real and lasting. In 1912 he would publish a translation of *De Re Metallica*, a sixteenth-century treatise on mining, and his pronouncements were to include phrases originating in the work of the radical sociologist Thorstein Veblen, who hoped that the mind of technology would triumph over less exact mentalities. But Hoover's mining practice was from the beginning a business practice as well. He was a mining entrepreneur in Australia and Asia and, by 1901, a partner in the prosperous London mining firm of Bewick, Moreing and Company.

If there was any principle of efficiency and order in Hoover's earliest entrepreneurial days, no evidence of it survives. He could be harsh not only toward his workers but toward the inanimate world. It was with no religious concept of stewardship over objects that, as has been reported of him, he wore out machinery in relentless usage. By the early twentieth century, however, he was becoming a public advocate of responsible business methods. He proposed requiring that management make available to investors abundant information about the state of their business; he spoke for bargaining with unions. Hoover may have been working from a plain sense of right conduct, or perhaps he was concerned with making business more orderly and respectable. Either motive would have befitted a Quaker.

Order, at any rate, increasingly became Hoover's special province. What is particularly notable of his relief projects—for Belgium during World War I and for Eastern Europe in its aftermath—was not their humanitarian intent but their scope, organization, and the swiftness with which they assembled a volunteer staff and collected funds for large-scale relief. They conformed precisely to a Quaker tradition of voluntary, organized, and efficient giving. After the United States's entry into the European combat, Hoover as food administrator organized the nation's food resources in support of a war effort that Friends faithful to their church's historic peace witness would have rejected. During the mid-1920s he was secretary of commerce, working to deepen the flow of international trade and promoting standardization of weights and measures.

Then, as president, Hoover made frequent use of the device that he had already employed as secretary of commerce. He held a series of conferences on such subjects as child welfare and education. The device was perfectly suited to the social doctrine Hoover had come to espouse, which was an unstable compound of progressivism—he was somewhere to the left within the Republican party, which does not put him very far to the left—and exaltation of entrepreneurial individualism. Since the conferences were voluntary in participation and had as their objective nothing more immediately coercive than the spread of awareness and ideas within the public, they comported with Hoover's belief in the primacy of individual effort. Yet the conferences did aim at collectivity of a sort: the awakening of a nationwide campaign. The conference device, suggesting the Quaker meeting, also peculiarly conforms to the Quaker spirit with its promotion of reasoned agreement and the arts of persuasion.[2]

Finance, commerce, and statesmanship as Hoover practiced them aimed particularly at rationalizing and composing, which was more appropriate to the Quaker Hoover than to the spokesman for rugged competition that legend and some of his own words make him out to be. It is in keeping with his career that in the Truman administration he was to undertake a major reordering of the federal government. But what of the inanimate realm of ores and machines that he had been trained to manage and, at least for a time, managed apparently with little care for preservation? Hoover had little to say of it. Commentators, however, noting that he is supposed to have been interested in the writings of Thorstein Veblen and recognizing ideological similarities, have linked them as contributors to a persuasion, known as technocracy, that had its moment in the optimistic 1920s. This was the conviction that the solutions to our problems lie not in political doctrines but in technical expertise at once hardheaded and humane—that is, an expertise that industrialism cultivates. Veblen was more a political radical than that. He pictured a silent struggle between business and technology for control of the industrial process. That struggle, according to his description, is not only a clash of self-interest. Business skills are the skills of advertising and enticement; the skills of the technician, disciplined to the intricate and impersonal processes of the machine and the natural world, are precise and respect fact. (Veblen conceded that much of business requires some schooling in objectivity, and technocrats wanted to bring administrators into the management of the new society.) A Friend could have found much to like in the writings of the relentlessly skeptical social scientist Veblen. The Quaker faith treats the world essentially as a workplace for tasks of industry and charity. Veblen despised the fatuous wordiness he associated with business enticement; Quakers once made a virtual part of their daily discipline the principle that words be exact and few.

Hoover as president turned repeatedly to the kind of good works that belonged to his Quaker heritage. His co-religionists were backers of his conference of 1929 on child welfare. The Indian bureau, seeded with his Quaker appointees, increased provisions for health, food, clothing, and schools. At the head of the federal prison system he placed the reformer Sanford Bates, who instituted a more liberal policy of parole. Civil liberties, a cause appealing to Friends in their dedication to freedom of conscience and their opposition to coercive government, should appeal as well to anyone who espouses, even as ambivalently as Hoover, a philosophy of individualism. In any event, his administration wrote a kind of epilogue to the story of the wartime repressions and the Red Scare, which were acts of a Democratic administration subsequently reversed by Republicans. He had the Justice Department investigate whether any penalties remained upon the victims, and he was able to report to the social reformer Jane Addams that the Republican White House had released all subjects of the Red Scare and had freely granted pardons to applicants. In a time when the most rigid social segregation was not only the law in the South but the custom throughout much of the country, the Hoover White House went at least mildly against the current, and southerners were infuriated at the gesture, trivial by any later standard, of including at tea the black wife of a congressman. The president also proposed an unQuakerly scheme, which his attorney general had him abandon as unconstitutional, for rushing federal troops by airplane to prevent threatened lynchings.[3]

These reforms do not add up to an articulate public policy. If they have a central connecting motive, it is simply the attitude that is generally termed humanitarianism, an ethic that does not normally require a precise philosophical or religious formulation. Hoover did not often speak of the reforms. There would have been little occasion for him to do so: prison reform offered no political advantage and needed no moral defense, and the humanitarian programs of Hoover's administration would interest neither liberals who have dismissed him as a Scrooge nor right-wingers who have admiringly perceived him as one of their own. Yet they suggest a lot about Hoover: his Quaker background and associations; the years of increasingly knowing himself, and being known, as a philanthropist; and beyond all this, perhaps, an engineer's and entrepreneur's appetite for doing things and fixing things. It may have been in part the humanitarian conscience in Hoover, along with a certain absence of mature and skeptical curiosity about himself and others, that flawed his understanding of the Great Depression and what to do about it. Voluntary relief measures, so far as his experience could tell, had always gone smoothly; there had always been so many people willing to give of their wealth and talent. Surely communities would mobilize to assist the stricken—but only, Hoover worried, if the government refrained from taking the initiative away from them. Thus, the president waited for a whole nation of Hoovers—successful, confident, and with cash, intelligence, and conscience to spare—to come to the rescue of the depression's victims. Among the many things he did not recognize is that direct governmental intervention, instead of stifling hope and initiative, can quicken them.

The primary concern here has been not to discover whether Hoover was consciously obedient to the Quaker faith in all its applications, but to inquire into the ways Quakerism might adapt itself to the habits of the world and the means of power, with Hoover's programs as illustrations of possibilities. There is a kind of Quakerism that would proceed differently from those merchants and reformers who have tried to subjugate some corner of this world to Quaker peace without crushing its full materiality and its variety of enterprises. This other sort would keep strictly to the Quaker disciplines and address the world by exhortation and symbolic nonresistance. To follow this course brings the strength and the strategic advantages of simplicity: it may also risk losing what real goods the world may offer, and it fails to put the Quaker disciplines to their fullest, most rigorous engagement with the world's rebellious appetites. Hoover, whatever may have been the nature of his faith, took the more complicated way, and his life combined austerity, in person and intellectual vision, with an embrace of the earthly project. William Penn, writing his *Preface to the Frame of Government of Pennsylvania* in 1682, suggested something of that compound:

> Government seems to me a part of religion itself, a thing sacred in its institution and end. For if it does not directly remove the cause, it crushes the effects of evil and is as such (though a lower yet) an emanation of the same divine power that is both author and object of pure religion . . . But that is only to evil doers, government itself being otherwise as capable of kindness, goodness, and charity as a more private society. They weakly err that think there is no other use of government than correction which is the coarsest part of it. Daily experience tells us that the care and regulation of many other affairs, more soft and daily necessary, make up much of the greatest power of government and [this] must have followed the peopling of the world had Adam never fell. . . . [4]

NOTES

1. West Branch *Local Record*, September 19, 1895; February 24, 1884; March 27, 1884; October 2, 1879; "Minthorn," Box XIII, Geneology, Herbert

Hoover Presidential Library (hereafter HHPL); Springdale Preparative Meeting, Minutes, June 23, 1883, West Branch Friends Church, West Branch, Iowa. For various accounts of John Brown among the Quakers see Jeanette Mather Lord, "John Brown—They Had a Concern," *West Virginia History* 20 (April 1959): 163–83; Frederick Lloyd, "John Brown Among the Pedee Quakers," *Annals of Iowa* 4 (April 1966): 665–70, (July 1966): 712–18, and (October 1966): 759–64; Irving B. Richman, "John Brown's Band," *The Palimpsest* 41 (January 1960): 16–22; and Errol T. Elliott, *Quakers on the American Frontier* (Richmond, Ind., 1969).

2. What is implicit in a meeting for worship is often made explicit in the meeting for business. D. Elton Trueblood, "The Quaker Method of Reaching Decisions," in S. B. Laughlin, ed., *Beyond Dilemmas* (Philadelphia, 1937). Martin Fausold's book, *The Presidency of Herbert C. Hoover* (Lawrence, Kansas, 1984), emphasizes Quaker influences on Hoover's term in the White House.

3. David Burner, "Before the Crash: Hoover's First Eight Months in the Presidency," in Martin L. Fausold and George T. Mazuzan, eds., *The Hoover Presidency: A Reappraisal* (Albany, 1974); report of Charles J. Rhoads to Senator William King, January 18, 1933, file 200, Taylor/Gates Collection, HHPL; Jane Addams to Lawrence Richey, May 29, 1929; Hoover to Jane Addams, September 9, 1929; Addams to Hoover, September 28, 1929—all in "Amnesty, 1929," box 63; Hoover to W. D. Mitchell, April 23, 1929; Mitchell to Hoover, August 23, 1929—both in "Justice, 1929—A and B," Presidential Papers, HHPL; Hoover to W. D. Mitchell, October 18, 1930, box 63, Presidential Papers, HHPL; *New York World*, May 9 and June 27, 1929; *Time* 11 (July 8, 1929): 14; *New Republic* 59 (July 10, 1929): 19; box 102, Presidential Papers, HHPL.

4. Quoted in Frederick B. Tolles, *Meeting House and Counting House* (Chapel Hill, N.C., 1948), pp. 54–55.

5

Neo-institutional History and the Understanding of Herbert Hoover

Ellis W. Hawley

We have learned a good deal about Herbert Hoover in recent years. New biographies have clarified what he said and did during a long public career. New monographs, articles, and dissertations have told us about the programs and agencies through which he tackled a whole variety of national problems. New and more persuasive characterizations of his personality have appeared, and new research has made possible a reconstruction of his "forgotten years" and "forgotten progressivism."[1] In the future, moreover, we seem likely to learn still more. The scholarship emerging from recent seminars and conferences is now being published, other studies are under way, and the rich holdings at the Hoover Presidential Library and the Hoover Institution continue to be tapped.

The more we have learned about Hoover, however, the less certain we have become about his role in U.S. history. In our earlier state of ignorance there was substantial agreement on this. He belonged, so we thought, among the champions of laissez-faire individualism, a figure who might be condemned as an outmoded ideologue or praised as a great libertarian, but one who was clearly outside of and opposed to the movements for an enlarged government, rule-making by bureaucrats, or collectivization of society. Recent scholarship has made this view increasingly untenable. It has revealed a man who was indeed the author of *American Individualism*, yet who was at the same time closely associated with expanding governmental agencies, bureaucratic growth, and new forms of collective action. If his story was intertwined with that of antistatism, it also seemed intertwined with the stories of how economic management, collective bargaining, and expanding welfare services became parts of the U.S. system.

A growing discrepancy seems to exist between the documented evidence and the conceptual framework that has been used to order and understand twentieth-century U.S. history. In other words, here is an important political figure acting in ways that make him neither a laissez-faire individualist nor a champion of welfare statism. Efforts to deny this, it seems to me, have become increasingly tortured and unconvincing. It will not do to see his departures from individualism as being reluctant concessions to powerful political enemies. Although this may explain certain moves in 1931 and 1932, there was no such pressure in the 1920s. Nor will it do to move him into the other category of historical action and make him a proto–New Dealer working to lay the foundations of a modern welfare state. There is too much evidence of a genuine antistatism manifesting itself in actions that are irreconcilable with this reading of his career.

I would strongly suggest that the typical categories of historical action obscure much that was important in shaping modern American life. The confusion about Hoover is part of a larger confusion stemming from the inability of our conceptual framework to order and make sense of new research discoveries; not surprisingly, recent years have witnessed numerous efforts to fit the evidence into new conceptualizations of our national past. The 1950s brought consensus history, with its emphasis on a national ideology that worked to realize both conservative and progressive ends. That decade also brought pluralistic or interest-group history, which was adapted largely from the models in vogue in political science. In addition, there were new efforts to apply a Marxist analysis, and accompanying these kinds of model-building have been works stressing the centrality of such phenomena as the status revolution, ethnic divisions, and traumatized psyches. Each of these has served as the centerpiece in new schemes for ordering the past and trying to integrate what has been recently learned into a new and more satisfying synthesis.[2]

Some of this reconceptualization, moreover, has been reflected in reinterpretations of Hoover's public career. There have been, in particular, efforts to fit him into a neo-Marxist analysis, seeing him not as a laissez-faire ideologue or as a proto–New Dealer but as the flower of a sophisticated corporate gentry, trying to overcome the systemic contradictions in a maturing capitalism.[3] There have also been efforts to fit him into a framework of changing reformism—seeing him, in this case, as an outmoded reform figure who applied a kind of reformism that was at least a quarter century behind the kind needed and demanded.[4] Among those impressed with psychohistory, or the shaping power of subcultures, or the myths and symbols revealed by cultural analysis, there have been still other efforts at reinterpretation. Hooverian actions and policies, as analyzed in these quarters, have been related less to objective social conditions than to the satisfaction of psychic needs, the easing of cultural strains, or the sense of duty and propriety instilled by Quaker nurture.[5]

In my judgment, however, such reinterpretations have not provided satisfying syntheses of the new knowledge about Hoover. They ignore or obscure much that has been learned about his social perceptions, his modernism, and his technocratic turn of mind. Like the efforts to keep him within the older conceptual framework, they miss much of the social context in which Hoover operated and with it much of the institutional and ideological development that gave his career meaning and significance. He cannot be understood, I would argue, without these missing pieces; it is to those who have been supplying them that we must eventually look for a more satisfying synthesis of current knowledge.

My thesis in this paper, in other words, is that the advance of a new institutional history and the understanding of Hoover's historical role and public career have been and are likely to remain mutually reinforcing. It is this that I hope to demonstrate. By way of doing so, I want to look in turn at the nature and discoveries of this neo-institutional history, the new analytical framework that it has been developing, and how our growing knowledge about Hoover, when fitted into this framework, does become more comprehensible.

By neo-institutional history I mean that body of recent scholarship concerned with America's move from a society of independent capitalists and traditional communities to one ordered by new bureaucratic and associational mechanisms.[6] It has focused, in particular, on the development of modern administrative and interest-group structures, the emergence of a new class of salaried professionals, and the unfolding and implementation of a new managerial culture. Unlike earlier conceptualizations of the more recent past, this new scholarship has recognized that these developments were genuine historical forces and not merely agencies through which entrenched interests and democratizing reformers continued their struggle for power. Furthermore, the scholarship has seen these developments as stemming less from the impulses of monopoly capital or the reactions of a suffering and outraged populace than they did from concerns about social and market disorder, a desire for greater system and predictability, or efforts to eliminate obstacles in the way of technical progress and economic growth. Behind them lay the breakdown of an older set of social institutions, and in operation they have been the prime shapers of modern America. They have given us an organizational society resistant both to upper class direction and to that emanating from market activity, electoral politics, and parliamentary deliberations.

For this body of scholarship the term "neo-institutional" seems appropriate in three differing senses. First, such studies have emerged from a new interest in institutional development that is set apart in time from an earlier wave of this kind of history. Second, the studies are concerned chiefly with a new kind of institution providing a new kind of social order, not with the history of institutions as a whole. Third, they reflect a new orientation differing markedly from that of an earlier institutionalism; their focus is on social development, not, as was the case with the older studies, on the evolution of governmental bodies toward higher degrees of liberalism. Neo-institutional studies owe their insights much less to lawyers, politicians, and political scientists than they do to organizational sociology, especially as that discipline had developed by the 1950s. They also have links to management studies, administrative history, and institutional economics, but their greatest and most direct debt, both conceptually and analytically, is to a sociological orientation rooted in Max Weber and Emile Durkheim and developed along different lines by such scholars as Talcott Parsons, Robert Presthus, and Robert K. Merton.[7] They have sought, above all, to illuminate the historic roots of an order being revealed through sociological inquiries, and in doing this they have attempted to integrate the history of power, culture, and economic activity into an enlarged conception of social history.

For current purposes we need not review these neo-institutionalist works in detail, nor do we need a detailed accounting of the past as they have reconstructed it. It does seem necessary, however, before narrowing our focus to the Hoover era and Hoover's public career, to note briefly how such studies have broken down the older categories of historical action, brought out the importance of what was once treated as ancillary or peripheral, and helped us to make sense of unexpected research discoveries.

One damaging blow against the older framework has come from the demonstration that businessmen and business groups have often been the forces behind modern state building rather than the intransigent and negative opponents of it. Another has come from the discovery of a growing managerial and professional culture that often exerts an influence over public policy far greater than that coming from popular protests or upheavals.[8] A third blow, perhaps the most damaging of all, has come from a showing that modern America has been created less through governmental action than through organizational activity in the private sector. This, to be sure, had to break through and accommodate itself to a legal framework reflecting pre-organizational ideals.[9] Having done this, however, it became not only the provider of a new social structure but the principal explanation behind new forms of governmental activity.

Such discoveries have greatly reduced the explanatory power of a history organized around lawmaking, popular revolts, or business-government conflict. Indeed, it now appears that this kind of history has obscured or misrepresented some of the most important forces and processes shaping modern America. While making this plain, the neo-institutionalists have also been developing an alternative framework that does allow us to see the roles played by these major forces and processes. In this framework, as perhaps its major defining characteristic, the focus is less on lawmakers, protesters, and would-be monopolists and more on those engaged in organizational and rationalizing activities, the accommodation of these to hostile elements in the culture, and the creation around them of legitimizing and prescriptive ideologies.

More specifically, the neo-institutionalists see the core of modern American society as having arisen from three interrelated and interacting processes. From the first of these have come new kinds of primary organizations that engage in activities such as implementing and administering new systems of production, marketing, and politicking. It has brought forth, in particular, new and much more bureaucratized forms of the business corporation, the trade union, the professional association, the social-service agency, the agricultural cooperative, and the organized pressure group. The second process has revolved around efforts to create another kind of organization, one that could perform coordinating or liaison functions that were no longer being effectively performed by the market or by traditional constraints and folkways. Out of this came interorganizational associations and federations, new kinds of governmental agencies, and such new forms of technocratic authority as the "think tank" or the council of experts. The third has been concerned with developing new agencies of socialization that are designed to reduce cultural strain or lag and to equip individuals with the skills, outlooks, and values appropriate to a modern organizational order. It has been manifested particularly in certain kinds of educational reform, media activity, and public-relations work.[10]

It is from the timing of these organizational processes, moreover, that the neo-institutionalists derive a new succession of historical periods. Initially, as the organizational revolution began, most of the activity was of the primary sort. By the 1910s it was moving into a second phase, concerned now with coordination, liaison, and socialization. This was a transition greatly speeded up by the war experience of 1917 and 1918, and while some of this new activity involved an expansion of government, the great bulk of it, initially, sought to develop private coordinating bodies, corporative structures, and extragovernmental authorities. The visions of social coordination that dominated the years from 1915 to 1935 were modeled essentially after the internal structures of the corporation, trade association, professional society, or civic federation. They were not visions of a planning or regulatory state or of direction by some new political elite. It was only after the resulting structures failed to prevent and deal effectively with the Great Depression that the country moved into a third period of organizational development, one in which the New Deal's broker, compensatory, and welfare state became a major feature of the coordinating and socializing apparatus.[11]

It was along this path, then, as the neo-institutionalists see it, that modern America took shape. Once we recognize this, we can begin to see the social context and historical developments that give meaning and significance to Hoover's career. In part the Hoover era was a time of extraordinary war measures followed by a "normalcy" period, during which politicians and social leaders reasserted the social value of self-interest and individual pursuits of gain and happiness. More significantly, it was also a period of organizational ferment and creativity, seeking better mechanisms through which individual initiatives could be translated into social good and making a new place for master organizers and administrators who could allegedly devise and build the needed mechanisms. Mixed with the demands for governmental retrenchment were efforts to create a new kind of organizational leadership and discipline. At the center of such efforts, heading public and private agencies engaged in this organizational task, was a remarkable group of business figures, most of whom had made fortunes in the early twentieth century, emerged as "industrial statesmen" and war managers during the Wilson administration, and then stepped into the roles of social saviors and engineers of social progress. For this phase of America's organizational revolution, they were the theoreticians and pioneers.

It remains an open question whether or not the designs and activities of this group should be seen merely as a transitional stage in the coming of the New Deal system. The New Deal won support largely because the structures developed during the Hoover era could not meet the social expectations they had aroused. But the most effective capitalist societies of recent years, so a number of writers have argued, have been those moving away from statist regulation and relying more on corporative structures and components.[12] It may be that our own society will be forced in this direction, and if such is the case the organization building of the Hoover period may eventually be seen not only as paving the way for that of the New Deal years but also as a kind of premature foreshadowing of modern America's organizational future.

With this framework in mind, then, let us now return to what recent research has been telling us about the life and career of Herbert Hoover. It has, as noted before, disclosed an important political figure who cannot be forced into the molds of laissez-faire conservative, progressive welfare statist, or alienated radical. Nor is there much gained by turning to the more recent categories of interest-group spokesman, status-minded activist, class-conscious sophisticate, or ethnic-group representative. Although those who fit these categories may have shared certain qualities with Hoover, he does not, on the basis of what we now know, fit well into any one of them. Where he seems to belong, increasingly so as research continues, is in those categories of historical action that neo-institutionalists have been identifying as crucial to the shaping of modern American society.

To begin with, Hoover was a part of the organizational society's "new class" of technocratic professionals, especially of those within this group who developed a degree of social consciousness and formulated social designs in which technocratic organizations served liberal and moral ends. He was also part of the continuing organizational process. He became, as his career advanced, a master organizer, administrator, and rationalizer, first of business corporations and other primary structures, and then increasingly of structures concerned with interorganizational coordination, intergroup liaison, and integrative socialization. In addition, he became a leading figure in efforts to bring the legal framework—especially the antitrust and industrial relations laws—into line with the new organizational and managerial ideals. Of the Wilsonian war managers engaged in postwar organizational activity, Hoover was the one who remained at the center of public life, built a new structure of guides and aids for economic decisionmakers, and committed governmental resources to the task of filling institutional and organizational gaps. He was not only a member of this central group but perhaps the central figure in it.

All of this could be spelled out in considerable detail. For our purposes, however, it should suffice to recall briefly the succeeding phases of Hoover's career, noting at each stage how he fits into the categories and processes that have been identified, and how these in turn illuminate and give meaning to much that has seemed puzzling or incomprehensible. In particular, let us look first at the nature of his prewar career and then at the war experience, the secretary of commerce years, and the presidential performance.

By 1914 Hoover was a well-known figure in the world of international business. Yet he cannot be understood as merely another self-made man of the kind idealized by Horatio Alger or even of the kind that Quakers were wont to admire. He had achieved prominence not so much as a merchant, manufacturer, financier, or philanthropist, but rather as the supplier of new professional services, first of a technical or administrative sort and then increasingly of the kind needed to devise and install new systems of corporate organization and management. He had become, in essence, an organizational rather than a mining engineer, a pioneer both in providing this kind of professional expertise and in developing the institutions through which it was delivered. Like a number of others engaged in such work, he had come to think of himself as having insights and skills that might be used to fashion or modernize other kinds of economic and social units. He and others like him, as they saw it, could become social engineers, helping to bring order and rationality to the organizational and associational activities going on around them; on occasion he had already involved himself in efforts to design new community structures, new mechanisms of social integration, and new disciplines for a creative but unruly individualism.[13]

It was with this preparation, then, that Hoover became a war manager or, more precisely, an organizational engineer in the service of a warring nation. He joined a new group of state-supported organization builders, people who moved into the institutional gaps created by war exigencies and sought to fill these with new planning, coordinating, and administrative structures. With this group he shared not a common personality, upbringing, or political allegiance but rather a common sense of elite responsibility, a common vision of how war needs were to be identified and met, and a common core of experience in organizational engineering and in securing concerted action from holders of private power.[14] Something approaching an elite corps of organizational developers and middlemen quickly emerged, not as the cream of an expanding civil service but as a directorate drawn from those portions of the private sector that the Wilson administration considered to be progressive, forward looking, and socially concerned. It was America's substitute for the high officialdoms, the party directorates, or the modernizing aristocracies that emerged at the centers of other organizational societies, and once formed it became an important part of the context within which Hoover's subsequent career would unfold.

Through the work of such men, moreover, a new kind of bureaucratic structure was created in 1917 and 1918, a structure that was part private and part public, but with the public or governmental side substantially distinct from the regular agencies of government. On this public side, the characteristic organization was the commodity division, which was technically a governmental agency yet was staffed mostly with people who were on temporary leave from positions in the private sector. On the other side of the apparatus, the characteristic organization was the industrial authority or war service committee, which was chosen typically through the industry's associational machinery yet endowed with regulatory power that had been delegated to it by the corresponding commodity division. In this new setup, federations like the Chamber of Commerce and the American Federation of Labor also assumed governmental duties. They became the certifiers and coordinators of private governmental units. Moving into another kind of coordinating role were a number of professional orders, especially the engineering societies and various scientific associations.[15]

The outcome was sometimes called war socialism, but the more appropriate label, as some contemporaries recognized, was war guildism or war corporatism.[16] Out of the wartime organizational experience, both in the United States and abroad, came movements to shift policy-making power from parliamentary institutions and governmental regulators to associational networks and corporative bodies arising out of the private sector. In this way, it was argued, capitalist societies could deal with social fragmentation and move toward the realization of progressive ideals without undergoing either socialist revolutions or some form of statist regimentation.[17]

In the forging and operation of the war system, Herbert Hoover was a key figure. He was not only the man in charge of organizing the foods sector but was also a major influence on the way that the rest of the system was organized. In the subsequent debate over how much of the system should be retained and adapted to peacetime needs and purposes, Hoover quickly emerged with organizational formulas attuned to the competing desires for social order and entrepreneurial freedom. While insisting that governmental or monopolistic encroachments on economic liberty must be rolled back and held in check, he became the champion of a new associationalism and a new kind of government, which taken together would allegedly provide the ordered freedom needed for continued economic and social progress. The associations would provide the machinery for securing constructive cooperation, curbing abuses of entrepreneurial freedom, and allowing trained professionals, especially engineers, social scientists, and planners of one sort or another, to reduce the irrational components in economic and social behavior. The government, as Hoover proposed to use it, would function not as a regulator but as an aide in developing the new private mechanisms, helping them to acquire a system of national consciousness and mobilizing them to deal with unforeseen developments.[18] In one sense it was a version of the "midwife state" found in corporative political theory. In another sense it was a state that looked much like Hoover's engineering firm or his wartime operations in Washington.

Much of Hoover's subsequent activity is best seen as an effort to realize the organizational visions set forth in his speeches of 1919, 1920, and 1921. As secretary of commerce he continued to see himself as the nation's organizational engineer, and as such he became deeply involved in three kinds of activity, all of which fit well into the reconstruction of this period now emerging in neo-institutional studies. He sought, first of all, to make the commerce secretariat into a kind of economic presidency, equipped with the tools needed for associational nurture and engineering. At the same time he worked energetically to block the initiatives of those who would deal with disorder and irrationality through statist controls or public ownership, and, while carrying on these campaigns, he made the Commerce Department the most active of the public and private agencies engaged in building new units of private government.

In part, Hoover's transformation of the commerce secretariat proceeded through bureaucratic annexations, personnel changes, and the assertion of bureaucratic hegemony over other departments and agencies. However, it is also important to note his success in taking over war-inspired organizational initiatives and putting together a new bureaucratic structure that was similar to the one that had existed during the war. Once again he developed a parallel structure of commodity divisions and industrial committees, the former staffed with individuals on temporary leave from the private sector and the latter entrusted with a variety of administrative duties. Once again linkages between group federations, professional orders, and this new "economic presidency" were to provide the machinery through which system-wide coordination could be improved. The new bureaucracy, as Hoover had developed it by 1928, was not the Peace Industries Board envisioned by some of the war managers in 1918 and 1919, nor was it the National Recovery Administration that would be established in 1933. Yet it bore marked resemblances to both, and it now appears to stand squarely in the middle of historical processes linking the two together and leading on to the organizational developments of the later 1930s.[19]

While developing this new bureaucratic structure, Hoover was also carrying on his celebrated battles with the antitrust authorities, the McNary-Haugenites, and the champions of federal development in the Tennessee Valley. In his terminology these groups were organization wreckers, price fixers, and socialists, all threatening the mechanisms and initiatives that could give Americans both liberty and progress. Yet it now seems clear that this was less a battle between reformers and standpatters than it was a battle between competing visions of governmental and social activism. The new bureaucracy was intended not only to protect work that was going on in the private sector but also to organize progressive solutions to such problems as monopolistic abuse, agricultural maladjustment, and misallocation of resources. It was to be an instrument of social change as well as social defense, and its use for the former purpose did produce a whole range of historical phenomena that the older understandings of Hoover have been unable to comprehend.

In the early 1920s, for example, these Hooverian initiatives produced an ongoing "war against waste," functioning primarily through simplification conferences, publicly endorsed standardization agreements, and cooperative conservation programs. They also produced a new system of commercial intelligence and trade promotion, an expanding network of statistical and informational exchanges, and new schemes for organizing labor participation and agricultural adjustment. In addition, they produced new rationalizing agencies for malfunctioning industries or other troubled areas of intergroup relations. At the macroeconomic level, they produced the federal government's first peacetime efforts to organize full employment and develop the planning agencies and countercyclical compensators needed for continuing stability.[20] Such initiatives are hardly compatible with the older conceptions of a rigid laissez-faire ideologue, nor can they really be understood as the frenetic activity of a man driven by the compulsions of his psyche and nurture. They were addressed to the real problems of an organizational order, and they seem best understood as the work of a man who had become a commanding, if not heroic, figure in the world of organizational engineering and who was fully confident that this world, and not those of politics or traditional entrepreneurship, held the keys to ordered liberty and continued national progress.[21]

In the later 1920s there was less urgency behind these Hooverian initiatives and, generally speaking, more of a tendency to gloss over their failings and weaknesses. To a greater degree than before, Hoover became the defender of an existing system rather than the would-be initiator of a new one. Yet even in this period, the initiatives were both numerous and important. They were, in part, responsible for a growing body of trade practice codes, for new welfare adhocracies concerned with such areas as child health and home ownership, and for a variety of efforts to deal with "sick," "chaotic," or "problem" areas of the economic system.[22] The initiatives moved into the area of "play" as well as work, seeking to develop new organizational mechanisms through which the use of leisure time could be rationally adapted to both individual and social needs.[23] Finally, by quickly occupying the organizational vacuums opened by natural disasters, in particular the Mississippi flood, Hoover and his corps of organizers put together an emergency mobilization and coordination system that was praised both for its efficiency and effectiveness and for its compatibility with national values and ideals.²⁴

In large measure, Hoover's activities as president can also be seen as basic extensions of the three kinds of activity in which he had been engaged as secretary of commerce. First, there was an effort to restructure the whole executive branch along lines resembling the commerce secretariat of the 1920s. It was an effort reflected not only in schemes of administrative reform but also in designs for a public-private directorate attached to the White House, in new presidential agencies charged with filling organizational vacuums, and in a new emphasis on equipping the presidency for organizational engineering and the securing of concerted private initiatives rather than for legislative, party, or mass leadership. Second, there was the continued production of organizational machinery in the private sector, much of which was concerned with promoting economic recovery or relieving depression distress, but some of it with providing new marketing structures for farmers, new rationalizing instruments for problem industries, new credit systems for borrowers, and new ordering mechanisms for the delivery of social services. Third and finally, there was the continuing line of battle against antitrusters, statists, and advocates of public ownership. This had become a line of intensifying conflict that reflected, in particular, mounting struggles over who was to fill the organizational vacuums opened by the depression and left open by the failure of Hoover's recovery programs.²⁵

For Hoover, of course, there would be no second term in the White House, and it was only in peripheral assignments that he would ever again serve as his nation's organizational engineer. The Great Depression marked the end of his role as a central figure in America's organizational development, just as it marked the beginning of a coordinating structure relying more heavily on statist institutions and governmental power. Clearly, however, in the light of what we now know, he cannot be understood as the kind of "rugged individualist" who resisted both the coming of an organizational society and the coming of a regulatory and welfare state. He belongs instead at the very core of the processes through which America moved from a society of independent capitalists and traditional communities to one ordered by bureaucratic institutions and collective bargaining. Had he succeeded in filling the organizational vacuums opened by the depression, as he had succeeded in filling others during his stints as corporate medicine man, war manager, and secretary of commerce, he might have remained at the center of these processes and perhaps steered them onto different paths.

Thus, a satisfactory understanding of what has recently been learned about Herbert Hoover must begin not with his antistatism, his psychological makeup, or his Quaker upbringing, but rather with a fuller knowledge of the changing social context that gave his career meaning and, in a sense, determined the problems with which he would be concerned, the roles he would play, and the ideals he would seek to realize. It is this knowledge that neo-institutionalist studies have been providing. Once Hoover is fitted into what they have been telling us about the making of modern America—that is, once it is recognized that he was, in succession, one of the new breed of organizational engineers, one of the select group of business figures who emerged from the private sector to become Woodrow Wilson's war managers, and one of the war chieftains who subsequently stepped into the role of social savior and engineer of social progress—then much that has puzzled us about his ideology, behavior, and political outlook begins to fall into place. In these respects he was strikingly similar to other first-generation organizational engineers, other Wilsonian war managers, and other New Era engineers of social progress, which suggests that he can be understood as a variant within an evolving and changing social type. It is chiefly by ignoring the historical importance of these groups and trying to connect Hoover to the more customary categories, particularly to conceptions of self-made men, Republican standpatters, or progressive reformers, that the present state of confusion has been reached.

This is not to say, however, that Hoover was entirely shaped by the social roles that he played, nor is it to say that his early years have no importance in explaining his later behavior. In his upbringing, I think, are clues as to why he was among those who filled the social roles identified above, why he deviated in various ways from others who filled similar roles, and why, in the face of failure and criticism, he became increasingly rigid and doctrinaire. But to see Hoover's career as an extension of the personality developed in his childhood strikes me not only as a gross distortion of his capacity for subsequent socialization but also as an exaggeration of the individual autonomy and power that he came to enjoy. Furthermore, to see the ideology that Hoover embraced and the kind of initiatives that he undertook as being basic manifestations of Quakerism or of childhood insecurity strikes me as an even greater fallacy. Other Quakers and other orphans did not develop in this way, and others who became "Wilsonian statesmen" and "social engineers" and who embraced essentially the same ideals and values and undertook essentially the same kind of initiatives, were, for the most part, neither uprooted orphans nor products of Quaker homes and meeting houses.[26]

My conviction is that the basic patterns and attributes of Hoover's career must be understood through sociological as opposed to psychological or subcultural analysis. My expectations, for reasons I have tried to explain, are that the advance of neo-institutional history and the understanding of Herbert Hoover and his career will continue to be linked and will remain mutually reinforcing.

NOTES

1. The two path-breaking biographies have been Joan Hoff-Wilson, *Herbert Hoover: Forgotten Progressive* (Boston, 1975), and David Burner, *Herbert Hoover: A Public Life* (New York, 1979). For other recent works, see Robert H. Zieger, "Herbert Hoover: A Reinterpretation," *American Historical Review* 81 (October 1976): 800–810; the bibliographical essay in Hoff-Wilson's biography; and Ellis Hawley, "Herbert Hoover and Modern American History: Fifty Years After," in *Congressional Record* 126 (February 27, 1980): 1927–32.

2. For a good discussion of recent efforts at reconceptualization, see John M. Carroll, "Reassessing America's Past," in Charles Bussey et al., eds., *America's Heritage in the Twentieth Century* (St. Louis, 1978).

3. See, in particular, William A. Williams, "The Central Role of Herbert Hoover in the Maturation of an Industrial Gentry," in his *Contours of American History* (Cleveland, 1961).

4. See, for example, Larry Grothaus, "Herbert Hoover and Black Americans," and Roger Corley, "Hoover's Judicial Appointments" (Papers given at the 1980 meeting of the Missouri Valley History Conference, Omaha, Nebraska). See also Albert U. Romasco, *The Poverty of Abundance* (New York, 1965).

5. See, for example, Kent Schofield, "The Public Image of Herbert Hoover," *Mid-America* 51 (October 1969): 278–93; Gerald Nash's essay in J. Joseph Huthmacher and Warren I. Susman, eds., *Herbert Hoover and the Crisis of American Capitalism* (Cambridge, 1973); David Burner, "Quaker in the White House," Hoover Seminar Papers, Herbert Hoover Presidential Library (hereafter cited as HHPL); and James P. Johnson, "Herbert Hoover: The Orphan as President," *U.S.A. Today* 108 (September 1979): 61–62.

6. See Louis Galambos, "The Emerging Organizational Synthesis in Modern American History," *Business History Review* 44 (Autumn 1970): 279–90; Robert D. Cuff, "American Historians and the Organizational Factor," *Canadian Review of American Studies* 4 (Spring 1973): 19–31; John Higham et al., *History* (Englewood Cliffs, N.J., 1965), pp. 230–32; Edwin J. Perkins, ed., *Men and Organizations* (New York, 1977); Stephen E. Ambrose, ed., *Institutions in Modern America* (Baltimore, 1967); and Jerry Israel, ed., *Building the Organizational Society* (New York, 1972). Key works in the emergence of such scholarship have been Samuel P. Hays, *Response to Industrialism* (Chicago, 1957); Alfred D. Chandler, *Strategy and Structure* (Cambridge, Mass., 1962); Robert H. Wiebe, *The Search for Order* (New York, 1967); and Louis Galambos, *Competition and Cooperation* (Baltimore, 1966).

7. Frequently used and cited have been such works as Robert K. Merton et al., eds., *Reader in Bureaucracy* (Glencoe, Ill., 1952); Talcott Parsons, "A Sociological Approach to the Theory of Organizations," *Administrative Science Quarterly* (June 1956): 63–85; Robert V. Presthus, *The Organizational Society* (New York, 1962); and W. Lloyd Warner, ed., *The Emergent American Society* (New York, 1967). See also Lewis A. Coser, ed., *The Idea of Social Structure: Papers in Honor of Robert K. Merton* (New York, 1975).

8. See especially such works as Robert Wiebe, *Businessmen and Reform* (Cambridge, Mass., 1962); Samuel P. Hays, *Conservation and the Gospel of Efficiency* (Cambridge, Mass., 1959); K. Austin Kerr, *American Railroad Politics, 1914–1920* (Pittsburgh, 1968); Samuel Haber, *Efficiency and Uplift* (Chicago, 1964); and Gerald D. Nash, *United States Oil Policy, 1890–1964* (Pittsburgh, 1968).

9. The influence of the antitrust framework is stressed in Alfred D. Chandler, "The Managerial Revolution in International Perspective" (Paper delivered at the 1979 meeting of the Conference on the History of American Public Policy, Harvard Business School), and in Philippe Schmitter and Donald Brand, "Organizing Capitalists in the United States" (Paper delivered at the 1979 meeting of the American Political Science Association, Washington, D.C.).

10. See Alfred D. Chandler and Louis Galambos, "The Development of Large-Scale Economic Organizations in Modern America," *Journal of Economic History* 30 (March 1970): 201–17.

11. Ibid. See also Ellis W. Hawley, "The New Deal and Business," in John Braeman et al., eds., *The New Deal: The National Level* (Columbus, Ohio, 1975).

12. See, for example, Ezra F. Vogel, *Japan as Number One* (Cambridge, Mass., 1979); Andrew Shonfield, *Modern Capitalism* (New York, 1965); G. Lehmbruch, "Liberal Corporatism and Party Government," *Comparative Political Studies* 10 (1977): 91–126; and Frederick Pike and Thomas Stritch, eds., *The New Corporatism,* (Notre Dame, Ind., 1974).

13. See Burner, *Herbert Hoover: A Public Life,* chapters 2, 3, and 4.

14. For some perceptive insights into the nature of the group, see Robert D.

Cuff, "We Band of Brothers—Woodrow Wilson's War Managers," *Canadian Review of American Studies* 5 (Fall 1974): 135–48.

15. On the war bureaucracy, see Robert D. Cuff, *The War Industries Board* (Baltimore, 1973); Burton Kaufman, *Efficiency and Expansion* (Westport, Conn., 1974); and Frederic L. Paxson, "American War Government," *American Historical Review* 26 (October 1920): 57–76. See also Murray N. Rothbard's provocative essay, "War Collectivism in World War I," in Ronald Radosh and Murray N. Rothbard, eds., *A New History of Leviathan* (New York, 1972).

16. See, for example, William Hard, "Socialistic Coal," *New Republic* 17 (November 16, 1918): 64–66.

17. See the essays in the *Revue Recherches* special issue on "Guerre, Fascisme, et Taylorisme" (September 1978).

18. See Ellis W. Hawley, "Herbert Hoover, the Commerce Secretariat, and the Vision of an 'Associative State,' 1921–1928," *Journal of American History* 61 (June 1974), 116–40. For Hoover's transition from Wilsonian war manager to one of Harding's "best minds," see Gary Dean Best, *The Politics of American Individualism: Herbert Hoover in Transition, 1918–1921* (Westport, Conn., 1975).

19. For a fuller description of how the department was expanded and reorganized, see Hawley, "Hoover, the Commerce Secretariat, and the Vision of an 'Associative State.'" See also Peri Arnold, "Herbert Hoover and the Department of Commerce: A Study of Ideology and Policy" (Ph.D. diss., University of Chicago, 1972).

20. In addition to the works cited above, see Carolyn Grin, "The Unemployment Conference of 1921: An Experiment in Cooperative National Planning," *Mid-America* 55 (April 1973): 83–107; Evan Metcalf, "Secretary Hoover and the Emergence of Macroeconomic Management," *Business History Review* 49 (Spring 1975): 60–80; Ellis W. Hawley, "Herbert Hoover and Economic Stabilization, 1921–1922," Hoover Seminar Papers, HHPL; Joan Hoff-Wilson, "Herbert Hoover's Agricultural Policies, 1921–1928," Hoover Seminar Papers, HHPL; Robert H. Zieger, "Herbert Hoover, the Wage Earner, and the New Economic System, 1919–1929," Hoover Seminar Papers, HHPL; and William Tanner, "Herbert Hoover and Standardization," National Endowment for the Humanities (NEH) Seminar Papers, HHPL.

21. For a perceptive analysis of Hoover's role in turning political questions into technical ones and thereby removing them from the older political arenas, see Peri Arnold, "Herbert Hoover and the Continuity of American Policy," *Public Policy* (Fall 1972): 525–44.

22. U.S. Commerce Department, *Trade Association Activities* (1927); "Five Years of the ACHA," American Child Health Association Papers, HHPL; "Better Homes and Decreased Costs," Building and Housing File, Commerce Section, Hoover Papers, HHPL; "Hoover as Secretary of Commerce," Commerce-Achievements File, Commerce Section, Hoover Papers, HHPL; Ellis W. Hawley, "Secretary Hoover and the Bituminous Coal Problem," *Business History Review* 42 (Autumn 1968): 253–70.

23. See Carl Krog, "Organizing the Production of Leisure: Herbert Hoover, Fishing, and Outdoor Recreation in the 1920s," NEH Seminar Papers, HHPL.

24. See Bruce A. Lohof, "Herbert Hoover, Spokesman of Humane Efficiency," *American Quarterly* 22 (Fall 1970): 690–700.

25. For an interpretation of the presidency along these lines, see Ellis W. Hawley, *The Great War and the Search for a Modern Order: A History of the American People and Their Institutions, 1917–1933* (New York, 1979), chapters 10, 11, and 12, and Ellis W. Hawley, "Herbert Hoover and American Corporatism," in Martin L. Fausold and George T. Mazuzan, eds., *The Hoover Presidency: A Reappraisal* (Albany, 1974).

26. Nor will the analogies sometimes drawn between the methods and concerns of Quakerism and those of Hooverism stand much scrutiny. The Hooverian conference, in its typical form, was not a meeting of elders, leading citizens, or people who listened to the promptings of their inner voices. It was a meeting essentially of the leaders or representatives of recognized interests and functional blocs, coming together to make social policy that they could implement through their organizations; it resembled not a Quaker meeting but rather the economic parliament, social council, and extragovernmental authority that were part of the corporative impulses of the period. Although Hoover did concern himself with matters in which Quakers had long taken an interest, such as the plight of Indians, blacks, prisoners, and underprivileged children, his solutions tended to be far more technocratic than Quakerly. They envisioned improvement less through social legislation or appeals to Christian duty and conscience than through the creation of new forms of organizational discipline that could serve both as character builders and as mechanisms for securing a more rational and more humane kind of social behavior. His attempted reforms in these areas were parts of larger schemes for organizing social evils away.

6

Herbert Hoover and the Two Great Food Crusades of the 1940s

Susan Estabrook Kennedy

Herbert Hoover's initial reputation in public life arose from his legendary success in feeding the victims of World War I. Already established as a successful consulting engineer, he had responded to overwhelming human need at the outbreak of the war and set up the Commission for Relief in Belgium to facilitate humanitarian responses to the dislocations of German occupation. From 1914 until the U.S. declaration of war in April 1917, Hoover administered a complex organization to raise funds, obtain food, and transport it to the needy. Along the way he negotiated and renegotiated with the warring governments, convincing them to permit his rescue operations. At the conclusion of the war, Hoover resumed international feeding with the American Relief Administration. During the 1920s, when he perceived need, he responded in the same fashion—in Russia from 1921 to 1923, for example, and again during the Mississippi floods of 1927.

These feeding, relief, and rescue operations made him one of the most beloved and admired men in the world. But that personal prestige was of small importance to Hoover, compared with the sense of satisfaction at having "saved the lives of 1,400,000,000 human beings, mostly women and children, who otherwise would have perished."[1]

In all of his rescue efforts, children represented Hoover's first concern. Orphaned himself by age ten, he showed a lifetime commitment to making sure that all children should have the opportunity to grow up with adequately nourished bodies and minds. In public life, his efforts may be seen in the White House Conference on Child Health and Protection; in private life, he and his wife, Lou Henry, engaged in countless hidden charities, providing for destitute families and educating needy youngsters. Each of Hoover's relief operations began with the concern for suffering children and then expanded to include mothers, other women, the aged, and, finally, able-bodied men.

However, Hoover's purpose stretched beyond mere feeding. He understood that the Four Horsemen of the Apocalypse rode together, and that Famine's grim companions could warp minds as well as bodies. Not often poetic, Hoover nevertheless printed this verse at the beginning of his great documentary study of his relief activities:[2]

> I am the stalking aftermath of all wars.
> Pestilence is my companion.
> Tumult and Revolution rise round my feet.
> We kill more than all of the guns.
> I breed fears and hates that bring to man more wars,
> From me comes no peace to mankind.
> My legacy is to Children of Famine—
> Stunted bodies and twisted minds.

The battle against starvation had critical long-term political and ideological aspects, since the hungry could not long defend themselves—or defend Freedom.

The outbreak of World War II in Europe in September 1939 immediately raised the relief question again. Within two weeks, in conversations with representatives of the Roosevelt administration, Hoover suggested centralizing all relief activities under a single agency, preferably the Red Cross. When invited to join the executive committee of the Red Cross, Hoover declared himself willing to accept only if the Red Cross would "take on the whole job," dealing with food, clothing, medicine, and other aspects of relief. Yet Norman Davis, head of the Red Cross, defined its role more narrowly, arguing that there was a fundamental difference between emergency relief—which had been the normal function of the Red Cross and which could be financed by private contributions—and the mass feeding and relief over an extended period which would require government financing. Hoover and Roosevelt's emissaries reached an impasse.[3]

To Hoover's mind, however, the job of civilian relief still needed to be done. If no one else would do it properly, he would—if he were asked. As early as September 16, 1939, the Polish government appealed for aid; Finland followed on December 3. Since Hoover estimated that the medical assistance of the Red Cross would assuage only 10 percent of the overall problem, he mobilized the same group that had formed the old Commission for Relief in Belgium and the American Relief Administration to handle food and clothing needs. The task of organization was made easier by the fact that men like Maurice Pate, Edgar Rickard, Perrin Galpin, Raymond Sawtelle, and William Hallam Tuck had remained together in the interwar period in a network of charitable and educational committees. Thus, the establishment of a functioning staff and headquarters organization became more a matter of adapting existing facilities to new needs than of beginning an entirely new operation.

Fund-raising and obtaining needed supplies at first seemed to present no problem. The exiled governments had adequate monies, supplemented by private contributions, to purchase whatever food they needed. Hoover also reckoned that the United States and other neutral nations produced sufficient surplus food to sell to them. Accordingly, Hoover and his colleagues organized the Commission for Polish Relief, Inc. on September 25, 1939, and the Finnish Relief Fund, Inc. on December 6, 1939.[4]

Nevertheless, the financial and organizational arrangements were not so simple. Hoover appealed to a variety of sources, such as newspapers and colleges, to establish relief funds, and asked governors to start statewide committees. A number of Democratic governors seemed reluctant to join his efforts, causing one columnist to speculate that perhaps they feared the re-emergence of a popular Herbert Hoover as a candidate in 1940.[5] At the same time, the press carried rumors that Hoover had refused an offer from FDR to become the general manager in charge of a centralized relief agency, precisely the organizational approach which Hoover had proposed and Roosevelt's messengers had rejected. But there had never been talk of Hoover heading such a group, and he resented the implication that he might be seeking a job from his successor. Hoover hastened to denounce those who would "poison the wells of charity" and affirmed his support of Norman Davis and the Red Cross.[6]

Behind the scenes, Davis and Hoover appeared to be in competition for relief funds. Publicly, they maintained that the two operations—Davis's Red Cross and Hoover's Polish and Finnish funds—drew on separate revenues and spent those monies for different things: the Red Cross for medical supplies and the Hoover groups for food and clothing. Privately, however, Davis tried to convince Hoover to transfer money from the Finnish Relief Fund to the Red Cross. "Don't send all your darn money over there," Davis said in a telephone conversation, "I want some of it." But Hoover believed that the increased revenues of the Red Cross as well as its $4 million earmarked for war emergency relief could adequately pay for whatever medical supplies Davis intended to send. Simultaneously, Hoover fretted over appeals from the Finns for money for arms and ammunition; he did not want his humanitarian efforts confused with Finnish attempts to prosecute the military aspects of the war.[7]

One area in which Hoover's relief campaign encountered no initial problem was in arranging delivery of food and clothing to Poland and Finland. Despite a British blockade the Chamberlain government, which lasted until May 1940, permitted relief shipments, and Germany granted immunity from submarine attack, provided that neutral vessels were used.[8]

In a limited sense, then, Hoover's relief for Poland and Finland in 1939 and 1940 could be counted a success. An important aspect of that success rested on Hoover's use of fund-raising speeches and rallies to remind Americans of the symbolism of Polish and Finnish freedom and independence, and to contrast them with Fascist and Communist rapacity. "The spirit of a great race does not die from oppression," he told a Pulaski Memorial Day audience in New York on October 11, 1939. "Poland is not dead. Poland will rise again." In an appeal for money for Finnish refugees on December 20, he recalled that "just 21 years ago this month the people of Finland had thrown off the Bolshevik yoke and established themselves as a free Republic." Yet, he concluded, "forces of primitive savagery have been unloosened upon the world," resisted only by the gallant Finns who, he said, constituted "a star illuminating the No Man's Land of civilization."[9]

If Hoover were to spearhead the drive to keep those heroic people alive, to nourish their children in order to ensure freedom in the next generation, he would have to expand his efforts in 1940, when Belgium, Luxembourg, the Netherlands, and Norway would add their calls for his help. Hoover would see that struggle as a great contest—not merely a contest between democratic peoples and totalitarian conquerors, but a contest between himself and Winston Churchill—a contest Hoover was not destined to win.

When the winter's Phony War gave way to the Lightning War of spring, bringing the devastation of Belgium, enormous refugee problems, and the fall of France, Hoover received appeals to extend relief activities to the Low Countries and responded by reviving the Commission for Relief in Belgium. As with the Polish and Finnish organizations, headquarters and staff were virtually in place at the outset, and the question of financing again seemed well in hand from funds of the fugitive governments augmented by charitable contributions. Sources of food also appeared to be a simple matter, and Hoover even believed that he could get a contribution of cereals from the Germans, since he had observed them stockpiling food during his 1938 European tour.[10]

If Hoover anticipated any problems at all, they would come from negotiations with the warring powers over delivery of the goods and distribution of relief supplies. In this new phase, Hoover used John Hartigan to lobby the Germans to permit relief operations. Hartigan later described his task as "walking a very thin chalk line and creating the impression of both distinctive objectivity and neutrality in negotiations," but even members of Hoover's group worried about Hartigan appearing too cordial to the Germans.[11] Meanwhile, Hugh Gibson worked in London with representatives of the Polish, Belgian, and Netherlands governments to persuade the British to allow relief materials to pass through the naval blockade which had been established to cut Germany off from the outside world.[12]

The fact that Winston Churchill had replaced Neville Chamberlain as prime minister of Great Britain made a significant difference in the deliberations, to Hoover's mind. Hoover bitterly described Churchill as "a militarist of the extreme school who held that the incidental starvation of women and children was justified if it contributed to the earlier ending of the war by victory," and he recalled that Churchill alone had opposed Belgian relief in World War I.[13] Over the next year, Hoover would come to link Franklin Roosevelt with Churchill as twin barriers to his relief plans.

During the summer of 1940, Hoover's agents hoped to convince the British of two key principles: that small tonnages of relief goods would not affect the blockade, and that airtight control of distribution would be possible to insure that the Germans would receive no military advantage from outside relief of the subject peoples.[14] Hoover himself joined the campaign in a press statement on August 11 in which he emphasized the monumental human need, called for relief "by a neutral nongovernmental organization as was the case in the first World War," and set out the conditions that would govern transport and distribution of relief, namely:[15]

> 1. That Germany agree: (a) To take none of the domestic produce of these people; (b) To furnish an equivalent of any food already taken; (c) To permit imports from Russia and the Balkan States; (d) To allow free passage of ships without attack; (e) To permit adequate control of

distribution by the organization, so as to enable it to assure that those guarantees are carried out.

2. The British to agree that ships carrying cargoes solely of food for these people should be allowed to pass their blockade so long as the guarantees are fulfilled.

Hoover felt considerable irritation that the section of his statement requiring German guarantees was not reported in the British press, and he believed that Churchill shamelessly misrepresented the case in his August 20 address in the House of Commons when he also ignored the promise to secure guarantees, implied that foods like milk could be used to manufacture munitions, and warned that German seizure of relief goods could prolong the war.[16] "It has been rightly said that truth is the first fatality of war," Hoover later observed, noting that it was sheer nonsense to claim that children's food could make armaments or that the Germans could seize more than a few hours' supply of food from the relief organization. But he refrained from public comment at the time, realistically judging that the middle of the Battle of Britain was hardly the propitious moment to air his caustic views.[17]

Moreover, the United States was about to enter the intensive phase of the 1940 presidential campaign, and Hoover hoped to avoid raising the relief issue as part of it. He believed that "Churchill's attitude was either approved or coached on by Washington," and he hoped that the replacement of the New Deal by a Republican administration would offer a more amenable situation at home when he revived his efforts. In the meantime, he intended to concentrate on building his organization.[18]

Hoover, however, did not have exclusive control over whether the debate would continue. British sympathizers took up the food issue in a press statement on October 6, which not only accused the Germans of removing food from conquered territories but scorned efforts by "private American citizens" to pressure the Allies to permit food ships to pass through the blockade, presumably to replenish supplies looted by the Nazis. Hoover privately contacted those who signed the statement, reiterated his plan, including the necessity for German guarantees, and stressed that it would not damage the British cause. Publicly, he emphasized the right of the Belgians, Dutch, Poles, and Norwegians to import food purchased with their own money and distributed under the supervision of the international organization.[19]

Meanwhile, Hoover continued to urge the opening of the blockade; he spoke to Lord Lothian, the British ambassador to the United States, on October 8. Contrary to Hoover's expectation, Lothian took a position very different from the official stand of his government. He not only acknowledged the need for relief but promised to plead the case of the Hoover group to Churchill when he returned to London within the week. On his return to Washington from London, however, the ambassador issued a flat rejection of the Hoover plan.[20]

Almost simultaneously, Hoover was forming a new relief organization. With the election past and FDR returned to the White House, Hoover moved to create the National Committee on Food for the Small Democracies, a vast organization to mobilize public opinion in favor of relief along the lines Hoover had proposed. Fourteen hundred prominent citizens served on the national body, including more than two hundred clergymen of fourteen denominations, two hundred educators, sixty journalists, and an impressive collection of former cabinet officers, ambassadors, governors, and military men. Parallel local committees were established in each of the states, with the broadest possible representation. The committees would not be relief organizations per se, but were intended to "raise a voice on behalf of the peoples of Finland, Norway, Holland, Belgium, and Central Poland so that agreements may be made by the German and British governments with a neutral organization" to protect the domestic food supply and to import supplemental supplies through the blockade in order to prevent starvation.[21]

With this propaganda arm behind him, Hoover was ready to press his case with the two belligerents. He knew that he needed an ironclad agreement with Germany,[22] and, at the same time, he needed a way to assure the British that they would not be hurt even if Germany were to violate its guarantee. Accordingly, in January 1941, Hoover decided to narrow the focus of his proposal to a test case: Belgium. Since local soup kitchens existed throughout the occupied democracies and lacked only food to be distributed, Hoover suggested that each month the Germans supply twenty-five thousand tons of cereals to those distribution centers, while another twenty thousand tons of meat and fats, condensed milk, and special foods for children be allowed through the British blockade. Local registration and rationing would ensure that the food went only to the needy. Hoover added that, if the imported food on hand in Belgium never exceeded ten thousand tons at any one time, the available supplies would constitute less than one day's supply for Germany, thus making it worthless for Germany to seize the small quantity of food; besides, if it did, it would gain virtually nothing from the violation except world contempt.[23]

The experiment still needed German and British cooperation, however. On January 30, 1941, the Belgian minister of foreign affairs tried unsuccessfully to convince the London government to permit the new plan. On February 4, Hoover himself presented it to the new ambassador in Washington, Lord Halifax, who argued that the responsibility for feeding the occupied peoples rested with Germany, that any food taken into the invaded area relieved pressure on Germany, that Britain would not lift the blockade, and that, in any case, Germany would never agree.[24]

Hoover kept up his efforts on two other fronts. On February 16 he addressed a mass meeting in Chicago, recalling the relief successes of World War I, detailing the "agonies of famine" about to strike winter-torn Europe, and explaining the terms of his latest proposal.[25]

At the same time his agents continued negotiations with Germany, and on February 26 they secured that government's agreement to permit an American relief group to operate in Brussels. Germany also pledged to refrain from "exportation or requisitioning any supplies furnished by the Hoover Commission or of equivalent domestic supplies" and offered to send bread, grains, and potatoes to Belgium. Hoover made copies of the agreement available to Hugh Gibson to present in London, and to the Belgian ambassador to give to the U.S. Department of State, which Hoover himself followed up in a meeting with Secretary Cordell Hull two days later. In Hoover's opinion, Hull appeared sympathetic or at least open-minded; but Under Secretary Sumner Welles more accurately reflected New Deal hostility to any relief operation under Hoover auspices.[26] The British responded by denouncing Germany, charging that adequate food surpluses existed within the areas of German occupation but that Germany refused to transport them to needy districts because the Nazis were using the means of transportation to carry troops and munitions in "the campaign against Britain." Hoover publicly challenged the assertion that adequate supplies existed in Europe, tried to offer the British a way out by suggesting that perhaps they had not been fully informed of his proposal, and repeated its details.[27] Privately, the British sent a representative to Hoover to emphasize that they regarded his proposals and propaganda efforts as anti-British, and Hoover's agents found the London government increasingly unwilling even to discuss the issue.[28]

Throughout the spring of 1941, Hoover and Hull exchanged long letters which produced no positive results. Finally, in June, Hull took the position that the responsibility for feeding rested with the Germans, since whatever shortages might exist were due to German removal of foodstuffs from the occupied areas.[29] Meanwhile, Hoover and the National Committee on Food for the Small Democracies continued their propaganda efforts. Hoover reasoned that a groundswell of American opinion would develop once the dire demographics of the current situation, and reminders of his World War I successes, could be presented to the people.[30] British opposition continued, now augmented by U.S. groups such as the Committee to Defend America by Aiding the Allies, and Fight for Freedom, Inc., as the food issue became inextricably entangled in the question of what the U.S. role should be in relation to Europe's war.[31]

Hoover himself had implied another sort of connection between the war and the relief problem from the beginning of his rescue activities in 1939. He constantly reminded audiences of the need to support freedom-loving nations and democratic governments in their struggles against totalitarianism. His early talks about Poland stressed the Communist menace, but he continued the rhetoric of democracy as Germany overran West European countries. Even the title of his national committee on Food for the Small Democracies underscored his essential point of view.[32]

As he continued to struggle to break the blockade in 1941, Hoover now encountered what, to him was the worst form of attack. Representatives of the very exiled governments he was trying to aid publicly denied that the European food situation was pressing, repudiated their requests for Hoover's good offices, accused him of taking the initiative himself, and charged that his attitude was pro-German. Hoover blamed Churchill and Roosevelt for putting pressure on the Belgians and tied each instance of rejection of him to a visit by a representative of that country to the U.S. Department of State, usually a conversation with Under Secretary Welles.[33]

Although he continued to collect and publicize evidence of overwhelming need by Belgian children and repeated his plan for a feeding experiment, Hoover was clearly beaten—as he had been virtually from the beginning. Several times aides hoped that he would close his campaign, and Hoover himself came to believe that the magnitude of the problem had grown too great for private efforts. With the attack on Pearl Harbor and the United States' official entry into the war, he suspended his own relief activities. When the Turks pierced the British blockade in 1942 to aid starving Greeks, Hoover privately tried to revive the cause of the small democracies, hoping that they might be fed under Swedish, Swiss, and Red Cross control; however, neither the Churchill nor the Roosevelt governments would agree.[34]

Hoover—out of power, lacking formal ties to his own government, and without even a sympathetic regime in Washington—had had little chance to press his relief plan successfully. He felt his illegitimacy deeply and tried to circumvent it by establishing a national propaganda group to exert pressure on behalf of his ideas. The lack of such a forum during the Great Depression must have taught him the potential value of that kind of ally. Nonetheless, in 1941 he and his supporters faced overwhelming odds, not only in antagonistic propaganda organizations but in the weight of the Roosevelt administration's philosophic, moral, and political commitment to the Churchill government. Hoover described his relief efforts during the Roosevelt years as "four years of frustration."[35] Small wonder, then, that he welcomed the end of that frustration when Harry Truman assumed the presidency and re-opened the doors of the White House to Herbert Hoover.

After elaborate negotiations, Truman and Hoover met in Washington on May 28, 1945. The president wanted to draw upon his predecessor's expertise as a food specialist,[36] but Hoover addressed such issues as Japan and the creation of a War Economic Council in addition to both the domestic and the European food situations. With regard to relief, Hoover pointed out that northwestern Europe faced a three-month food crisis until its fall harvest, and he recommended that the War Department be directed to control emergency feeding, since it had access both to food supplies and to means of transporting them. Following Hoover's suggestions, a million tons of food were delivered each month during the emergency.[37] Hoover personally wanted to avoid heading a relief operation at that point—partly to escape being regarded as a petitioner for a job, but primarily because he believed it was too late for a civilian agency to help.[38]

Hoover was once more available to the national administration, if not as a general adviser, at least in his old role as food expert. As such, he established a complementary working relationship with Secretary of Agriculture Clinton P. Anderson and urged that Anderson be given sufficient powers to institute a program of conservation in order to decrease domestic waste and increase the amount of food available for export to famine-ridden Europe and Asia.[39] Hoover publicly supported the Truman administration's February 1946 plea for voluntary food conservation in the United States,[40] but he became acutely aware of internal divisions on methods when he joined the Famine Emergency Committee the following month.

Hoover wanted to follow through on his offer to help Truman on food matters. Therefore, he interrupted a Florida trip to become honorary chairman of the Famine Emergency Committee. He would have preferred that power be lodged with the secretary of agriculture rather than in "a large and cumbersome committee" that would "sit around and give advice." Furthermore, the committee immediately divided on the best means to accomplish food conservation. On the one hand, Hoover, Anderson, and committee chairman Chester Davis urged Truman to pursue voluntary saving of food—for example, by asking the American people to reduce wheat consumption by 25 percent until Europe's next harvest. On the other hand, Herbert Lehman (who had just resigned as head of the United Nations Relief and Rehabilitation Administration [UNRRA] in protest over Truman's appointment of Hoover without consulting him) and Secretary of Commerce Henry Wallace pressed for the reintroduction of rationing, which had been abolished at the end of the war. Hoover caustically wondered what might happen during the two months it would take to print ration cards and re-establish rationing boards.[41]

Fortunately, Herbert Hoover's personal role in the great postwar food crusade did not become hopelessly mired in the swamp of domestic squabbles. He would soon be launched on an international venture much in keeping with his historic activities after World War I.

According to statistics gathered by U.S. Agriculture Department experts, the world food situation in 1946 was nothing short of catastrophic. UNRRA aid to Eastern Europe could not be expected to do more than 20 percent of the feeding job, if that, and Hoover expressed strong concern that so much of the effort was being expended in the Communist sector, to the apparent neglect of what he called "the seat of Western civilization."[42] The only other feeding source of note was the Combined Food Board, which consisted of the United States, Great

Britain, and Canada. However, Great Britain lacked surpluses to export, and even if the resources of the two other major surplus countries—Argentina and Australia—were added to the output of Canada and the United States, and if certain Scandinavian, East European, and African nations could be reclassified as "self-sufficient," the adjusted figures still left a world situation in which 313 million people would have to feed 1.4 billion. In cereals alone, the fifteen million tons available would fall eleven million short of the estimated requirements; fats would not come within three million tons of those needed; and the shortages of other foodstuffs could not even be calculated. In reviewing these figures with Dr. Dennis FitzGerald of the Department of Agriculture, who also served on the Combined Food Board, Hoover concluded that "it now appeared that we could not prevent mass starvation among over 800,000,000 people." Nevertheless, he was prepared to try.[43]

Hoover recommended to Truman that the president act immediately to establish a "solid world front in this fight against world disaster."[44] The State Department suggested an international conference in Washington, but Hoover argued against diplomatic delays and persuaded Truman to send a mission to Western Europe and perhaps even around the world to galvanize governments: the needy to reassess their requirements, and the surplus countries to conserve on domestic consumption and make exports available to the starving—even to those who had so recently been enemies. Truman, in turn, asked that Hoover take on the job.

Although he was 71 years old and spoke of his reluctance to leave his commitments to a variety of charitable and educational committees in the United States, Hoover impressed friends as energized by the prospect of the trip. This venture would have a legitimacy which he had not enjoyed in thirteen years: he would be traveling as the official representative of the president of the United States. Moreover, he would again be operating at the international level, where his personal prestige had not suffered the devastation of the domestic Great Depression, and where he could, for the duration of the trip, at least function relatively free of the restrictions of American partisan politics. Finally, he rapidly assembled an efficient, compatible group of companions, manifestly loyal to himself, to whom he could delegate critical parts of the investigation ahead. Dennis FitzGerald brought the latest food and agriculture data available through the U.S. Department of Agriculture. Veterans of Hoover's World War I relief activities included Hugh Gibson,

William Hallam Tuck, Perrin Galpin, and Maurice Pate; Gibson would handle logistics, Galpin local programs, and a relatively new colleague, Frank Mason, would deal with the press.[45]

As soon as news of the mission became public, representatives of foreign delegations clamored to meet with the man who had fed the world a generation earlier and who was again going to try to battle international famine. For the hectic weekend of March 9–11, the heads of virtually every European embassy in Washington paraded through his suite at the Mayflower Hotel, extending invitations to visit their countries and usually attempting to plead their case in advance. The Poles and Yugoslavs carefully balanced their invitations with conferences with their Communist-dominated home governments; by the end of the weekend, nearly everyone except the Soviets had climbed aboard the bandwagon of the Famine Survey Mission.

On March 17, 1946, Hoover and his companions left New York aboard a C-54 plane (playfully named the "Faithful Cow"). In this first major phase of their world journey, they would travel more than thirty-five thousand miles in fifty-seven days, visiting twenty-five countries and gathering information on another five. They would endure a pace of activity which exhausted the younger men and left them amazed at the stamina of the indestructible Hoover. He, however, was having a wonderful time, doing what he did best: coordinating a mind-boggling enterprise and waging war on the forces of famine, which he regarded as the root of so much political and social disaster.

Hoover's administrative talents and decisive efficiency governed the venture. At each stop, Hoover and his colleagues had arranged in advance for the U.S. embassy or military occupation forces to assemble the latest data on food requirements and availability. After a briefing by the American staff, members of the Famine Survey would meet with local agricultural and food ministers and technicians, conduct their own research through long-standing personal associations (many dating from the last war), check actual conditions in rationing agencies and public feeding institutions, and talk with representatives of labor or industry or other groups not directly involved with feeding.[46] Each man had a task; Maurice Pate, for example, specialized in the conditions of children and the aged. Occasionally, Hoover would send part of the team on a side trip to assess particular local situations, such as FitzGerald's flight to French North Africa to review the impact of the previous year's drought. These masses of information were digested on the spot, with Hoover and FitzGerald then trying to calculate what level of imports would be needed each month to sustain a daily minimum of 1,500 to 1,550 calories for each urban resident (on the assumption that farm people would usually hold back enough to feed themselves). Hoover would then discuss the proposal with local food officials, solicit their view on the estimates, but make no commitment until he had the opportunity to assess the larger picture.

In Paris, Rome, Geneva, Prague, Warsaw, Helsinki, Stockholm, Oslo, London, Brussels, The Hague, Copenhagen, Berlin, Vienna, Belgrade, Athens, and Cairo—the pattern repeated itself. In some cases, Hoover encountered surpluses rather than pleas for imports. Switzerland, for example, could offer thirty thousand tons of cereals during each of the summer months and was willing to share its small extra amounts of meats and fats with France and Italy.

In each capital, as well, Hoover would meet with the press or deliver a brief broadcast summarizing his findings. These 42 press conferences and 24 public addresses were fully reported in the United States, since a significant part of the Hoover mission involved raising American awareness of the international problem, with the expectation that it would encourage Americans to limit their own food consumption in order to make more available for export. Along similar propaganda lines, members of the excursion welcomed the Spartan meals served in lieu of elaborate banquets, although their hosts frequently lamented the lack of prewar cuisine. Hugh Gibson explained to one embarrassed Frenchman that it would have been disastrous for an unfriendly reporter to see the Famine Surveyors sit down to a luxurious meal.[47] Indeed, they often sat at tables set with an empty chair and plate for the "invisible guest," reminiscent of the World War I reminder that hunger lurked at so many tables. Hoover would later mention his discomfort at the contrast between the seven-course dinner given by the Polish communist government and the appalling evidences of malnutrition among Polish school children.[48]

The propaganda aspect of the Hoover mission had such importance that, when the group reached Cairo, Hoover received an appeal from President Truman to return to the United States "in order to bring directly home to the American people your eye-witness account of the necessity for greater assistance from this country."[49] Hoover, however, argued that a world report would have more impact than a European one and, instead, agreed to broadcast to the United States from Cairo on Good Friday, April 19. In this address he made a dramatic distinction between the 3,200 calories per day consumed by the average American, the 2,800 in Great Britain, the 2,200 estimated by experts as "the minimum at which public health and progress can be maintained," and the findings of his mission. Thirteen countries were currently feeding less than 1,900 calories; another six less than 1,500 calories; and millions of people did not eat even 1,000 calories each day. The greatest need, he said, was for cereals, and he appealed to the United States, Great Britain, the Soviet Union, and Latin America to try to fill the gap. Typically, he underscored the plight of "the smaller liberated nations" who had "suffered most" and whose "domestic resources are more limited than others." He concluded that the gift of food would not only save human lives and "return the lamp of compassion to the world," but would be "part of the moral and spiritual reconstruction of the world," a theme he would express again and again.[50]

On they flew—to Baghdad, Karachi, Bombay, Bangalore, Bangkok, Manila, Shanghai, Nanking, Seoul, and Tokyo. Hoover found Mohandas Gandhi much more interested in the human side of feeding than Jawaharlal Nehru, whose concerns centered more around politics.[51] From China, he passed along reports of UNRRA corruption, and in Japan, he gathered data to try to prepare the American people for the task of feeding their recent enemy.[52]

Over the Pacific, Hoover and his colleagues prepared their report, which they delivered to President Truman on May 13,[53] and which formed the substance of Hoover's address to the nation from Chicago four days later. (A month earlier, in a two-minute telephone conversation from Cairo, Hoover had persuaded Truman that Chicago would be a better location than New York for a speech aimed at the nation's farmers and housewives.)[54] Again, Hoover delivered a twofold message: farmers must increase production while the consuming public must reduce purchases of fats by 20 percent and breadstuffs by two pounds a week. He reiterated and dramatized the gravity of the crisis, and again spoke of moral and spiritual reconstruction.[55]

Hoover's travels did not end with his return to the United States and his report to the president and the people. As he put it, "the famine-relief clock was now striking 11:00";[56] it would not be enough to survey the damage and ask Americans to be generous. On May 25 Hoover and his cohort (with Julius Klein replacing Tuck) left for Latin America. Although they visited eleven countries, their major objective was Argentina. Since the U.S. State Department opposed Juan Perón, the embassy discouraged Hoover's efforts to do business with him. But Perón controlled Argentina, and Argentina had a surplus of grain. By a charming diplomatic sleight-of-hand, Hugh Gibson drew upon his connections in Roman Catholic circles to establish access to Perón by way of the Mexican embassy. Meanwhile, the Pope had also interceded, in fulfillment of a promise made when Hoover had visited the Vatican. Perón, meeting with Hoover, expressed his sympathy for the starving people of Europe and even agreed to give them grain on credit, but only if Hoover would persuade Truman to drop restraints on Argentine gold and trade that the State Department had imposed. Both men fulfilled their promises, and Latin American breadstuffs appeared on European tables.[57]

Back in the United States once more, Hoover reported to Truman on June 20 and held a press conference summarizing the results of his fifty-thousand-mile journey to coordinate the needs and contributions of 38 countries. He believed that he had reduced the gap between requirements and available supplies by more than seven million tons and concluded that world disaster could be averted until the next harvest, even if vast numbers of persons had to exist on 1,000 or 1,500 calories a day.[58] Contemporary and later critics quibbled with Hoover's figures, claiming that FitzGerald's statistics contained miscalculations,[59] but few could question the enormous impact of the trip. FitzGerald himself thought that most of the data could have been gathered from Washington but that the public relations job depended solely on Hoover, the one man who could command such monumental world attention.[60]

Hoover illustrated that impact when he addressed the Canadian Parliament in Ottawa on June 28, 1946. He spoke of the end of the war, the horrors of its aftermath, the need to restore order and peace, and the requirements of economic reconstruction. Using the same words he had broadcast from Cairo and repeated in Chicago, he concluded with a call for "the return of the lamp of compassion to the earth." That, he said, "is a part of the moral and spiritual reconstruction of the world."[61]

Throughout his travels, Hoover had constantly emphasized the critical ideological aspect of the famine problem, whether he was commenting on Communists in France or expressing concern that the Iron Curtain had come down over major food-producing areas in Europe. Just as he had lauded the love of liberty in the small democracies in 1941, and as he would plead for the restoration of German industry in

1947 so that Germany could become a partner in democracy rather than a continued burden on U.S. taxpayers,[62] he never forgot that the underlying reality extended far beyond mere physical deprivation. Starvation of the soul follows quickly upon malnutrition of the body. At age 40 or at 71, with the sponsorship of his government or without it, if necessary, Herbert Hoover would combat that enemy. War, Famine, Pestilence, and Death had been superceded by Destruction, Drought, Fear, and Revolution, he said. Throughout his life, Hoover did everything in his power to deprive the Children of Famine their legacy of stunted bodies and twisted minds.

NOTES

1. Herbert Hoover, *An American Epic*, vol. 1: *Introduction, The Relief of Belgium and Northern France, 1914–1930* (Chicago, 1959), p. ix.

2. Ibid., p. vii.

3. Hoover, memorandum of meeting with Myron Taylor, September 11, 1939; Hoover to Norman Davis, September 15, 1939; Davis to Hoover, September 22, 1939; Hoover to Davis, September 24, 1939—in Postpresidential Individual File (hereafter cited as PPI): Norman Davis, Herbert Hoover Presidential Library, West Branch, Iowa (hereafter cited as HHPL).

4. Lewis Strauss to Bernice Miller, March 21, 1946, PPI: Strauss, HHPL; Hoover, *An American Epic*, vol. IV: *The Guns Cease Killing and the Saving of Life from Famine Begins, 1939–1963* (Chicago, 1964), pp. 2–3.

5. Paul Mallon, "The News Behind the News," *New York Journal American*, December 16, 1939.

6. *New York World Telegram*, December 14, 1939; *New York Times*, December 15, 1939; *Christian Science Monitor*, December 14, 1939.

7. Norman Davis to Hoover, December 16, 1939; Hoover, transcript of telephone conversations with Davis, December 19, 1939, January 8, 1940, and March 22, 1940; Hoover to Davis, May 14, 1940—PPI: Davis, HHPL; Hugh Gibson, confidential memorandum, March 27, 1940, PPI: Gibson, HHPL.

8. John Hartigan, memorandum, November 9, 1942, PPI: Hartigan, HHPL; Hoover, *An American Epic*, vol. IV, p. 8.

9. Hoover, *Further Addresses Upon the American Road, 1938–1940* (New York, 1940), pp. 227–35. *New York Times*, October 12 and December 21, 1939. Hoover, draft of *An American Epic*, chapter 3, in Hoover to Lewis Strauss, October 10, 1960, PPI: Strauss, HHPL.

10. William Hallam Tuck to Hoover, memorandum on Food Situation, May–July 1940, Tuck papers, HHPL; *New York Times*, May 16, 1940; Hoover, *An American Epic*, vol. IV, p. 18.

11. John Hartigan to Colonel Rosser L. Hunter, November 25, 1942, PPI: Hartigan, HHPL.

12. Maurice Pate to Hugh Gibson, August 12, 1940. PPI: Edgar Rickard, HHPL.

13. Hoover, *An American Epic*, vol. IV, p. 17.

14. Edgar Rickard to Hoover, August 8, 1940, PPI: Rickard, HHPL.

15. Hoover, *Addresses Upon the American Road, 1940–1941* (New York, 1941), pp. 117–18; *New York Times*, August 11–18 and September 1, 1940.

16. House of Commons, Parliamentary Debates, 5th series, vol. 364, August 20, 1940, pp. 1159–62.

17. Hoover, *An American Epic*, vol. IV, pp. 20–21.

18. Hoover to William R. Castle, August 21, 1940; Castle to Hoover, September 4, 1940—PPI: Castle, HHPL.

19. *New York Times*, October 6 and 13, 1940; *New York Herald Tribune*, October 7, 1940; Hoover, *Addresses, 1940–1941*, pp. 119–20.

20. *New York Times*, December 11–12, 1940. Hoover had taken the precaution of asking former undersecretary of state William R. Castle to be present at the October 8 meeting. When Lord Lothian died shortly after issuing the formal rejection of Hoover's proposal, Hoover asked Castle to write a memorandum of the conversation. Hoover to Castle, December 13, 1940; Castle to Hoover, December 18, 1940—Castle Papers, HHPL; Harlan Fiske Stone to Hoover, December 16, 1940, PPI: Stone, HHPL.

21. *New York Times*, December 9, 1940; Hoover, "Feed Hungry Europe," *Collier's* 106 (November 23, 1940): 12; Hoover, *An American Epic*, vol. IV, pp. 29–31.

22. Hoover to Nicholas Roosevelt, December 6, 1940; Roosevelt to Lawrence Ritchie, December 7 and 10, 1940; Roosevelt to Hoover, December 13, 1940—Nicholas Roosevelt Papers, George Arents Research Library, Syracuse University.

23. Hoover, *An American Epic*, vol. IV, pp. 34–35.

24. Hoover, memorandum of conversation at the British Embassy, February 4, 1941, PPI: Lord Halifax, HHPL.

25. Hoover, *Addresses, 1940–1941*, pp. 147–55.

26. Memorandum, February 28, 1941; Hoover to Cordell Hull, March 5, 1941; Hull to Hoover, March 14, 1941—PPI: Hull, HHPL; Hoover, *An American Epic*, vol. IV, pp. 40–43.

27. *New York Herald Tribune*, March 10, 1941.

28. Hoover, memorandum of conversation with Sir Gerald Campbell, March 16, 1941, PPI: Campbell, HHPL; William Hallam Tuck, memorandum of meeting with Helm, March 27, 1941, PPI: Lord Halifax, HHPL.

29. Hoover to Cordell Hull, March 27, 1941; Hull to Hoover, April 11, 1941; Hoover to Hull, April 24, 1941; Hull to Hoover, May 10, 1941; Hoover to Hull,

June 3, 1941; Hull to Hoover, June 28, 1941—PPI: Hull, HHPL; Cordell Hull, *Memoirs*, vol. II (New York, 1949), p. 1052.

30. Hoover to Dare Stark McMullin, October 24, 1941, PPI: McMullin, HHPL; Milton M. Brown, oral history memoir, HHPL, pp. 6–10; Hoover to Roy W. Howard, April 2, 1941, PPI: Howard, HHPL; Hoover to William Philip Simms, April 30, 1941; Simms to Hoover, May 3 and 6, 1941; Hoover to Simms, May 6, 1941—PPI: Simms, HHPL; Hoover to Gardner Cowles, May 1, 1941, PPI: Cowles, HHPL; Hoover to Wheeler McMillin, May 7, 1941, McMillin Papers, HHPL.

31. Hoover to William Allen White, April 5, 1941, PPI: White, HHPL; William Hallam Tuck to Carter Glass, June 5, 1941; Glass to Tuck, June 9, 1941—Glass papers, University of Virginia.

32. Hoover, *Addresses, 1940–1941*, pp. 117–61 passim.

33. Hoover, *An American Epic*, vol. IV, pp. 68–71.

34. Ibid., pp. 90–97; Hoover, *Addresses Upon the American Road, World War II, 1941–1945* (New York, 1946), pp. 324–38, 353–56; Harold Manchester Fleming, notes on interview with Hoover, November 18, 1942, Fleming Papers, HHPL; Unsigned memorandum, January 8, 1943, PPI: Lord Halifax, HHPL.

35. Hoover, *An American Epic*, vol. IV, pp. 1–97 passim.

36. Harry S. Truman, *Memoirs*, vol. I (New York, 1955), p. 344.

37. Hoover to Truman, May 30, 1945, PPI: Truman, HHPL; Hoover, *An American Epic*, vol. IV, p. 105.

38. Hoover to Lewis Strauss, April 24, 1945, PPI: Strauss, HHPL.

39. H. W. Parisius to Leo T. Browley, May 26, 1945, Truman Papers, HHPL.

40. Herbert Hoover, *Addresses Upon the American Road, 1945–1948* (New York, 1949), pp. 49–53; Hoover, *An American Epic*, vol. IV, p. 114.

41. Hugh Gibson to William Hallam Tuck, March 3, 1946, Tuck Papers, HHPL; Hoover, *Addresses, 1945–1948*, pp. 165–66; Hoover, *An American Epic*, vol. IV, pp. 114–15; Henry A. Wallace, oral history memoir, Columbia University, p. 4596.

42. Hoover, *An American Epic*, vol. IV, p. 116.

43. Ibid., pp. 116–20; "Food: Hand of Politics Weighs on the Starving," *Newsweek* 27 (April 1, 1946): 40–42.

44. Hoover, *An American Epic*, vol. IV, p. 122.

45. This and subsequent data about the 1946 trip are taken from Hoover, *An American Epic*, vol. IV, pp. 101–9, and the "diaries" kept by Maurice Pate, Hugh Gibson, and Frank Mason on the journey. Mason's account, in the form of the "Dear Julius" letters, was intended to maintain contact with Julius Klein, who coordinated details in Washington. Copies of the Pate, Gibson, and Mason manuscripts appear in several collections at HHPL including Post-Presidential Subject File: Famine Emergency Committee.

46. Louis Paul Lochner, oral history memoir, HHPL, pp. 6–7; Lucius D. Clay, oral history memoir, HHPL, pp. 2–6; Eleanor Lansing Dulles, oral his-

tory memoir, HHPL, pp. 1–2, 5; Louis Paul Lochner, *Herbert Hoover and Germany* (New York, 1960), chap. 10.

47. Gibson diary, March 21, 1946.

48. Hoover, *An American Epic*, vol. IV, pp. 146–47; *New York Times*, April 1, 1946.

49. Truman, *Memoirs*, vol. I, p. 521; James F. Byrnes to Truman, March 12, 1946; Truman to Byrnes, March 13, 1946; William Hallam Tuck (for Hoover) to Truman, April 18, 1946; Truman to Hoover, April 18, 1946; Tony Vaccaro to Charles Ross, n.d.; Hoover to Truman, April 21, 1946; Truman to Hoover, May 7, 1946—in Truman Papers, HHPL.

50. Hoover, *Addresses, 1945–1948*, pp. 193–98.

51. Perrin Galpin, oral history memoir, Columbia University, p. 34; William Hallam Tuck to Irene de Beughen, April 27, 1946, PPI: Tuck, HHPL.

52. Hoover to Patrick J. Hurley, May 15, 1951, PPI: Hurley, HHPL; Hoover, *An American Epic*, vol. IV, pp. 191–93.

53. Hoover et al. to Truman, May 13, 1946, PPI: Truman, HHPL; *New York Times*, May 13–14, 1946.

54. Hoover, *An American Epic*, vol. IV, p. 173.

55. Hoover, *Addresses, 1945–1948*, pp. 221–28.

56. Hoover, *An American Epic*, vol. IV, p. 203.

57. Gibson diary, June 6–10, 1946; Hoover, *An American Epic*, vol. IV, pp. 210–14; Frank Mason, oral history memoir, HHPL, pp. 21–24; Walter Hoving, oral history memoir, HHPL, pp. 1–2; *New York Times*, June 7–11, 1946.

58. *New York Times*, June 20–21, 1946.

59. Harold Weston, "The Inside Story of the Hoover Report," speech, May 22, 1946, cited in Allen J. Matusow, *Farm Policies and Politics in the Truman Years* (Cambridge, Mass., 1967), pp. 33–36.

60. FitzGerald, oral history memoir, HHPL, p. 7.

61. Hoover, *Addresses, 1945–1948*, pp. 193–98, 221–28, 259–66.

62. Theodore A. Wilson and Richard D. McKinzie, "Save Wheat, Save Meat, Save the Peace: The Food Crusade of 1947," *Prologue* 3 (Winter 1971): 136–52.

7

Herbert Hoover and the Great Debates over Foreign Policy, 1940–1941 and 1950–1951

Gary Dean Best

For twenty years Herbert Hoover was the only ex-president of the United States in American life. There is no clearly defined role for former presidents, although there have been various proposals of ways in which their experience might be utilized by the government. In the absence of a defined role, former U.S. presidents have pursued their postpresidential lives in a variety of ways. Most have sought a dignified retirement from public life, surfacing, if at all, only to lend their support to major causes. Few have pursued a public life with the energy that Hoover did. This is surprising, because there was every reason to expect that Hoover would be little heard from once he left Washington in March 1933. Blamed by many for the depression and faulted by many others for not having done more to relieve its misery, Hoover left the White House under a cloud that would have inhibited many men from ever again taking an active public role. Moreover, whereas an open-minded administration in Washington might have sought his multifaceted expertise in domestic and foreign affairs and thus have kept him active in public affairs, the Roosevelt administration ignored him for twelve years after he left the White House, except for unofficial contacts with him during the war years. Even in his own Republican party organization Hoover was a man with little following. He had never been popular with the party regulars and was anathema to the progressive wing. Everything, then, seemed to militate against his reappearance in public life.

For two years, in fact, Hoover did largely withdraw from public life. From his home on the Stanford University campus came few public statements, and these did not take issue with the policies being pursued by the Roosevelt administration. Privately, however, Hoover was in anguish over those policies and his correspondence was filled with denunciations of the direction in which Roosevelt seemed to be taking the United States. Publicly Hoover remained silent, primarily for two reasons. First, since his own policies had been repudiated by the voters, Hoover felt that the Roosevelt administration deserved the chance to test its policies free of the kind of opposition that could lead to charges that the opponents had sabotaged recovery. Hoover believed that in time the policies would fail and the Roosevelt administration would be repudiated. Second, Hoover also felt—wrongly as it turned out—that there was no interest among Americans in what he might have to say on the issues.[1]

Despite all of the forces working against his reappearance in public life, there was good reason to expect that Hoover would not remain silent or inactive for long. For one thing, he was a restless man who craved activity and was bored by retirement. For another, he desperately sought vindication. Hoover honestly believed that his own policies had turned the tide of the depression in the summer of 1932. He was convinced that continuation of his policies, without the uncertainties introduced by the presidential campaign and election of 1932 and the lack of confidence in the president-elect during the months between his election and his inauguration, would have continued to produce recovery without the alterations in the American system that his successor seemed to be introducing. Roosevelt blamed Hoover for policies that had virtually brought the American economy to a dead stop in the banking crisis that existed on inauguration day; Hoover blamed Roosevelt's election for having aborted the recovery of the summer of 1932 and Roosevelt, himself, for the deterioration of the situation during the early months of 1933. From this and from the philosophical differences between the two men, it was virtually inevitable that Hoover would at some time go on the attack against Roosevelt's policies. Once on the attack, Hoover found that his fears that there would not be an audience willing to listen had been groundless.

Hoover possessed numerous and devoted followers who had been attracted to him by his intellect, his humanitarian activities, and his public philosophy. In addition to those who were devoted to Hoover personally, his attacks on the policies of Presidents Roosevelt and Truman appealed particularly to four groups in American life: those who for partisan reasons desired to defeat the Democrats in Washington; those who opposed the changes being made in the American system on philosophical grounds; those who did not oppose the Democratic rule in Washington on political or even philosophical grounds but viewed the New Deal policies, or the manner in which they were carried out, as detrimental to economic recovery; and those who opposed the foreign policies of Roosevelt and Truman as dangerous to the United States. It was Hoover's appeal to this last group that I shall examine.

Hoover had little to say on the subject of foreign policy until international affairs began to loom important in the late 1930s. It should not be surprising that he took an active role in the foreign policy debates because, in addition to the reasons already given, Hoover was in every sense a world figure. Even ignoring his four years as president of the United States, Hoover possessed an expertise concerning foreign lands that was equaled by few inside or outside of the government. Most of his early mining career was spent overseas, and his emergence into public view came as a result of his activities with the American Relief Committee in London in 1914 and his leadership of the Belgian relief effort before the United States entered World War I. During the armistice months of late 1918 and well into 1919, Hoover served as the virtual economic czar of much of Europe for the Versailles Peace Conference. Back in the United States in late 1919 and 1920 he was a leading figure in the fight for ratification of the Treaty of Versailles and U.S. entry into the League of Nations. As secretary of commerce under Presidents Harding and Coolidge, he was intimately involved in America's economic relations with foreign countries.

As a result of these experiences, added to his four years at the head of the U.S. government during a trying time in foreign relations, Hoover's views on foreign policy were well informed. In addition, at the time of the two most important debates over foreign policy—in 1940–1941 and 1950–1951—Hoover possessed recent intimate, first-hand knowledge of the nations concerned and their leaders, derived from travel in those lands and conversations with the heads of governments. His opposition to U.S. participation in World War II came after extensive travel through Europe in 1938, during which he conferred with Hitler and other European leaders.[2] He was also well acquainted with the leading figures in Japan, and was visited at his home on the Stanford campus by Matsuoka Yōsuke and Konoe Fumimarō.[3] These two, as foreign minister and prime minister, respectively, would occupy important positions in the government during the deterioration of relations between the United States and Japan in the late 1930s and early 1940s. Hoover's later opposition to the stationing of U.S. ground forces in Europe during the 1950–1951 debate came after extensive travels through Europe and Asia on behalf of the Famine Emergency Committee after World War II.

To the decades of experience that Hoover possessed in the international arena and to the direct contacts he had with the leaders and conditions of the countries involved must be added his scholarly interest in the causes of war. This led him to establish what was originally the Hoover War Library at Stanford University and to acquire documents from all over the world for its collection.

All of this meant that Hoover was one of the best informed men outside of the government concerning the issues raised in the great debates and that his qualifications rivaled even those within the government. Yet it is true that informed judgments are not necessarily more correct than uninformed or ill-informed ones. It should be kept in mind, too, that Hoover was free of the responsibilities of actual decision-making—responsibilities that might have caused alterations in his views had he been in a position of authority. Nonetheless, Hoover's qualifications mean that historians would be well advised to give his arguments attention.

In looking at these two great debates, I will concentrate primarily on two of Hoover's speeches, with some elaboration. The first speech is that of June 29, 1941. Since 1938, Hoover had taken a leading role in arousing U.S. public opinion against the policies that he feared were leading the nation to follow once again the 1917 experience of needless and useless involvement in one of Europe's chronic power struggles.[4] In the beginning he advocated American concentration on defense of the Western Hemisphere. He argued that U.S. intervention elsewhere would be only "an attempt to maintain the *status quo* in national boundaries all over the world," and to do so would involve the United States in endless conflicts. Moreover, the U.S. record of expansion in North America was far from clean. Hoover predicted: "We cannot become the world's policeman unless we are prepared to sacrifice millions of American lives—and probably some day see all the world against us. In time they would envisage us as the world's greatest bully, not as the world's greatest idealist." World War I had demonstrated the folly of trying to "make the world safe for democracy."[5] As the situations of Great Britain and China grew more desperate in 1940 and 1941, he favored the extension of aid to those countries.[6] He opposed Lend-Lease, however, as an unneutral step reminiscent of those that the United States had followed in 1917. Then, in June 1941, the German military machine turned from its pressure on the British Isles and launched an invasion of the Soviet Union—a move Hoover had predicted in conversations with Secretary of State Cordell Hull because of impressions he had gained in Germany in 1938.[7]

With the pressure on Great Britain relaxed and Germany launched in mortal combat with another totalitarian dictatorship equally repugnant to many Americans, the principal argument for U.S. interventionist policies seemed to have been removed. Yet to Hoover's surprise the movement for U.S. intervention gained greater force now that American friends of the Soviet Union were converted from noninterventionists into dedicated interventionists. These new converts to the interventionist cause increased its shrillness and intemperance.

For Hoover, Senator Robert Taft, Senator Harry Truman, and others, there was nothing to choose between Nazi Germany and Communist Russia.[8] The Soviets, by their nonaggression treaty with Hitler in 1939, had permitted the Germans to launch their invasion of Western Europe, had participated themselves in the rape of Poland, and had invaded Latvia, Estonia, Lithuania, and Finland. If totalitarianism was the issue, the Soviet Union was as totalitarian as Nazi Germany; if aggression was the issue, the Soviet Union seemed equally guilty with the Germans. By whatever standard of judgment, the United States did not belong in the war on the side of Stalin any more than it did on the side of Hitler.

Senator Taft was the first to make these points in a speech,[9] but Hoover followed a few days later with his address of June 29, 1941. He told his audience he found it curious that, while the German invasion of the Soviet Union had lessened the threat to Great Britain, which all had been concerned about, it had also intensified the "propaganda of fear or hate" designed to force the United States into the war. He recognized that it was sensible for Great Britain to cooperate with the Soviet Union since they were at war against a common enemy, but he argued that the new situation made it clear that U.S. intervention could not be justified as a crusade for freedom against tyranny. In Hoover's view, U.S. intervention would, instead, win for Stalin "the grip of communism on Russia, the enslavement of nations, and more opportunity for it to extend in the world." Instead, he advocated a policy of "watchful waiting, armed to the teeth, while these men exhaust themselves." The United States should "give every aid we can to Britain and China within the law, but do not put the American flag or American boys in the zone of war. Arm to the teeth for defense of the Western Hemisphere, and cease to talk and to provoke war." Instead of seeking to impose freedom on other nations by force, the United States should seek to make an example of itself for the rest of the world. Then, when the warring nations were exhausted from the conflict, the United States, with its own resources unimpaired, could promote a just and permanent peace.[10] Thereafter, Hoover continually reiterated the point that U.S. intervention in the war served only to "make the world safe for Stalin."

Hoover was much encouraged by the response to his speech. His office wired him that there had been an "avalanche of enthusiastic comments" and a "flood of requests for copies." W. K. Kellogg, the cereal king, sent $5,000 to underwrite distribution costs.[11] Surveying the reaction, Hoover concluded that the speech had received a greater response than any he had delivered since leaving the White House. According to a close Hoover friend, the former president's mail indicated that he had turned many minds against intervention.[12] Between June 29 and July 9, the Gallup Poll showed an increase in the percentage of those opposed to going to war with Germany and Italy from 75 to 79 percent.[13]

Through July and August Hoover cooperated with other noninterventionists outside of Congress in putting together and issuing a statement opposing what they called the "step-by-step projection of the United States into undeclared war." The statement was issued early in August and signed by Hoover, Alfred Landon, Charles Dawes, John L. Lewis, Felix Morley, Robert Hutchins, and a number of other prominent Americans. The statement reiterated Hoover's position that the United States should concentrate on the defense of the Western Hemisphere, make aid available to the democracies "at our seaboard," and preserve freedom and democracy in the United States. It also pointed to the changed nature of the war now that Germany had invaded the Soviet Union.[14]

During the remaining months before the attack on Pearl Harbor, Hoover continued to protest his policies that he saw leading the United States into the war. His task was complicated by the fact that, while public opinion polls continued to show the American people opposed to participation in the war, they also showed support for the very policies of President Roosevelt that Hoover viewed as leading inevitably to intervention. He found also that his subsequent speeches on the subject did not evoke the response of the one on June 29, and that some leading Americans did not take kindly to his position. Hoover wrote one friend late in August that John D. Rockefeller "has cut me off his social list completely and violently because I do not want to go to war."¹⁵ Nonetheless, he explained to columnist Boake Carter that he intended to "go on making nasty remarks until Congress finally declares war—even though it may only be a confirmation of a declaration of war."¹⁶ He realized that his speeches "had better not be too frequent and must be properly timed." As he wrote one congressman:

> You will remember that when we used to boil maple syrup as youngsters and the syrup reached the point at which it was about to crystallize, it would begin to sputter. The old New England custom was to pour in a few drops of cold water and it would calm down. If I can be of that kind of service, I will have reached the only point of usefulness that I care about.¹⁷

Hoover's final attempt to pour a few drops of cold water on the sputtering situation was his speech of November 19. In it he still identified the Soviet Union with Nazi Germany and Fascist Italy as an enemy of freedom, and he told his listeners: "We want the end of these evil and brutal ideas of Nazism, Fascism, and Communism." Hoover asked for assurances from Roosevelt that no U.S. expeditionary forces would be sent overseas without the approval of Congress, and he also called for planning to begin immediately for the peace conference that would follow the end of the war.¹⁸ Less than three weeks after this speech the bombs fell on Pearl Harbor and the United States was in the war.

I might add, parenthetically, before going on to the other great debate, that the bombs had scarcely fallen before Hoover began to follow his own advice with regard to planning for the peace. In collaboration with Hugh Gibson, Hoover set forth a plan for peacemaking that included U.S. participation in an international organization after the war, and he played a major role in rallying the Republican party to support American entry into the United Nations.

Once World War II ended, Hoover was quickly returned to official public life by President Truman. Subsequently he traveled for the president on behalf of famine relief and then took on duties as chairman of the so-called Hoover Commission in dealing with reorganization of the executive branch of the federal government. In the midst of these latter activities, the United States negotiated the treaty that established NATO in 1949. Preoccupied with the work of the commission and sensitive to the desirability of avoiding controversy while seeking to get the reforms recommended by the commission put into effect through presidential orders and congressional legislation, Hoover was not in the beginning a vocal critic of this gradual evolution of a U.S. commitment to the defense of Europe.

By May 1950, however, Hoover was concerned over America's seeming lack of a foreign policy and the "overstrained" U.S. economy, which, because of the expenditures for the Marshall Plan, military aid to Europe, and America's own defense spending, made it impossible to give Americans the "services and relief of taxes that they should enjoy."[19] Pointing to the puny military strength of the West European nations in comparison with that of the Soviet Union, Hoover insisted that before the United States appropriated more money to aid their defense, it should find whether they were unwilling to do more to defend themselves.[20]

Hoover's concern over the strains on the U.S. economy was heightened in June 1950 when the United States went to the aid of South Korea. That struggle also confirmed him in his suspicions that the United Nations was proving ineffective as a device for preserving the peace and that Western Europe lacked the will to stand with the United States to repel communist aggression. Hoover calculated that the manpower and industrial capacity of West European nations was greater in 1950 than before, but that they had only one-fifth the army divisions that they had put onto the field for the two world wars. With such numbers a successful ground war could not be fought against the military might of the Soviet Union, he insisted, and the United States must rely on air and sea power to defend itself.[21] In a speech in October 1950, Hoover questioned whether the Europeans, outside of Great Britain, had "the will to fight, or even the will to preparedness." The United States should be willing to provide aid, but "if Western Europeans want defense from the communist tide, they must do most of it themselves—and do it fast." He expressed opposition to the stationing of ten U.S. combat divisions in Europe, since that could result only in "a slaughter of American boys unless many times that number were standing by their sides. We should say, and at once, that we shall provide no more money until a definitely unified and sufficient European army is in sight. And further that ten American divisions will not be landed until then."[22]

Hoover's major speech of the great debate in 1950–1951 was on December 20 and was nationally broadcast. He regarded it as one of the most important addresses of his life, ranking with the June 29, 1941, speech discussed above. As he wrote to Raymond Moley and others:

> In an "emergency" on June 29, 1941, I made an appraisal of the forces moving in the world. I advised arming to the teeth and a policy of watchful waiting before we committed ourselves. I pointed out the obvious disaster if we jumped in. I was to be proved right after infinite losses to our country.[23]

The speech he was to give in December, he predicted, was "likely to be no more welcome than the one ten years ago."[24] He wrote to Senator Robert Taft that he did not "expect our Eastern seaboard press to be any more enthusiastic about this" speech than they had been about the one in 1941.[25]

The speech in 1950, delivered as U.S. forces reeled back in disarray in Korea before the onslaught of Chinese Communist "volunteers," began with a survey of the imbalance in military forces between the communist and the free world. From this Hoover reiterated his conclusion that there existed no possibility of victory in a land war against the Soviet Union and its satellites. Moreover, the U.S. economy was already strained to its limit. As he had in the first great debate, Hoover advocated American concentration on the defense of what he called the "Western Hemisphere Gibraltar of Western Civilization," but also, through the use of air and sea power, the defense of the Atlantic and Pacific oceans, with Great Britain as the frontier of American defense in the Atlantic and with Japan, Taiwan, and the Philippines as the American frontier in the Pacific. This meant that the United States should build powerful air and sea forces rather than maintain a large army.

Not only was this the only feasible means of defense against the enormous communist ground armies, it was also less expensive. After the initial large outlay for planes and ships, the United States would be able to cut military expenditures, balance the budget, and free itself "from the dangers of inflation and economic degeneration." Economically strong, the United States could then continue to feed the hungry of the world and assist other countries in arming themselves for defense against communism. However, before the United States extended any further military aid to Europe, those nations must demonstrate their own determination to defend themselves by organizing and equipping combat divisions in sufficient numbers to "erect a sure dam against the red flood." That must be done before the United States landed "another man or another dollar on their shores." To do otherwise would only encourage another Korea, and that "would be a calamity to Europe as well as to us." The U.S. policy toward Europe should "be confined to a period of watchful waiting." His policy was not isolationism, Hoover argued, but just the opposite.[26]

Hoover's office reported a "tremendous, favorable response" after the speech, with the telephone ringing continually and a flood of telegrams that began even before Hoover had returned to the office from delivering it. Not one message received was unfavorable.[27] A check through the *Congressional Record* for a comparison of congressional comment on the 1950 speech with that in 1941 found that there had been little comment over the earlier speech by contrast with the amount of attention the more recent speech was receiving in the *Record*.[28] Hoover was confident that his position would arouse support among American public opinion. He wrote to Senator H. Alexander Smith that he suspected "Congress is going to get a jolt of public opinion such as it has not seen for a long time!"[29]

Hoover was not far wrong, as members of Congress were inundated with mail and wires in support of his doctrines. Senator Richard Nixon wrote him that he had "already received over 100 wires this morning indicating enthusiastic approval of your speech last night." Nixon added that he was sure Hoover's comments would "have an excellent effect in developing a more realistic approach to the critical problems we face today."[30] Raymond Moley, who supported the Hoover doctrine in his newspaper column and in *Newsweek*, wrote the former president that he did not think any speech had ever so clearly reflected the feeling of the country.[31] Felix Morley expressed enthusiastic approval and added: "If the Europeans have any real desire to unite for self-preservation your speech will stimulate it. If they have no such desire, you have at least pointed to the course that we shall eventually have to follow."[32]

As Hoover expected, the Eastern press did not welcome his speech. The *New York Herald Tribune* admitted that his position was not "isolationist," since it embraced the Western Hemisphere as well as Great Britain, Japan, Taiwan, and the Philippines, but it coined a new term to describe his policy: "retreatism." The doctrine had gained "increased stature," the newspaper admitted, because of Hoover's advocacy of it, and it represented a "body of opinion that must be reckoned with in the formation of American policy" because it appealed "to the angry frustration which events in Korea have aroused and because it offers what purports to be a cheaper way to defend America than by assisting allies."³³

President Truman wasted no time in reiterating his position that Western Europe's defense was vital to the security of the United States. John Foster Dulles, Republican adviser to Truman's State Department, was trotted out to give a speech that was widely hailed as the administration's reply to the Hoover address. Despite the ballyhoo attempted by newspapers like the *New York Times*, however, the Dulles speech scarcely caused a ripple in the public, and even the *Times* confessed that the response to Dulles' speech was "meager." It reported that a sampling of congressional mail had found response to the Dulles speech to be "insignificant" and "disappointing," in "sharp contrast to the heavy public response resulting from the Hoover speech."³⁴

Hoover's position was quickly echoed, with some modifications, by Senator Taft and others, but it also attracted the predicted smears and distortions. One such smear, circulated by the Democratic National Committee, accused Hoover and Taft of being "false prophets of doom" who were now advocating policies as "wrong" as those they had fought for in 1941. Two men who had been so completely in error a decade earlier could certainly not be judged competent, the argument went, in the present circumstances.³⁵ Hoover addressed himself to this type of criticism in a speech on February 9, 1951.

In that speech, Hoover recalled that in his address of June 1941 he had questioned the wisdom of the United States aligning itself with Soviet communism against German nazism, and added: "Need I remind you that the grip of communism in this decade has spread slavery from 200,000,000 to 800,000,000? And we have no peace." In 1951 Hoover reiterated the "stark realities" on which U.S. policies must be based, and again advocated that the American contribution to the defense of the free world be limited to a powerful navy and air force. The air threat to the Soviet Union, he insisted, was "far more powerful than pouring American divisions into the reach of this Asiatic horde." A ground war, moreover, must be a defensive war, whereas in the air the United States could go on the offensive. Moreover, the concentration of U.S. resources on airpower would be less of a strain on the economy.

Hoover had altered his doctrine since the December speech, however, and his position was now closer to that of Senator Taft and air power advocates like Major Alexander P. de Seversky. Although his December address had emphasized defense and included only the Atlantic and Pacific oceans and the areas in those oceans that could be defended by air and sea power, he now contemplated, as did Taft, the use of U.S. air and sea power in an offensive role to aid Western Europe if it were attacked by the Soviet Union. Where before he had resisted an American commitment to NATO unless the NATO countries rearmed to an adequate level, he now embraced that commitment but offered U.S. air and sea power in place of ground troops for an offensive role against the Soviet Union rather than a defensive one. Hoover argued correctly that what he now proposed was neither retreat nor withdrawal. "The essence of this program I have proposed is to effectively restrain our enemies from attack upon our allies or ourselves . . . It is the best chance of peace—even if it is an uneasy peace."[36]

Despite Hoover's opposition, the U.S. Senate did permit, by a vote of 49–43, the stationing of four divisions of U.S. ground troops in Europe, subject to the condition that President Truman did not increase that number without the approval of Congress. It appeared that Hoover had lost the second great debate as resoundingly as he had the one in 1941. There was some consolation in the fact that U.S. defense policy came increasingly to rely on the strategy of "massive retaliation," especially with the Eisenhower years. But this did not replace, as Hoover had intended, the maintenance of a sizable army and the stationing of ground troops overseas, and so the reduction in military expenditures that Hoover had envisioned did not materialize.

After both of these great debates, subsequent events convinced Hoover that he had been correct in his positions. World War II did end with the grip of communism fastened on many more nations and peoples than before the war, and the willingness of the United States to commit ground troops to the defense of Western Europe did appear to lessen the sense of urgency among NATO nations to build their own defense forces adequately. Hoover, of course, was less than objective in his appraisal of the results and always sought vindication for his positions. Yet other people, too, who might be considered more objective, have begun to question the inevitability of the events I have described and the desirability of the policies embraced by the United States in 1941 and 1950–1951. For example, Robert Sherrill, Washington editor of *The Nation*, wrote in 1979:

All admirers of Roosevelt, and even many of his critics, will contend that how or why he manipulated us into World War II really doesn't matter because it was inevitable that we would eventually get in, and the sooner the better, for the cause was just and the results noble. It is time we begin seriously to question that old argument. Far from being noble, the results of World War II, like the effluence of Love Canal, have poisoned our earth seemingly forever. Most of the negative forces that make our national life so unhappy and irrational—the military-industrial waste, the impenetrable federal budget, the "national security" hysteria that is supposed to excuse FBI excesses, the covert insanity of the CIA, the incredibly unwieldy federal bureaucracy, the flatulent patriotism of our educators—became permanent fixtures with World War II.[37]

It would also not be difficult to assemble a pile of American complaints about the NATO allies' unwillingness to take up the burden of their own defense that echo Hoover's own observations of 1950 and 1951. Such complaints have become particularly numerous and acute in recent years because of NATO misgivings over the stationing of Pershing II missiles and nuclear cruise missiles in Europe and the unwillingness of the NATO powers to follow the U.S. lead in applying sanctions against Poland. My favorite observation, though, is that by Hedley Donovan in *Time* magazine:

It is indeed remarkable and in some ways outrageous that we keep a large American army in Germany 36 years after the end of World War II, and make a greater defense effort (by most measurements) than the prosperous countries we are helping to defend, while even in the most responsible European conversations one sometimes catches an implication that NATO is somehow more to our interest than theirs.[38]

In fairness, however, it must be added that just because Hoover's predictions came true it does not follow that his proposed policies would have yielded a better result or, because of present disillusionment with the results of our policies, that the policies we did follow were wrong. Considering 1941, for example, one may well question whether it would have been a better world with Nazi Germany in possession of the vast territories and resources of the Soviet Union, able to link up with Japan in the east and to threaten India and the Middle East from the north, or with the Soviet Union victorious against Germany and in possession of all of continental Europe. Yet those were the possible consequences if the United States had followed Hoover's advice. Considering 1950–1951, one can only speculate, without knowing the minds of the Kremlin leaders in these intervening 30 years, whether the presence of U.S. ground troops in Europe restrained the Soviet Union or not. All that can be said for sure is that this country did not reap the happy results from the policies of 1941 and 1951 that their advocates claimed would follow, and that the critics of those policies deserve more attention and a fairer hearing than they have received. This is particularly important since history has a disturbing habit of repeating itself.

Notes

1. Gary Dean Best, "Herbert Hoover as Titular Leader of the GOP, 1933–35," *Mid-America* 56 (April–July 1979): 81–97.

2. Accounts of this trip may be found in Suda Bane, "Mr. Hoover's European Trip, 1938," and Perrin Galpin, "Through Europe with Mr. Hoover," in the Hoover Papers, Post-Presidential Subject Files, Herbert Hoover Presidential Library, West Branch, Iowa (hereafter cited as HHPL).

3. Hoover to William Castle, April 6, 1933; Prince Konoe Fumimarō to Hoover, June 7, 1934 and December 11, 1936—Hoover Papers, Post-Presidential Individual Files (hereafter cited as PPI), HHPL; John Callan O'Laughlin to Hoover, April 3, 1933, O'Laughlin Papers, Library of Congress.

4. See, for example, his speech before the Council of Foreign Relations in February 1939, reprinted in Herbert Hoover, *Further Addresses Upon the American Road, 1938–1940* (New York, 1940), pp. 93–103.

5. Article in *Liberty* magazine, April 1939, reprinted in Hoover, *Further Addresses*, pp. 104–15.

6. For Hoover's support of aid for the democracies, see his speech of June 25, 1940, before the Republican National Convention, in Hoover Papers, Public Statements, 1940, HHPL.

7. For Hoover's discussion with Hull see "Memorandum of a meeting with Hull at 9:30 on February 28, 1941," PPI: Cordell Hull, HHPL.

8. For Truman's position see *New York Times*, June 23, 1941.

9. "Broadcast by Robert A. Taft over CBS, 6-25-1941," PPI: Taft, HHPL.

10. Hoover speech of June 29, 1941, in Hoover Papers, Public Statements, 1941, HHPL.

11. Arch Shaw to Hoover, telegram, June 30, 1941, PPI, HHPL.

12. Edgar Rickard Diary, June 30, 1941, HHPL.

13. George Gallup, *The Gallup Poll*, vol. I (New York, 1972), pp. 286, 288.

14. The statement appeared in the *New York Times*, August 6, 1941.

15. Edgar Rickard Diary, October 21, 1941, HHPL; Hoover to Joseph Scott, August 27, 1941, PPI, HHPL.

16. Hoover to Boake Carter, July 14, 1941, PPI, HHPL.

17. Hoover to Congressman Woodruff, July 14, 1941, PPI, HHPL.

18. The speech is in Hoover Papers, Public Statements, 1941, HHPL.

19. Hoover to Senator Kenneth Wherry, May 6, 1950, with memorandum, PPI, HHPL.

20. Senator Homer Ferguson to Hoover, July 17, 1950; Hoover to Ferguson, July 20, 1950—PPI, HHPL.

21. Speech to the Bohemian Encampment, in Hoover Papers, Public Statements, 1950, HHPL.

22. Ibid.

23. Hoover to Raymond Moley, December 18, 1950, Moley Papers, HHPL.

24. Hoover to Neil MacNeil, December 19, 1950, PPI, HHPL.

25. Hoover to Taft, December 18, 1950, Taft Papers, Library of Congress.

26. In Hoover Papers, Public Statements, 1950, HHPL.

27. *San Francisco Examiner*, December 21, 1950.

28. Arthur Kemp to Hoover, undated (probably December 1950 or early January 1951), PPI, HHPL.

29. Hoover to H. Alexander Smith, December 27, 1950, PPI, HHPL.

30. Richard Nixon to Hoover, December 22, 1950, PPI, HHPL.

31. Raymond Moley to Hoover, December 21, 1950, PPI, HHPL.

32. Felix Morley to Hoover, December 27, 1950, Morley Papers, HHPL.

33. *New York Herald Tribune*, December 22, 1950.

34. *New York Times*, January 3, 1951.

35. *New York Herald Tribune*, January 28, 1951.

36. In Hoover Papers, Public Statements, 1951, HHPL.

37. Robert Sherrill, "Backdoor to War," *Inquiry* (May 14, 1979): 28.

38. *Time* 120 (August 10, 1981): 74.

8

Hoover and FDR: Reminiscent Reflections

Frank Freidel

President LeShana, distinguished fellow guests, enthusiastic followers of Herbert Hoover research. It is a delight to be here this afternoon. Officially my task this afternoon is to comment on those two fine papers that we heard this morning, so good that I think any comments of mine can do little except underscore the important points that they made. Also, since I am speaking to you after lunch, it was felt that it might be well for me to make some more general remarks, so I do want to assure Professors Kennedy and Best that I will not or have not forgotten them. I will come to their papers shortly, but first of all I would like to put Mr. Hoover in his setting.

This was an amazing man, doing strenuous things when he was 71 years old and still tart and sharp at 85. I saw the pictures of him in the Herbert Hoover Academic Building a few minutes ago as I am sure the rest of you did. You may well wonder, and I shall be personal about it, how I could possibly be interested in both Herbert Hoover and Franklin D. Roosevelt, those two notable antagonists. Well, if the truth be known I started out with Herbert Hoover as my boyhood hero. I was brought up feeling that here was a man of greatness, a thought that has stayed with me, I must say. I had admiration, as I have to this day, for Herbert Hoover as one of the great figures of modern America, indeed of the modern world. At the same time may I say, because I am not partisan about these things, that I also consider—for all of his shortcomings and weaknesses—Franklin D. Roosevelt as one of the great fig-

---

Frank Freidel's original assignment was to comment on the papers of Gary Dean Best and Susan Estabrook Kennedy at Hoover Symposium III, February 20, 1982. When illness made it impossible for Robert Burke to appear for his scheduled luncheon address, Professor Freidel was asked to expand his commentary as he wished and to speak at the luncheon. The result was this extemporaneous excursion over several decades of research and recollection. Professor Freidel has generously consented to the publication of his informal address, very much as spoken and recorded.

ures of modern times. So you will have to put up with my prejudices such as they are.

For many years Hoover was overshadowed because of his misfortune, getting into the White House just in time for the Great Depression. Because of that we tended to forget the brilliance of the man and the assets he brought to the White House. As a person who has been a historian of presidents, the more I think about Hoover the more I am convinced that the only reason he did not become one of our greatest presidents was simply because he could not cope with the depression. Mr. Roosevelt largely did not cope with it either. But Hoover did bring about a good bit of the modern presidency. In some respects he was the major planner in the White House. He was the last of the old and the first of the new—a transitional figure of enormous importance. Much more than that, for the reasons that Susan Estabrook Kennedy made so amply clear in her paper, Hoover was a man of transcendental world importance as a humanitarian who could so well organize the resources of the world to keep people from being hungry. Twice he helped alleviate widespread famine, first during and after World War I and then after World War II. One could point to him also as the man who was able to achieve what no one had previously been able to do, when he brought about a reorganization of the U.S. government in the Truman administration.

Herbert Hoover was a man of conspicuous assets and some liabilities, a thoroughly humane man, and a man of absolute Quaker honesty. He was also a man guided, as any good Quaker should be, by the inner light, the feeling that he had to do what was right whether it was popular or not. To that extent I think the inner light could create problems for anyone trying to function as a politician with the problems of accommodation that go along with being a politician. Hoover was a man with a dedication to public service, another Benjamin Franklin. Like Franklin he made a fortune, ceased to work for income when he was 40, and devoted the rest of his life to public service. However, I must say I doubt if Hoover entirely had the kinds of insights into himself that made Franklin so remarkable. On the other hand, he was not as blatantly a showman as Franklin often was. There were differences between those two men. Hoover was, above all, an organizer of the new technology, a man who would be totally at home in the computer age and would be thinking of new ways in which computers could be used. He was an expert fact finder, one of the first great fact finders we had.

He was ready to grant an important role to the government when individual initiatives or enterprise could not work, although he prized individualism and is well known for his tiny but famous book published in the 1920s, *American Individualism*. Consequently, while he wanted the government to do things that individuals could not do, he was afraid of overcentralization in the government. He was a man of faith in the future of American abundance. Finally, in all these foreign-policy matters as Gary Dean Best has pointed out to us, Hoover was a man who had a world approach to problems—not a narrowly parochial Iowan, Oregonian, or even American approach, but a world approach. Both the papers brought that point out very well.

I would be a bad historian if I did not somehow deal with Hoover's liabilities. The fact is that many of these traits of his, such as his Quaker honesty, could create problems for him in trying to reach accommodations and trying to reach consensus. He was not well equipped to be a consensus kind of a person and, in fact, at times could carry dogmatism to an amazing degree. As a precision-oriented engineer, he often believed he was precisely right and any slight variation was wrong. There was, for example, the emergency banking legislation, which was a very conservative piece of legislation that Roosevelt put through after he took office in March 1933. It had been drawn up by Hoover's own treasury people, especially by Arthur A. Ballantine, a loyal Hoover man. Privately, Hoover was unhappy about it and considered it a disastrously dangerous piece of legislation; yet if Hoover would have stayed on, it would have been his own legislation. There is this side to Hoover, and we have to face up to it and to the fact that it was often impossible to budge him beyond a limited point. He could budge, but was slow to budge. Thus, there is not any list of liabilities as compared with the list of assets, but there are things about Hoover that make him an intensely human man. He should not be thought of simply as such a great figure that he did not share the emotions of the rest of us.

He was a man of considerable compassion and sensitivity who could, when with his friends who loved him, show himself to have a magnificent sense of humor and be the best of companions. Those who worked for Hoover never forgot the experience. I can cite the names of Democrats who worked under him and who felt the same way as the Republicans did. It would have been a joy to have known Hoover well and to have been one of those who called him "the Chief." There are enigmas connected with Hoover that make him a continuing fascination to historians. Two of these historians we have met today—Professors Kennedy and Best. They are studying the period after he left office, when he was still a relatively young, energetic man, dedicated to service and bringing rare assets to the aid of the United States and the world. It has been too easy to look on this as a rather negative period in Hoover's life, when the best was behind him, and to think of him primarily in his younger, more adventuresome years.

I had to be informed by Susan Estabrook Kennedy of how much Hoover had achieved in 1946, although I lived through it, as did a good many of you here. I was reminded of certain of Hoover's traits, one of which was, of course, how expert he was as a master of public relations. In managing, in timing, and in getting his message before the public, he proved himself one of the great craftsmen of the art. I was also reminded of his strong sense of right and wrong; this kept him from being a routine politician. The story Professor Kennedy tells is such a dramatic one in its basic outline of Hoover versus Churchill and, presumably, Hoover versus Franklin D. Roosevelt, as our subject tried to get food to the helpless in Europe. World War I, World War II, and I suppose every modern war is to a great extent a war against the helpless, against women and children. All of us particularly feel for the war that is going on in El Salvador today because of what is happening to those helpless ones. Yet Churchill, that man whom we all respect and admire so much, could suggest that milk should be turned into munitions. It is a sad story.

As you know, my main task this afternoon is to serve as a commentator on these papers. One thing that bothers me is that Hoover gives a figure of the people he saved from starving as being a billion four hundred million people. I was going to say dollars because it sounds more like dollars than people, which seems to be nearly the entire population of the world in 1946. I don't know quite how that got in there and I hope Professor Kennedy will elucidate that for us before her book comes out in the future. Another minor point that I noted and you the audience would not have because I have read her paper, was that when she talks about Hoover crossing swords with Norman Davis, who was the head of the Red Cross, Hoover had a transcript of a telephone conversation with Davis and she quotes from that. By the way, I quoted likewise in my fourth volume on FDR from a transcript of a telephone conversation between President Hoover and President-elect Roosevelt that Hoover had down. I mention it to you partly just to amuse you that now you can see the headlines, "Professor Kennedy exposes Hoover tapes," though I am sure it was a stenographer sitting there copying down what was said. I suggest, too, that too much fuss has been made in the last few weeks about tapes, that it is a pretty common practice, and that a man who is as totally upright as Hoover could and did engage in this practice, much to my benefit and I know to Professor Kennedy's benefit. As a matter of fact the conversation that he had recorded with Franklin Roosevelt put his case far more firmly than anything he had been able to tell me when I had asked him about the question involved.

I do hope that someone can get to the base of the British feeling that food must not go to those suffering children and their mothers in Europe. Why was there a switch from Chamberlain's policy to Churchill's policy? Why had Churchill taken such a firm view during World War I? We historians all know that this was basically the British policy and that Churchill and Hoover had locked horns over it. The British had the feeling that anything that went to feed anybody within the German territory would somehow release food or would release something that could be made into munitions to aid the German cause. They felt that it was the only way to counter the German submarines. As for the Americans going along with it, this was only an indication of the extent that they had become co-belligerents with the British. Today we have the feeling that it is unfortunate Hoover was not in a position to go into the White House to talk to Roosevelt, who was also a humanitarian, and then go forth with Roosevelt's blessing and negotiate with the Germans. Hoover had international status as did no other American, even in Germany, although I am sure not with Hitler. Even in Germany Hoover was totally respected, as was the American Friends Service Committee, because of the relief activities in World War I and thereafter. He was respected as a person who could be counted on to be absolutely neutral on behalf of saving the lives of these people suffering from the misfortune of war. Within the United States he could touch two groups that Roosevelt badly needed to have touched. He could touch both the humanitarian conscience of the American people and he could touch various groups of people whose relatives were in Holland, Belgium, Norway, Poland, and other countries as they came to be overrun.

What a great change it was when Harry Truman came in and was able to make use of Hoover for the very task that Roosevelt would not assign him. I shall come back to this point later; it is my main concern with these two papers.

What a magnificent organization Hoover had, how good he was at picking people, how smoothly they operated. Few people were as expert administrators as Hoover. We have called him the Great Engineer; he was really the Great Administrator. The years he spent before World War I had largely been in London and as an administrator at the international level where he was so remarkably talented. The interesting thing, by the way, so far as 1945 is concerned, is that Roosevelt at the time of his death was aware of the food crisis and worried about it. He had written, for example, just a few days before his death to Queen Wilhelmina of Holland, saying to her, "I am afraid that there is not going to be enough food. I am going to see to it as much as possible that it goes to the Dutch people. I have sent word to Eisenhower that this is to be done. They are not to be too lavish with the Germans. We are to think about people like your people and the Belgians first." Would Roosevelt have done more than that? Of course he would not have made use of Hoover to dramatize what needed to be done. He would not have had perhaps as good an organization as Hoover's, although I must add that Roosevelt was also good at picking people and good at sending the right people on missions.

Truman, of course, lacking the great credibility with the American people that Hoover or Roosevelt had and being a relatively unknown at that time, needed Hoover badly and Hoover needed Truman. So this strange alliance developed and held up fairly well. The rest of his life Truman said much nicer things about Hoover than he said in private about Roosevelt, which is rather interesting. I give this to you as an illustration of how such things could work politically—that these two men could make good use of each other and the public would and did enormously benefit. I have a curious question in my mind, and that is, did the shipment of U.S. food in 1946 really keep large numbers of people from going hungry? There have been various things written about this. Professor Kennedy, of course, only had 40 minutes in which to tell us a vast amount, but perhaps later she can give us a few remarks on that point. I also wonder if at home it helped send prices up, take meat from the butcher shops, and create the shortages that so irritated the American people in the summer of 1946; this helped bring about the removal of the price ceilings and the Republican landslide in the election of 1946. Finally, I want to mention that the great coup in Argentina might be considered an illustration of how Hoover back in power could act differently than Hoover out of power. Here was Hoover in Argentina ready to deal with the sinister dictator for a very good reason: to get food to those hungry people. I think Hoover was absolutely right, but I wonder if Hoover out of power would not have been pretty critical of somebody dealing with a man as unsavory as Perón.

I will turn now to Gary Dean Best's paper on the great debates on foreign policy. The thing that I think fascinates me the most about this paper is that, while there are some important differences at certain points between Hoover and Roosevelt and Hoover and Truman over foreign policy, there is such an enormous area of consensus. This is what Professor Best has given us and given us so well that I cannot do much more than underscore certain points. The paper is a study in consensus in foreign policy with little deviations here and there. The differences between Hoover and Roosevelt really were not very great. In the campaign of 1932, for example, Roosevelt thought first of presenting a foreign policy and then decided not to. He remarked to Raymond Moley, as Moley remembered it, "Old Hoover is good on that. We won't talk about that at all." I cannot imagine that he used the word "old," because the truth of the matter is that Hoover was only about ten years older than Roosevelt, which was not very old at that time. Philosophically, Hoover and Roosevelt were not very far apart. I think the sad thing is that they were not able to form a solid front on foreign policy and only disagree occasionally, as presidents of the present time try to do normally. On various occasions today the president will try to get a former president of the different party to stand side by side with him on a national matter in which it is important to show solidarity.

Certainly Roosevelt would have been delighted if he had had the chance to talk with Hitler as Hoover did. Roosevelt also hoped as much as Hoover to be able to do business with people like Prince Konoe and Matsuoka. One of my great regrets is that Roosevelt did not manage in the months before Pearl Harbor to get to the Pacific and have a conversation with Konoe, although I think things were really in the hands of the militarists in Japan then and it would not have changed the course of events. Of course, the great difference was that Hoover was free of responsibility and that FDR and Truman were in power. One wonders if Hoover in power would have found himself acting differently. Hoover's speeches interest me, because the split on foreign policy really only comes about the time of Lend-Lease (in March 1941). Roosevelt was determined to keep the United States out of war as best he could. He was serious when he said at Chautauqua in 1936 that he had seen war and he hated it. He was not the enthusiast that he had been as a young admirer of Theodore Roosevelt.

The split thus came about over Lend-Lease, and that was a fairly technical split. A more serious split came on the question of the difference between Nazis and Communists, in which Hoover went one direction and Roosevelt and Churchill went another. It is interesting, by the way, that Churchill—who was in power in England at a time of the German attack on Russia in June 1941—offered Ambassador Maisky everything he wanted, when he could have driven hard bargains during those first few weeks of the invasion. Why? Well, it is a tough question. May I say first of all, since I am old enough to remember all of this and yet was young enough at the time to face the prospect of going into the armed forces, that my view at the time was *totally* Herbert Hoover's view. Believe me, I did not want to see us get into World War II. I have come in later years as a historian, in fact I came before the war was over, to feel that I had taken the wrong position. I changed my mind. But these were powerful sentiments, and the selection that Professor Best read from Robert Sherrill does indicate the poisons that came out of the war; people, even young people like me, were aware of what could come after a war. We did not look forward to the prospect of the United States being a garrison state. Yet I can't envisage—any more than Professor Best can—that it would have been advantageous to have let the Nazis fight it out with the Communists. There seemed every likelihood that Communists and the Soviet Union would be destroyed as a basic fighting power within a few months. The expectation of our general staff, I believe, was about six weeks. Of course they were wrong, and Harry Hopkins brought back amazing news to Roosevelt from Moscow— namely, that he thought the Soviets could hold out and that it would be worth our while to start sending materials of war to them and to include them in Lend-Lease. He was going against most accepted military opinion of the time.

Why then should we have chosen Stalin over Hitler? I think what Churchill and Roosevelt had in mind was perfectly simple: the Germans were by far the greater menace. For example, Roosevelt and Churchill already knew that an atomic bomb was feasible and that the Germans were working on one. They did not know that the Soviets—either then or shortly thereafter—would also be working on one, but they knew that the Germans were. Picture what the world would have been if Germany, if Hitler, had produced the atomic bomb first. I give that simply as an illustration. The fact is that the ability of the Nazis to turn out new weapons of war of various sorts—not just the atomic bomb but also such equipment as jet airplanes, snorkel submarines, special kinds of marine mines, and bombs—showed that their technical ability was a threat to the United States. Here is the real difference between Roosevelt, Churchill, and Hoover. Hoover in power probably would have listened to enough generals for it to have made a difference. I think it made a great difference to him in his old age, sitting in the Waldorf Tower with Douglas McArthur two stories over him. They spent a good bit of time together, and the Hoover of the period of the Hoover-McArthur friendship sounded very different to me than the earlier Hoover. May I say I much preferred the earlier Hoover. It is an interesting thing to talk about, this business of letting them fight it out to the point of impotent deadlock. It is logically appealing, you see, and goes back to Wilson's "peace without victory" view; that of course is the early Hoover. Yet it was a sad slogan—to make the world safe for Stalin—and that was the last thing any of us wanted. But we had no choice and had to take the lesser evil. There is no question that, since we are alive and well here today, we made the right decision. We would not have had a happy choice if either Germany or the Soviet Union alone had come out the victor. Instead, the Western world gained because the United States did join the war.

I could say much the same thing about the 1950 debate, except that I had the feeling that much of this in the end did not amount to a great deal. To us at the time this was *the* great debate over foreign policy, and yet in the end what did we do? We sent four divisions to Europe at that time, a little more later. Our troops are hostages, really, to Western Europe to show them that we mean business and that in case of a Soviet attack we would be involved in it with them. They are hostages; they are not a group that can defeat the Soviet land forces. This is why the question always comes up: would the United States use its nuclear devices? This question is still with us as it was in 1950. If Dulles' speech of late 1950 was meant as a refutation of Hoover, it was a rather ridiculous thing for Dulles to do, because the Dulles formula became massive retaliation. The Republicans were actually urging a rollback at that time because they could get Polish-Americans and other groups with sympathies toward Soviet satellite states enthusiastically behind them.

I think the prime Hoover quarrel, although he did not recognize it, was actually with members of his own party. They are the ones who created the situation in which the Hungarians arose thinking the Americans would come in, and yet of course it was impossible for them to intervene.

There was less difference, I would propose to you, between the Truman and Hoover viewpoints than there was between Hoover and what became Secretary of State Dulles and President Eisenhower's viewpoint. What I am suggesting is that there could have been a symbiosis between Hoover and Truman, and it is unfortunate that at times they did not recognize this a little more than they did. Nevertheless, I think even the foreign policy criticism helped Truman because he needed help in prodding the West European nations to arm. The fact that a man they admired so much as Hoover, who was in the opposition and yet taking this view, did not go unnoticed in Western Europe.

Finally, then, the whole relationship between Hoover and Roosevelt has interested me a great deal. It is a curious and interesting problem. Hoover and Roosevelt had much in common and had been good personal friends; how had this terrible falling out taken place? What they had in common was very simple. They both had served Woodrow Wilson during World War I, and both of them appeared to be people who were efficient and good administrators. Hoover had a world reputation, and although Roosevelt was not so widely known, he was well regarded and was considered a person of consequence in Washington. They used to meet about once a month. (When the Hoovers were in Washington, they would join a little club in which eight or ten people would go to one another's house on Sunday evening. At the end everybody would be served scrambled eggs out of a chafing dish.) Both were men of great dedication to Wilson and his principles. Hoover wrote a book on his warm admiration of Woodrow Wilson—Hoover was, remember, a staunch Progressive.

Roosevelt said how much he hoped that Hoover would be a candidate for president on the Democratic ticket. (The cause of my own falling out with Hoover was that I suggested in a book of mine that it was logical for Roosevelt and the Democrats to want to nominate Hoover for the presidency. Hoover, having forgotten that he said in 1920 that he was an independent Progressive and only belatedly saying that he was a Republican, wrote me very tartly that he had never been anything but a Republican. I can well understand that he remembered things that way. This was the only thing I ever did so far as I know that upset Hoover.)

I think it was very much to Hoover's credit that he was such a Wilsonian that people thought he might be the heir of Wilson; even FDR thought he might be the heir of Wilson. Nevertheless, though Hoover decided in 1920 he would be Republican, the friendship endured so that when Roosevelt got the nomination for vice president Hoover sent him a charming and warm little note of congratulations, which is in the Roosevelt papers. Then, while Hoover was Secretary of Commerce, Roosevelt—after his polio attack was out of the limelight—headed a trade association in which Hoover was interested, called the American Construction Council. On occasion Hoover and Roosevelt sat together on the same platform. They had a considerable correspondence that does not amount to a great deal but is marked by cordiality, at least up to 1926 or 1927.

Suddenly, in 1928 everything seemed to be different. That year Hoover ran for president and Roosevelt for governor of New York. I know that Roosevelt was interested in backing Al Smith for president, but I never knew just what had gone wrong. Then, a couple of years ago, I was in the Hoover library, and I have here a photocopy of what I picked up. It is part of a memo from Hoover on September 26, 1958, entitled "My Personal Relations with Mr. Roosevelt." Here is an old man, mellowed, who is writing a touching account and granting in 1958 what he would not grant when he talked to me some years earlier—that he and Roosevelt had been friends and had often seen each other. In fact, he had said to me earlier, "I never really knew him well. I only saw him once in a while. I didn't take him seriously." But in 1958 he says they met socially during the Wilson years and were good friends. Its tone is precise and careful: "In September 1919 I returned from Europe and tried to bring about the ratification of the Treaty of Versailles. I had a number of pleasant meetings with Mr. Roosevelt." I give you this just to show that Hoover was human; in other words, he had a bad memory at certain points. He says that, when Roosevelt got polio, "I greatly admired the courage in which he fought his way back to an active life in which he overcame the handicap which had come to him." He goes on in 1958 about these exchanges and even includes the congratulations that Roosevelt as governor of New York sent to Hoover when he was inaugurated, saying "Mrs. Roosevelt and I also send you and Mrs. Hoover personal congratulations and good wishes." These are the sorts of things that you would find between old friends in different political parties.

Continuing his memorandum, Hoover says, "Subsequent to the

election, the following letter came into my hands which seemed to indicate less than fair play and political debate from a personal friend." This is a form letter, which I do not think was written by Roosevelt himself, but by Louis Howe, who carried out political correspondence of this sort. The letter says that the best way to fulfill the ideals of Woodrow Wilson would be to put Al Smith in the White House, rather than—please note this—"the materialistic and self-seeking advisors who surround the other candidate." That hurt Hoover to the quick. People who have been old friends can be extremely sensitive, and Roosevelt several times during the campaign said that he never criticized Hoover. But he did criticize the Republicans in Washington and said they were materialistic and so forth. So perhaps he wrote that letter, but it makes no difference; I am just showing you how trivial this seems to be, given how politicians are.

On the Roosevelt side of the split, it is equally trivial and untoward; Mrs. Roosevelt told me this story—in fact she told me this a couple of times. When FDR was governor of New York, he was the leading candidate for the Democratic presidential nomination in the late spring of 1932. He was also the chairman of the governors' conference in Richmond, and the governors had come up for a reception at the White House. There was a good deal of talk going around that this man was a cripple who was not capable of being president, that he could not take it. It was a hot day. He had steel braces, and of course he gave the impression of walking when he could not walk. He would hold onto the arm of his son James and stiffly move along with his braces locked; it hurt to stand very long. He came into the White House with the governors, but Hoover was not there. The president was busy and so Roosevelt stood; the perspiration started to run down his face and Hoover did not come, but he remained standing. Several people said to him, "Governor, do take a chair," but Roosevelt refused. He was absolutely convinced, and so was Mrs. Roosevelt, that Hoover was purposely staying away to make him stand as an endurance contest to try to prove that Roosevelt would collapse and was not capable of being president. Well, now, that is absolutely preposterous. Yet I am talking about honorable people, decent people, humanitarians all of them. The touchiness of Roosevelt was like that of Hoover. Hoover was obviously tied up with all of the affairs that go with being president and was not able to get to the governors' reception quickly. If he had any notion of what was going on I am sure he would have cut everything short to get out there and be the decent, kind man that he was.

It was over pathetic little things like this that the relationship became so bitter. There was real hostility between the two of them, to such an extent that when they rode to Roosevelt's inauguration there was not much of anything they could say to each other. Hoover did ask if Roosevelt could get a job for his secretary, who was of course going to be out of a job; Roosevelt said he would, and in fact two months later when a commission had a vacancy in which a Republican had to be appointed he appointed this man, Newton, to the commission. Nonetheless, Jimmy Roosevelt still remembers to this day that, sitting in front of the car, he was amazed when he heard his father break the grim silence by saying to Hoover as they rode by the new Interior Building where the girders were up, "Isn't that beautiful steel?" Apparently there was nothing much they could find to converse about as two old friends. The point to this pathetic story is, of course, that we were all the losers. Hoover lost and Roosevelt lost. This helps to explain, I think, why Roosevelt did not enlist this remarkable man for purposes that would have suited them both and been to the common good of the American people.

I especially like the conclusion of the 1958 memorandum by Hoover. Concerning foreign affairs, he goes on to say, "In my speech on June 29, 1941, I said that in the last seven days that call to sacrifice American boys for an ideal has been made as a sounding brass and a tinkling cymbal." He had urged Americans "to stand on the sidelines while those demons Hitler and Stalin destroyed each other . . . Once the United States had become involved in the war, like every other American I gave such assistance as I was permitted to win the war. I offered my services to the President in any way or position where my experience could be useful. He made no reply. He frigidly declined any association with me . . . I did not blame him for this attitude, as my speeches and opposition to his foreign activities were probably hard for him to bear." I end on this note because I think it is something so totally admirable. May I say I think one of the hardest things for Herbert Hoover to do was to be so generous toward someone who had hurt him so badly.

Thank you.

NOTE ON SOURCES

The prime base for these remarks is the papers of Gary Dean Best and Susan Estabrook Kennedy upon which I was commenting. On the foreign policy views of Hoover and Roosevelt, see the biographies of Hoover by David Burner and Joan Hoff-Wilson; Robert H. Ferrell, *American Diplomacy in the Great Depression: Hoover-Stimson Foreign Policy, 1929–1933* (New Haven, Conn., 1957); Robert Dallek, *Franklin D. Roosevelt and American Foreign Policy, 1932–1945* (New York, 1979); and Wayne S. Cole, *Roosevelt and the Isolationists, 1932–45* (Lincoln, Neb., 1983). On the Hoover-Roosevelt relationship, see a paper of broader scope, Frank Freidel, "Hoover and Roosevelt and Historical Continuity," in Arthur S. Link, ed., *Herbert Hoover Reassessed* (Washington, D.C., 1981), pp. 275–91. For details and documentation, see Freidel, *Franklin D. Roosevelt*, vols. 1–4 (Boston, 1952, 1954, 1956, 1973). See also the F. D. Roosevelt file in the Hoover papers at the Hoover Library, West Branch, Iowa. I am grateful to the directors and staff of both the Hoover and Roosevelt Libraries for much assistance.

9

Hiram Johnson Looks at Herbert Hoover

Robert E. Burke

Hiram Johnson and Herbert Hoover were surely California's major contributors to national politics in the first half of this century (just as, I suppose, Richard Nixon and Ronald Reagan have been to the second half). Johnson and Hoover, once they had sized each other up during World War I, came to look upon one another (in Senator Robert Kerr's classic phrase) with "minimum high regard." Theirs was animosity based in part on their opposing positions during the war, when Food Administrator Hoover was a leading light in the Wilson regime and Senator Johnson became one of Wilson's most relentless critics. To this one must add their foreign policy differences in 1919, when Hoover defended the League of Nations and Johnson was one of the leaders of the opposition. Finally, the two became bitter personal enemies in 1920, when Hoover proclaimed himself a lifelong Republican (to the surprise of many Democrats, including his colleague and supporter Franklin Roosevelt) and permitted his friends to enter his name against Johnson in the California presidential preference primary. This was exceedingly unpleasant for Johnson, whose chief opponents had decided to avoid a contest with him in his native state. The Hoover forces concentrated on the League of Nations issue and won a substantial vote in southern California, although the Johnson delegates won. After he lost the nomination to Senator Warren Harding of Ohio, Johnson helped to persuade his old poker-playing buddy to take a basically isolationist position, kept him in line when he began to waver under pressure from internationalists such as Hoover, and in the end campaigned for him. Hoover abandoned "100 percent Wilsonism" (if indeed he ever believed in it), became a mild reservationist, and sought to make one out of Harding; he, too, ended up a Harding supporter in 1920.

Against Johnson's vehement advice, Harding appointed Hoover to his cabinet. As secretary of commerce, Hoover was able to enhance his own already-significant personal following and to become one of the idols of the business world. Johnson got some patronage from Harding, but the Hoover group got more and aligned itself with the Old Guard Republicans of California. In 1922 these forces ran a strong candidate against Johnson in the Senate primary; although they could not deny him renomination, they demonstrated that Johnson had a great deal of opposition, especially in Los Angeles. Two years later, Johnson's second run for president was effectively halted by the same Hoover–Old Guard forces, who humiliated him by carrying California for a Coolidge delegation on the strength of big majorities in the south.

Although Johnson's presidential ambitions were thwarted, he did not lose his power base in California. In 1926 he helped his old colleague C. C. Young win the governorship away from the Old Guard. In 1928 Johnson was renominated without opposition after his friends worked out a "nonaggression pact" with Hoover's friends. For his part, Johnson was required to endorse Hoover. This may have been a bit humiliating, but it was not too difficult since he despised Democrats generally and Al Smith in particular. The Hoover-Johnson animosity emerged once more as soon as Hoover was in the White House. Johnson opposed him on every major policy, domestic and foreign, and in 1932 endorsed and campaigned for FDR. So long as Johnson's love affair with FDR lasted, Johnson's dislike of Hoover remained intact. Only after he, too, had become a critic of That Man in the White House did Johnson begin to see that Hoover had some redeeming features after all. Yet if his memoirs can be believed, Hoover continued to hold Johnson in "minimum high regard."

Granting that the Hoover-Johnson political rivalry was a natural occurrence—even the great state of California could not provide space for two stars of such magnitude without fireworks—how can one account for its intensity and duration, long after Johnson's presidential ambitions were thwarted and long after there was much hope that Johnson could be dislodged from his Senate seat? Were their differences so fundamental that they couldn't have worked out a modus vivendi beyond the short-lived 1928 truce? Although Johnson never gave up his isolationism, Hoover never seriously attempted to alter the Harding policy of U.S. noninvolvement with the League of Nations. Both men moved politically somewhat to the right in the 1920s, Hoover much more than Johnson, although Johnson moved enough in that direction to lose many of his former progressive supporters.

Policy differences between the two were important, but it seems that even more important were matters of pride and power. Both men were exceedingly thin-skinned, never having acquired the usual officeholder's protective hide. Both had hot tempers, and both suffered fools with only the greatest reluctance and ill-grace. The Hoover letters I have seen are not especially revealing of Hoover's private feelings, and I believe it is safe to say that the Hoover scholars are agreed that Hoover managed to keep his private thoughts very private indeed. On the other hand, Johnson's private thoughts did get onto paper: he was a fluent and prolific letter writer with a gift for invective as well as crystal-clear prose. His pride, insecurity, and near-paranoia are all revealed in some of his letters, especially those to his sons in California, Hiram, Jr. (Jack) and Archibald, who were San Francisco lawyers. When he entered the Senate in 1917 Johnson began a series of letters to them, sometimes addressed to both, sometimes to Jack's wife Amy (who died in the fall of 1918), sometimes to Archibald (who died in 1933), but most often to Jack. Some 5,000 pages of these letters, written from 1917 to 1945, have been made available in facsimile edition by Garland Publishing as *The Diary Letters of Hiram Johnson*.

This diary affords a good look at the inside of the world of Hiram Johnson, who entered the Senate at age 50 and was a hopeful for the presidency. His record as a brilliant lawyer, a spell-binding reform governor, and the running mate of Theodore Roosevelt on the Bull Moose ticket in 1912 made him a real contender. Instead, he had to settle for 28 years in the U.S. Senate. He had occasional triumphs—for example, the high tariffs on California specialty crops, the Boulder Dam, and the once-famous Johnson Act, which prohibited loans to nations in default on their war debts. He also had some genuine moments of bliss, especially in the early days of the New Deal, when he finally found a president who cared about him, consulted him, and rewarded him—indeed, who did just about everything Johnson wanted except to become a true isolationist. This bliss did not last, of course; after 1937 Johnson became once again the naysayer he had been most of the time before 1933.

This paper inspects the Hoover-Johnson relationship from Johnson's viewpoint, mainly by noting what he said in his diary. Although both men were California residents, Hoover had lived abroad most of the time since his graduation from Stanford in 1895, and they apparently never met (or at least had any extended conversation) until 1917. Johnson, as governor, must have been aware of Hoover's vigorous if unsuccessful campaign in London in 1912–1914 to get the British to take part in San Francisco's world's fair, the Panama-Pacific International Exposition of 1915.[1] Johnson must have also known of Hoover's work to rescue Americans from the war zone in 1914 and of his great work for Belgium relief; these were highly publicized and made Hoover a celebrity.

Soon after Johnson arrived in the Senate in 1917, just in time to vote for the declaration of war, Hoover returned from Europe to become food administrator. The measure authorizing this position and granting great power to Hoover, the Lever Act, did not become law until August and then only after a brutal battle, particularly in the Senate. In view of their later hostility, Johnson's support of Hoover and his consistent opposition to every effort to water down his authority through modifications in the Lever Act may seem surprising, especially in a senator already noted for his suspicion of Woodrow Wilson and his policies. When Jim Reed, Democrat of Missouri, attacked Hoover "by doubting his status as American voter, if not citizen," Johnson called Hoover "a distinguished world figure . . . particularly fitted for the task."[2]

While the Lever Act was going through Congress, Johnson wrote to his son:

> I dined with Hoover recently and talked with him at length. With my lack of knowledge, I am utterly unable to check the accuracy of his statements, but if he is accurate in his assertions—and he seemed to me to be a man of very great ability—autocratic powers over our food supplies apparently are necessary, not only that, scientifically, we may feed our allies, but that our own people shall not seriously suffer. I am not clear in regard to what comes to us from the Administration either. The fact is that the picture is being painted in darker and darker colors each day.[3]

A few weeks later he wrote his sons of the work he and a Pennsylvania Republican colleague were doing for the Lever Act: "Knox and I have undertaken to do the best we can for the measure and I have no doubt at all of its success."[4] Johnson's actions were a great help to Hoover, especially since the historian of the wartime Congress noted that Hoover "had no political following and thus presented an easy target for senators nursing a grudge against the administration."[5]

Johnson tried in vain to persuade Hoover to make use of his old California friend, Harris Weinstock, a well-known agricultural reformer and advocate of cooperative marketing.[6] He told Weinstock in early June 1917 that he had pressed Weinstock's case on Hoover and would do so again when the Lever Act was passed:

I will do this because he is really an overworked and overwrought man at present. He is endeavoring to perform a great patriotic work. He is meeting with something of that with which you met in California—violent opposition in certain quarters from men who don't understand and who have not sufficient brains, when told, to understand. I am quite anxious for you to work with him because what he is going to undertake, in my opinion, will be far-reaching and revolutionary.[7]

Six weeks later Johnson had to confess that he had not passed on Weinstock's suggestions to Hoover: "He has an absolute and an unbounded confidence in himself, which will either make him the greatest success of the world in the work he is about to undertake or will break him in six months."[8] A few days later he reported "a perfect pilgrimage of Californians to Hoover" and promised to try to take up Weinstock's case again but admitted: "The only difficulty is—that he has grown so great and received so much publicity and adulation, that it is hard for an ordinary man to talk to him."[9]

Thus, even before the final passage of the Lever Act, Senator Johnson found out that he was not going to have much influence with Hoover. There are few references to Hoover in the diary letters for the duration of the war; the most interesting is a reference to profiteering in wartime: "Armour's man Cotton is Hoover's confidential man."[10] In January 1919 Johnson was one of eighteen senators to vote against the Food Appropriation Act.[11] He told his son: "The ugly snout of big business I think I discerned in this . . . The packers wanted to get rid of their surplus stock, and apparently Hoover had agreed with them that this method of pretending to feed starving Europe was an opportune way."[12]

In 1920 many leading Democrats hoped that Hoover would be their party's candidate for president; he had endorsed Wilson's call for a Democratic Congress in 1918 and had been a leading figure in the Wilson administration. As FDR told a mutual friend: "He is certainly a wonder and I wish we could make him President. There couldn't be a better one."[13] But Hiram Johnson saw Hoover as a threat to his own candidacy for the Republican nomination long before March 30, when Hoover announced himself as a Republican in order to permit his delegation to go on the ballot against Johnson. As early as January he had analyzed the situation in a letter to his southern California manager:

The Hoover candidacy is assuming form. It, doubtless, means a fight in California. I am glad it is in the open. I knew it was coming, but, of course, everybody said I was pessimistic when I suggested it. The petition for his candidacy is one singular combination of Los Angeles *Times*, Food Administration, and League to Enforce Peace. But the list of names, I concede readily, is formidable. Hoover has been a candidate for President from the very instant he came to Washington as Food Administrator. This was the reason he surrounded himself with such a tremendous publicity bureau, and this is why Hoover, "the miracle man," "the wonder spirit of babies," etc., were made household terms, and this is why the publicity of the National Food Administration consisted more of laudation of Hoover than of anything else. He has now the greatest press bureau of any man in the Nation, and he has, too, a compact political organization in his Food Administration. He is an antagonist to be feared. First, because of his cleverness and his own personal wealth; secondly, because he is backed by the great powerful business interests to which he pandered while he was Food Administrator; and thirdly, because he is probably backed by the great international forces that wish a league of nations; lastly, because he is believed by our people to be a saint before whose shrine all must bow. If he can beat us in California, of course, that is the end. If the *Times* and the League to Enforce Peace men can break me from my eastern work and make me come to California in an intensive fight, that probably is the end as well. However, the strange thing about it is that this has been in my mind ever since I started. I have never doubted that my great troubles were to come from my own State and from the people there.[14]

As soon as the Hoover slate had filed, Johnson wrote from his campaign train en route to Detroit: "The Hoover people are beginning to boast of California, although apparently it is unnecessary for him to step inside the State or do more than communicate his lordly assent to accept the highest honor in America and the world." It especially angered Johnson that Hoover had moved over to the Republicans and become a reservationist on the League:

> The fact is England wants this League and will take any reservations. Hoover has simply followed Lord Grey, never mentioning reservations until Grey did. For once, Hearst is entirely right. Hoover represents Great Britain and what makes me sick is California is on her knees to this man who sells his country.[15]

Johnson worried about the California May primary—at one point he seriously toyed with the idea of returning to the state to campaign. But he could scarcely do so without damaging his chances in the Midwest and East, and it would have been galling for him since Hoover never campaigned at all and never went near California. Although Johnson's ticket won by a big margin—371,000 to 210,000—as David Burner notes Hoover's campaign may well have attained what may have been his real goal: "to spoil Johnson's campaign for the presidency."[16] It seems doubtful that Johnson could have won the Republican nomination in 1920, since he was far to the left on domestic issues and a bitter-end isolationist at a time when the American public was not yet willing to accept the view that some kind of collective security system was unattainable. It is certainly true, however, that Herbert Hoover did his full share to see that Johnson's presidential bubble burst in his face.

Johnson gave his sons a vivid account of his interview with President-Elect Harding, which sums up both his views of Hoover and his own attitude toward his old Senate friend:

> I was told last evening, confidentially, by Judd Welliver, who is now with Harding, and has been ever since the campaign, and will remain with him until the 4th of March, that there was a possibility of Hoover's appointment to the Cabinet. I said to Harding today, in our interview, that I wanted to say to him the sort of thing I seldom said, but that I did it that he might be fully informed. I then told him that the appointment of Hoover would be most unfortunate from our standpoint; that we had our fight in California, and had divided; that we had won, and were the dominant faction; that we had learned the character of Mr. Hoover in that fight, and his selection for the Cabinet after that struggle would be considered by us in California most unfortunate. He replied that he could not say to me that he could not appoint Hoover, and he would not say he would; that he believed he had to be considered psychologically, and that many people were pressing for his selection. I responded that while he (Harding) had ample ability to look out for his own interests, nevertheless, from his own point of view, he would be putting in his Cabinet a selfish, calculating, untrustworthy candidate for president, and from our point of view, he would be selecting one who had demonstrated his own unworth and whom our people had repudiated.
>
> I have not attempted to repeat all of the fulsome and honeyed phrases of Harding, nor if I tried, could I paint the oleaginous picture presented. No one could have been more friendly, none more flattering. But, in the two instances I have related, you can understand something of Harding's position. He is seeking in every possible way to unite every

hostile element. By flattery on the one side, and by offer of position on the other, he hopes to unite in sweet concord the cacophonies of the Republican Party. The principle of anything he is incapable of understanding. He wants to move smoothly along the path of least resistance, and in order to do so, will make, I think, to us, as well as to others opposed to us, all sorts of concessions. His talk about the League fills me with misgivings, and his lack of frankness concerning Hoover's appointment is quite significant. I will go with him, if it is possible to do so. If a break is to come I hope it comes early. I don't want to glide along here for a year or two by fooling our people, and so I am praying that if he is going wrong, is unfaithful to the promises that he made, that he will make this very clear even before his inauguration.[17]

Hoover, of course, did go into Harding's cabinet as secretary of commerce, and Johnson was not amused. Johnson reported to his sons that at a dinner and poker party at the White House, Harding said:

"Do you know, Johnson, I really think Hoover's going to make good."
I won't analyze this statement, because we, believing as we do that he did not wish to appoint Hoover, but was forced to by Morgan and Company, can smile at an all-powerful President justifying a bad choice on the theory that he *might* make good.[18]

Soon after this he told his sons that, "I believe now he is rather proud of having a part of him, and particularly under him men like Hoover, whom some think the greatest on earth."[19] When C. C. Moore of San Francisco, an old friend of Hoover, entered the senatorial primary against Johnson in 1922, the senator was convinced that there was a cabal of the old eastern standpatters with the Hoover forces to destroy him:

Hoover has an ambition that o'erleaps itself. He is perfectly mad to be President. He and his friends have come to the conclusion that so long as I am politically powerful or hold my present position, I present an insuperable obstacle to his ambition. He believes, and so do our standpat brethren of the East, that I am a standing candidate for President, and I have never thought the matter of sufficient importance, nor have I cared sufficiently for what they thought, to say that my ambitions in that direction were forgotten in 1920. But Hoover, and his friends, claiming California as Hoover's residence, do not think they could ever obtain a delegation from there unless I am broken. Outside of the

State, therefore, there is the sentiment very real in New York, some parts of New England, and in the Middle West, among the old standpatters that I must be rendered incapable of ever conducting another presidential fight, and the determination on the part of Hoover and his people that I must be literally destroyed politically, in order that his ambition may see its fruition.[20]

In the summer before he left Washington to take part in the August primary, he reported on a friendly lunch with the president: "I have been very careful to tell him that I asked nothing, and wanted no pronouncement in my favor, and that I was perfectly willing to fight Mr. Hoover again in California, but that, of course, I did not like to fight Mr. Hoover disguised as Mr. Harding." Johnson was renominated with ease, but his majority was only 75,000, whereas his ticket had won by 161,000 in 1920. Hoover, incidentally, did not get openly involved in this race; Harding told Johnson that Hoover had told him he did not approve of the challenge to Johnson.[21] While Hoover may have been telling Harding—and/or Harding telling Johnson—what the other wanted to hear, it is reasonably certain that the Harding administration did not try to "purge" Johnson in 1922. Johnson, in turn, made it clear that he would not oppose Harding's renomination in 1924.[22]

The death of President Harding in San Francisco on August 2, 1923, after an exhausting trip to Alaska on which he was accompanied by Secretary Hoover, occurred while Johnson was in Washington, shortly after his return from his only trip to Europe. Johnson, encouraged by many friends to enter the 1924 race, told his son that "the entire political situation is in the air." Already, however, he was warned about Hoover: "Nobody here knows what Hoover is going to do. The consensus of opinion is, however, that he will stick in the Cabinet, that Coolidge is going to utilize him, and that Hoover will be the residuary legatee of Coolidge as he expected to be of Harding."[23]

For once Johnson's "consensus of opinion" had it right, but Johnson went ahead with his own candidacy, overestimating his own strength and underestimating the appeal of "Silent Cal." The result was Johnson's political humiliation; he won only a single primary (South Dakota) and even lost California by 50,000 votes to a Coolidge slate backed to the hilt by Hoover's California friends. The Republican National Convention in Cleveland, to which Johnson listened on the radio, afforded him some consolation, as he wrote to his son:

As the last roll call on vice president was taken, and the first five or six states, including California with its twenty-nine votes, were cast for Hoover, my emotions were mixed, but when as the roll call progressed, Hoover was overwhelmed, I was delighted. I made an open fight for the presidency and was badly beaten, but I stood my ground and made my fight. This sneak Hoover has been trying to crawl into power in any fashion he could, first with Wilson, then with the Democratic Party, then with the Republican Party, then with Harding, then with Coolidge, and as all of us have known in the last few days, mad to be vice president. The administration tried to put him over on this last ballot, but the boss-ridden Republican Convention rebelled and revolted at the skunk and would not stand for him. While these twenty-nine Californians thought they were chosen against me for president, their selection was unable to render any real service to Hoover, and they came away from Cleveland a defeated bunch.[24]

Johnson's greatest battle in the Senate in the 1920s was for passage of the Swing-Johnson bill authorizing a high dam at Boulder Canyon on the Colorado, to be built with federal funds, for the purpose of providing irrigation water and hydroelectric power (chiefly for southern California). Congressman Philip Swing, who had long crusaded for it, persuaded Johnson to take the lead in the Senate, where it had intense opposition (particularly from private power companies, Arizona, and some of the "upper basin" states).[25] Although Secretary of Commerce Hoover had negotiated and then renegotiated the Colorado River Compact, which helped to clear the way for a dam, he had no enthusiasm for public power. Suddenly, however, in late March 1926 both Hoover and Secretary of the Interior Hubert Work endorsed the Swing-Johnson bill, but Treasury Secretary Andrew Mellon opposed it. The senator wrote his son: "The administration has been playing fast and loose with us. Hoover and Work favor our bill, and Mellon, apparently, is against it. This situation may be straightened out, but I have little confidence in what any of these gentlemen may say."[26]

A year later, Johnson got the bill on the floor but lost a motion for cloture, 32 to 59, when several of the bill's strongest supporters refused, in principle, to shut off debate.[27] He told his son that Vice President Charles M. Dawes had been of help but that Hoover only "pretended to be for it."[28] In the spring of 1928 Johnson again had the bill before the Senate and again blamed Hoover for its failure: "Whenever we uncover a power trust rogue, we find Hoover. California believes, if it believes anything or cares, that he is for our bill. Every individual with him is against us. The rottenness of the system nauseates me and I'm sick of it."[29] Nevertheless, Johnson got Dawes to make the bill the first order of business when Congress met in December (after the election); this time the compromise version of the bill was passed after an exhausting fight, and it was signed by President Coolidge.[30] It was one of Johnson's finest hours and he was in no mood to share the glory with Hoover, whom he continued to look upon as an obstruction.

That was also the year of the Johnson-Hoover nonaggression pact. After Coolidge announced that he did not "choose to run" in 1928, Johnson was soon convinced that Hoover would win the nomination. He wrote his son that "the Coolidge utterances and Hughes withdrawal put Hoover in the very front rank of the candidates."[31] Johnson was up for re-election himself in 1928 and clearly did not want to give up his Senate seat to challenge Hoover, even though he told his sons in February 1928: "There is a tremendous undercurrent against him, and in my opinion, if any one man could break through and denounce him as he could be denounced, he could be stopped."[32] Two old Johnson supporters wrote about a meeting with Hoover representatives, at which they agreed to support Hoover if Johnson were unopposed. Johnson wrote of this to his sons:

> I received from Bert Meek and from Theodore Roche letters in which they detail what was endeavoring to be done politically in California. Both of them I deem very good friends and I have for them, as you know, a very great affection, and their loyalty, unlike that of many others, is undoubted. They hope by aiding Hoover to aid me. *They* have a singleness of purpose, I think. Nearly all of the others who are engaged in the endeavor are kindly and friendly, but naturally they want their place in the political sun, and no act of mine, and no political principle of theirs, would deter them from actively supporting Hoover and shining in the reflected light of the Hoover campaign. That you may know exactly my attitude, I enclose to each of you herein a copy of my letter to Bert Meek. I felt that there was nothing for me to do, and nothing I could do, and I wrote him, therefore, that while I would not enter into any political bargains of any sort, I assumed my friends would pursue such course as they deemed appropriate. I think the thing for you to do is what I have done. Let matters take their own course. We could not shape them, if we would, and we could not influence nine out of ten who have been with us politically in the past in the attitude they desire to assume.[33]

The rather testy letter to Meek pointed out that the presidential primary was in June, leaving time for a double cross before the senate primary:

> I recognize that if those I have been associated with, enter into any agreement at all, that agreement will be scrupulously observed, and I would wish my friends to carry it out in the utmost good faith. I am perfectly free to say to you that, with a few exceptions, I doubt if those with whom you enter into an agreement would observe the like good faith. I recognize, too, that there is no possible way in which you could be certain of what will happen. The presidential preference primary occurring in May, the incentive for an agreement will be gone, and the gentlemen, who, in the past have violated every tenet of fair warfare will have no reason, when they have accomplished their purpose, save of course, good faith, which they have never observed, to perform their part, I beg you to believe that I am not writing you in bitterness or in hostile criticism of our opponents but I am under no illusions about what will happen this year, and I do not wish you, and a few others, for whom I have an abiding affection, and who I love to think have a similar affection for me, to be under any illusions either.[34]

The nonaggression pact held, even if neither partner actually signed it. By May Johnson had to admit to his sons that he agreed with an old friend and supporter who told him he would have to endorse Hoover after the convention or he would have to "retire permanently from the game."[35] In early June he was still expecting to be double-crossed by Hoover. He wrote his sons that "immediately after his nomination, his organization in the state of California, and it is the only organization probably of any volume, will develop a candidate for United States Senator and enthusiastically support that candidate."[36] Former governor Friend Richardson, one of Johnson's bitter enemies, withdrew from the Senate out of deference to Hoover, leaving him with only nominal opposition in the primary.[37] Johnson had a long conference with Hoover in California before the primary and after that campaigned for him, going so far in late October to call Hoover "one of the world's greatest leaders."[38] The two enemies had been forced by circumstances into one another's arms.

Unfortunately for us, Johnson was in California and thus not writing letters to his sons describing his real feelings at the time. But his envy comes through in letters he wrote in February 1929: "Everything here is in preparation for the inaugural. The skies will be all overcast until the fourth of March, and then God will reign";[39] "I do not need to tell the thoughts that course through my mind when the greatest Californian who has ever existed is about to be inaugurated into the Presidency of the United States."[40] His account of the inaugural is Johnsonian invective at its best:

> I pass over the inauguration with you, simply saying that almost directly in front of me sat yesterday in the senate chamber the outgoing and the incoming presidents. I would have given much to have been able to sketch their countenances. Two more dour, forbidding, and disagreeable faces it would be hard to conceive. Every lineament was sour and disgruntled, and no human expression once illumined these stony faces. The little man who left at once for Northampton is eating his heart out; the other man, who, despite his enormous publicity and the advertising of his modest and shrinking ways, feels himself practically a dictator, and will pursue his ruthless and relentless course in the next few years.[41]

Johnson kept his distance from the new president, although he did attend a White House dinner for the California delegation. He told his sons:

> Last night we received an invitation to dine at the White House next Wednesday night. There were but two courses to pursue: One the conventional course and accept, and the other, the course that simply is not done, of snubbing the President. Personally I should have liked to decline, and to have written a letter, which might have been published, giving my reasons, but such a letter could be met with universal condemnation, and might have involved your Mother in unpleasant social consequences. We'll dine, therefore, with god next Wednesday night, if we live. Dining with Hoover has neither attractions nor terrors for me. I have lived long enough now, and have had sufficient experience to feel perfectly at ease with any individual, no matter what his position, nor how omnipotent he may be.[42]

After the dinner was over he sent his sons an amusing account of the event and described Hoover's political use of White House meals:

> Mother was tremendously exercised about the affair all week. It turned out, however, as I had expected that it would, as a perfectly innocuous

occasion, neither particularly enjoyable nor at all unpleasant. Mrs. Hoover, at whose elbow I sat, rather interested me. She talks like a tragedienne, and I rather imagine she thinks she looks like Ellen Terry. If one were to shut his eyes and listen to her, he could imagine a phonograph running, and a voice attuned to the multitude in mellifluous accents endeavoring to charm. I must say, however, that the dinner was better than the usual Coolidge dinner, and that the Hoovers entertain really better than the Coolidges. The Hoovers have luncheons every day and a dinner every night. They scour the town for arrivals who may be of value politically, and from the publicity standpoint, and mingling these newly arrived individuals with members of the press they utilize to the full the presidential napkin. A New York Representative last Sunday rather wittingly said, "The White House no longer in reality represents the national administration, but the Food administration;" and some of us have dubbed the innumerable newspaper people who have been permitted to stretch their legs under the White House mahogany as the "Knights of the Napkin." It has its results, however. You can imagine the individual coming, for instance, from Kalamazoo or Pinole, who in his community is a paragrapher of note and read by at least a hundred people, suddenly finding himself on a brief visit to Washington, invited to lunch or dine at the White House. Forever after he calls the president Herbert, and he speaks with intimacy of the confidential communications passing between him and the great executive of the nation. The universality of commendation exists everywhere, save in the senate.[43]

Johnson soon became one of the most consistent opponents of Hoover's program. Soon after the Great Crash he wrote to his son:

You have observed that "god" in the White House is going to invite the great financiers here, to solve all of the problems that confront the financial world. Of course, it is merely a part of the regulation bunk that prevails. The newspapers, undoubtedly, in the next week or two will pour forth columns about the constructive energy and ability of the marvelous engineer, and how they have been brought into play in behalf of the financial wreck, and finally have rescued all the imperiled, and again put the world upon the path of prosperity.[44]

Three months later he wrote that, "Notwithstanding the efficient engineering genius in the White House, there is scarcely a thing that he has touched that has not been botched"[45] and, a week later, "It is the universally accepted opinion here that there never has been a President so utterly lacking in leadership or decision . . . His worst characteristic is that none believes in him, and none believes him."[46] In the summer of 1930 he turned down an invitation from the majority leader to a bill-signing ceremony: "I said to him I thought it better for both that I should fulfill a long-standing engagement this morning, which rendered it impossible for me to be on hand. I am now fulfilling that engagement."[47] In December he reported that Hoover was "practically friendless" on the Republican side of the Senate and, if his World Court proposal were put to a secret ballot there, "I do not believe that Hoover would have five votes."[48]

Johnson, like the rest of Congress, was able to spend most of 1931 at home, since Hoover refused to call a special session.[49] On his way back to Washington in November, Johnson told reporters that Hoover "would have the undying gratitude of the Republican Party" if, like Coolidge, he announced that he did not choose to run for re-election. He told his sons that "everybody here was laughing at it, and of course the Hoover papers just went wild," but at the same time every Republican in Washington agreed with him. He reported that there was much speculation about Johnson's own candidacy: "Of course, I have no such intentions as are attributed to me, but I haven't any objection to worrying the yellow man in the White House."[50]

Early in 1932 Johnson made it clear to his sons just why he would not himself challenge Hoover for the nomination:

> From Mr. McCormick, the proprietor of the *Chicago Tribune*, down to a lot of small-fry politicians here, I have been importuned day and night to go into the presidential preference primaries. Were I twenty years younger, and were I in the clear financially, I would not hesitate for a moment; but my years and my poverty make it well-nigh impossible. Of course, the result would not be ultimate success in a nomination, but a demonstration of the unpopularity of Hoover, and probably the prevention of his nomination. Assurances that have come to me from the State of Illinois are simply astounding, and among them all, there is not the slightest doubt of what the result would be there. The contest would entail, however, a similar contest in the State of California, and the very thought of coming into California in a fight for delegates to a national convention for myself personally is simply nauseating. After we had finished with these primaries, we would have about twenty percent of the delegates, and while I probably would

have succeeded in breaking Hoover, somebody else would be the nominee, who could not be worse, of course, but might not be very much better.⁵¹

Johnson loathed the Democrats in Congress, wondering whether their conservative performance might not help Hoover: "I am not sure whether the resentment against Hoover is so intense that nothing will remove it. Certainly, if anything can alter the situation, we may count upon the Democrats to furnish that something. In truth, however, they are a pretty contemptible lot."⁵² Governor Franklin Roosevelt struck Johnson as the Democrats' best choice: "He is really the only man in the offing that seems to have nationwide support, and I think he is the only certainty of defeating Hoover."⁵³ This, incidentally, is the first mention of FDR in the diary letters. He was further encouraged when the Democrats rebelled against their leaders and rejected a national sales tax. When Hoover supporters in the Senate claimed that Democratic disarray would help Hoover's chances, Johnson told his sons that they would have to make even more mistakes "to rehabilitate the fallen fortunes of the great Californian who was born in Iowa, matriculated from Oregon, and lived his life in England."⁵⁴ Although Johnson was upset when Roosevelt was defeated in the California primary and Hoover got a large vote there, he consoled his sons with the latest Hoover story:

> Here is the latest story of Hoover. Perhaps you have had it, and it is an old tale to you now, but only recently has it come to me. Hoover was suddenly kidnapped the other day, and his kidnappers left a ransom note. This note said "If we do not receive $500,000.00 within two hours, we'll bring him back." The tale can be told with all of the embellishments that are possible in Washington. For instance, one of our brethren rushed to a little group of us during the week, apparently out of breath, saying that Lawrence Rich[e]y, White House secretary and detective, had just advised him of the terrible deed, and then recited the note left by the kidnappers.⁵⁵

Johnson felt that the convention that renominated Hoover was "a flop" and picked up on the Prohibition plank to characterize the president: "Hoover, as usual, adopted a prohibition plank, which is the bunk. You can take that plank of the platform, look at it intently, as you gaze into a crystal, and you have a perfect picture of the Hoover mind—

timid, weak, vacillating, uncertain, ambiguous, indirect, deceitful, uncandid, and dishonest."[56] He was determined not to support Hoover in 1932 but was suspicious of the Democrats. In May he wrote:

> This campaign is going to present quite a problem to the old man. I can't support Hoover. I would not want to support a Democrat, who represented exactly what Hoover represents, and I can see the possibility of being a hard working lawyer during the campaign. Of course, this means substantially retirement from politics two years hence, but I am afraid I have been in this job so long I am not fit for any other.[57]

He rejoiced when Roosevelt was nominated, telling his son:

> I was interested in your statement that you were 100 percent for Roosevelt. I think there is no comparison between the two men who are candidates, as men. I thought there was something fine about Roosevelt flying to the Democratic Convention, and immediately expressing his views, and I said so publicly. I have been abused like a pick pocket by the Hoover press, because of this expression, and it has been taken in most quarters as indicative of a bolt upon my part.[58]

However, he was uncertain that Roosevelt could defeat the forces that would be arrayed against him:

> At Chicago, every crooked interest in the country was trying to break Roosevelt. During the campaign, the power trust, the rotten international bankers, and all of those who fatten off of government by robbery of the people will be in the Hoover campaign, and their strength, and power, and influence, can not be overestimated. The majority of the electorate, however, are the other class of our people, and the problem will be whether they will be for Roosevelt, or lukewarm in the campaign.[59]

In the course of the campaign Johnson was one of the Republican Progressives who bolted their party. He campaigned for Roosevelt, and the Democratic National Committee distributed, in leaflet form, his letter to southern California Republican editors who asked him to endorse the ticket. In it he portrayed himself as a progressive and Hoover as a standpat conservative: "The Progressive thinks in terms of human beings; the standpatter has little thought or concern for them." He contended that "the Republican Party is not at stake in this campaign. It is only the ambition of one man who but a little more than a decade ago did not know which was his party, and who before that had no American party at all . . . I cannot and I will not support Mr. Hoover."⁶⁰ Although he considered Alfred Landon a poor candidate, Johnson refused to give in to Roosevelt's repeated requests for re-endorsement in 1936. "I sent my absent voter's ballot yesterday, and voted for [Landon], although with many misgivings," he told his son.⁶¹

Hoover's name disappeared from the Johnson diary letters for several years. Early in 1940 the senator, coming up for what would be his last election, kept Hoover at arm's length. In a revealing letter to his son he wrote:

> I will say to you, confidentially, that Hoover has made several attempts to talk to me, but I have kept away from him, and refused to make any appointments with him. It is not so much that I distrust Hoover, for I am bound to believe his repeated protestations that he is not a candidate, but I simply do not want to get mixed up with him. I know how I would feel if I were in his shoes toward one, who had been guilty of the political sins, or what are looked upon as political sins, I have committed. I made up my mind in the beginning, therefore, and I have stated the fact to very many people, that I would have nothing to do with the selection of delegates to the National Convention, and would confine my gigantic energies to my own fight.⁶²

The last few mentions of Hoover in Johnson's diary letters are surprisingly favorable. In September 1940, after the choice of the Republican State Central Committee, he told his son "I do not think that it was quite just that Hoover should be kicked around in the manner that he was."⁶³ Johnson, who had endorsed Wendell Willkie after he himself had won the Democratic as well as the Republican nomination for senator, was angry when his party's titular leader did not speak out against the Lend-Lease bill. He wrote to his son: "Where is Mr. Willkie? His voice is not heard, although I am very glad to say Hoover's, Dewey's, Landon's, and many others' have been heard."⁶⁴ The last mention of Hoover in the diary letters comes in the summer of 1944, a little over a year before Johnson's death. He told his son that he had listened on the radio to all the speeches at the Republican National Convention: "Those of Hoover, Bricker in retiring as the presidential candidate, and Dewey, I thought were excellent."⁶⁵ Hoover did have some redeeming features after all and Johnson, in private at least, was at last willing to recognize them. We thus start out and end up with Johnson thinking highly of Hoover, but in between it was quite another story. It would be nice to know what Hoover really thought of Johnson.

NOTES

1. Craig Lloyd, *Aggressive Introvert: A Study of Herbert Hoover and Public Relations Management, 1912–1932* (Columbus, 1972), pp. 19–36.
2. Frederic L. Paxson, *America at War, 1917–1918* (Boston, 1939), p. 82.
3. Johnson to Archibald M. Johnson, June 8, 1917, Johnson Papers, Bancroft Library, Berkeley, California. This and all subsequent letters from Johnson to his sons are available in Robert E. Burke, ed., *The Diary Letters of Hiram Johnson*, 7 vols. (New York, 1983).
4. Johnson to sons, July 2, 1917.
5. Seward W. Livermore, *'Politics Is Adjourned': Woodrow Wilson and the War Congress, 1916–1918* (Middleton, 1966), p. 52.
6. A sketch of Weinstock's important career is in Grace Larsen, "A Progressive in Agriculture: Harris Weinstock," *Agricultural History* 32 (July 1958): 187–93.
7. Johnson to Harris Weinstock, June 6, 1917, Johnson Papers.
8. Ibid., July 17, 1917.
9. Ibid., July 26, 1917.
10. Johnson to Hiram Johnson, Jr., August 18, 1918.
11. *Congressional Record*, 65th Cong., 3d sess. (January 24, 1919), pt. 2: 1996.
12. Johnson to Hiram, Jr., January 24, 1919.
13. David Burner, *Herbert Hoover: A Public Life* (New York, 1979), pp. 150–51.
14. Johnson to Meyer Lissner, January 24, 1920, enclosed in letter to sons, same date, Johnson Papers.
15. Johnson to sons, April 2, 1920.
16. Burner, *Herbert Hoover: A Public Life*, p. 154.
17. Johnson to sons, December 7, 1920.
18. Ibid., September 10, 1921.
19. Ibid., October 29, 1921.
20. Ibid., June 23, 1922.
21. Richard Dale Batman, "The Road to the Presidency: Hoover, Johnson, and the California Republican Party, 1920–1924" (Ph.D. diss., University of Southern California, 1965), p. 217.
22. Robert K. Murray, *The Harding Era: Warren G. Harding and His Administration* (Minneapolis, 1969), p. 425.

23. Johnson to Hiram, Jr., August 10, 1923.
24. Ibid., June 13, 1924.
25. The best account of this affair is Beverly Bowen Moeller, *Phil Swing and Boulder Dam* (Berkeley, 1971).
26. Johnson to Archibald, March 27, 1926.
27. *Congressional Record*, 69th Cong., 2d sess. (February 27, 1927), vol. 68, pt. 5: 4898–4900.
28. Johnson to Hiram, Jr., March 11, 1927.
29. Johnson to sons, May 8, 1928.
30. Ibid., December 18, 1928; Johnson to Archibald, December 24, 1928.
31. Johnson to Hiram, Jr., December 10, 1927.
32. Johnson to sons, February 3, 1928.
33. Ibid., January 23, 1928.
34. Johnson to B. B. Meek, January 16, 1928, copy in Johnson Papers.
35. Johnson to sons, May 12, 1928.
36. Ibid., June 5, 1928.
37. *New York Times*, July 8, 1928.
38. Ibid., July 22 and October 26, 1928.
39. Johnson to Archibald, February 9, 1929.
40. Johnson to Hiram, Jr., February 9, 1929.
41. Johnson to sons, March 5, 1929.
42. Ibid., May 18, 1929.
43. Ibid., May 30, 1929.
44. Johnson to Archibald, November 16, 1929.
45. Johnson to sons, February 22, 1930.
46. Johnson to Hiram, Jr., March 1, 1930.
47. Johnson to Archibald, July 4, 1930.
48. Johnson to Hiram, Jr., December 12, 1930.
49. For the basic study of Hoover and Congress, see Jordan A. Schwarz, *The Interregnum of Despair: Hoover, Congress and the Depression* (Urbana, Ill., 1970).
50. Johnson to sons, November 22, 1931.
51. Ibid., January 9, 1932.
52. Ibid., March 6, 1932.
53. Johnson to Archibald, March 21, 1932.
54. Johnson to sons, April 2, 1932.
55. Ibid., May 7, 1932.
56. Johnson to Archibald, June 19, 1932.
57. Johnson to Hiram, Jr., May 1, 1932.

58. Ibid., July 9, 1932.
59. Ibid.
60. Hiram Johnson, "What Every Progressive Owes His Country," copy in Warren G. Magnuson Papers, University of Washington Library, Seattle.
61. Johnson to Hiram, Jr., October 24, 1936.
62. Ibid., February 14, 1940.
63. Ibid., September 29, 1940.
64. Ibid., January 11, 1941.
65. Ibid., July 12, 1944.

10

Herbert Hoover's Indian Reformers Under Attack: The Failures of Administrative Reform

William G. Robbins

Cycles of reform, retrenchment, and reaction have characterized the formulation and administration of federal Indian policy in the United States. Government bureaucrats and legislators have alternated between an aggressive pursuit of assimilation bent on integrating Indian people as quickly as possible into the dominant society, and a program that advocates some attention to preserving the Indian's legitimate cultural heritage along with a less aggressive, though still decidedly assimilationist ideology. The imperial powers of Western Europe, likewise, pursued sometimes ambivalent colonial schemes that equivocated between the stark cause of assimilation and one that permitted a greater degree of cultural autonomy. Whether the colonial design be British, French, or the Indian policy of the U.S. government, however, its identifying characteristics were paternal: a denial of traditional native political structures and a circumstance whereby indigenous people were dependent on nonnative political structures and resources.[1] This dichotomy has characterized Indian reform in the United States in the first half of the twentieth century. Most often reform programs represented superficial, administrative change that left the substructure of Indian policy intact and preserved the paternal relationship between federal government and native subject.[2]

Three sustaining assumptions characterized efforts to reform federal Indian policy in the early twentieth century: (1) that Indian people desire and should be thoroughly integrated into the dominant society; (2) that the immediate social and economic conditions of Indian people should be ameliorated; and (3) that the federal government is the agency best fitted to determine and carry out such programs. For the first twenty years of the new century, reformers showed little interest in Indian affairs, a phenomenon that suggests something about the narrowness of progressivism. Indeed it was not until the 1920s, a decade supposedly devoid of reform, that one hears the first rumblings about changing the federal administration of Indian policy. For many years after the passage of the General Allotment (or Dawes) Act in 1887, it was widely assumed that Indians were being successfully integrated into U.S. society and that the government's assimilation program would soon be a resounding success. By the 1920s, however, it was apparent to many that not all was well in the field, that somehow assimilation had failed to achieve its goals.[3] Finally, in 1929 the administration of Herbert Hoover, in addition to its commitment to bring the benefits of its New Era reforms to the majority of white Americans, also promised to extend those blessings to the American Indian.[4]

The General Allotment Act was predicated on the assumption that individualizing the Indian pattern of collective landholding would speed the erosion of tribalism and its cultural trappings, promote assimilation, and lead eventually to the full integration of Indian people into American life. An odd assortment of special interest groups had combined to force congressional passage of the measure: railroad and cattle spokesmen who wanted to break up the reservation system in the American West, reclamationists who wanted access to reservation water, and a strong assimilationist-minded group of Christian reformers centered in the Indian Rights Association.[5] As the years passed it became glaringly obvious that the allotment policy was perpetuating Indian poverty, contributing to ever-worsening health conditions, and accelerating the alienation of Indian people from their land base.[6] These matters were made public in the 1920s when a number of reform organizations publicized Indian health conditions and the continued fraudulent acquisition of land by non-Indians. The most notorious series of incidents centered around the Pueblo land controversy and the subsequent efforts of reformers to bring an end to the allotment policy.[7] During this period the reformers were united against the forces of tradition and an entrenched Indian bureaucracy.

The struggle to determine the direction of Indian policy in the 1920s produced knights in shining armor, crusading reform organizations, and a sprinkling of first-rate villains. Two hold-over officials, Charles H. Burke and Edgar Meritt, who had been appointed by former secretary of the interior Albert B. Fall, held the offices of commissioner and assistant commissioner of Indian affairs until Herbert Hoover replaced them shortly after his inauguration in the spring of 1929. Burke, a former congressman from South Dakota, had continued the breakup of the reservations under the allotment act and was contemptuous reformers like John Collier and his American Indian Defense Association (AIDA). As a consequence, the more aggressive activists contended that Burke and Meritt were reactionaries and should be removed from office.[8] Early in 1929 Harold Ickes, then an ambitious Chicago attorney, castigated the Fall appointees for perpetuating a "shameful record" in their treatment of American Indians.[9] Undoubtedly, the association of Burke and Meritt with Fall and their seeming reluctance to consider even the mildest of policy changes sharpened the differences between them and the Indian reformers. It remained to be seen, however, if a new administration would bring any dramatic new direction in Indian affairs.

Jealousy and ideological differences over the substance and speed with which assimilation should be carried out further muddied the reform scene of the 1920s. As part of an effort to engage the expertise of social scientists to help solve the government's persisting Indian problems, Secretary of the Interior Hubert Work commissioned the Institute for Government Research and an investigative team headed by Lewis Meriam of the University of Chicago to make a survey of economic and social conditions among American Indians. Popularly known as the Meriam Report and published in 1928, the study was a scathing indictment of health conditions, educational policy (especially the off-reservation boarding schools), and virtually every other aspect of the government's Indian program. The allotment policy was singled out as a special case for failure, not because it was bad policy but because it had failed to "individualize" Indian people and make them into self-supporting members of the communities in which they lived.[10]

The Meriam Report provided ample grist for groups and individuals with reform ambitions, especially because its publication came in the midst of an election year. It proposed a limited reform program, although it recognized the need to improve the condition of Indian people. But all indicators suggest that neither Indian affairs nor the publication of the Meriam Report was a major election issue in 1928. There is evidence, however, to suggest that Republican party campaign strategists may have withheld distribution of the report until the adjournment of Congress to avoid the onus of having failed to act on its own recommendations.[11] What confuses the issue is the fact that the leading Republican candidate was the energetic secretary of commerce, Herbert Hoover, a man who enjoyed wide public identification with humanitarian and reform causes. Moreover, Secretary of the Interior Work, the person chiefly responsible for handling federal Indian affairs, resigned his cabinet post to assume duties as Hoover's campaign manager.[12]

David Burner, a Hoover biographer, has claimed that Hoover "had strong reasons for addressing himself to the problems of American Indians" because of his long and intimate association with Indian people through childhood experiences, relatives in the employ of the Indian service, and the "Quaker tradition of fair treatment for Indians."[13] The claim is unfounded and misleading. If anything, an examination of the Hoover presidency shows that the chief executive had little interest and a surprising lack of familiarity with Indian affairs. Even the significant Meriam Report, for instance, seems to have escaped Hoover's attention for some time. As late as August 1928, Hoover's press secretary, George Akerson, responded to an inquiry about the Meriam Report: "Mr. Hoover has not yet seen the report . . . and of course since he is still Secretary of Commerce it would not be proper for him to comment upon the report of another Department."[14]

In early October 1928 the AIDA addressed questionnaires to both presidential candidates outlining the continuing "violation of obligations" to Indian people, the "misuse and misapplication of property held in guardianship," and the "arbitrary and tyrannical denial of the fundamental safeguards of life, liberty, and property." The democratic nominee, Al Smith, evidently responded immediately to the request and according to one Hoover supporter promised "everything under the sun." A Hoover sympathizer and member of the AIDA asked Hoover to respond to prevent "what seems now obvious—namely, the advice of the Executive Committee to vote for Smith upon the basis of the reply which is already in our hands." Hoover's subsequent reply to the questionnaire was ambivalent:

> Your letter of October 6th has been called to my attention. I am not in position to confirm or deny the assertions which have been put forth in your communication. If they are true they warrant and demand immediate remedy. Investigation was made, as you state, at the request of the Republican Administration, and I have no doubt of its desire to do its duty in these matters. My own connection in activities for the assistance of children has led the association of which I am head to interest themselves in Indian children during the past few years and this should be sufficient indication of my interest in these matters.[15]

From the outset it seemed obvious that Herbert Hoover would not be an activist reformer on behalf of Indian people; his reluctance to act on controversial Indian issues during his presidency supports this assumption.[16] To a certain degree, therefore, the Hoover administration's reputation for reform in Indian policy rests with the successes and failure of cabinet and Indian service appointees and not with the chief executive.

In keeping with the paternal and colonial nature of the relationship between Indian people and the U.S. government, the predominantly white activist organizations lobbied with the federal government (and vied with each other) to influence the direction of Indian policy. The Indian Rights Association, which had been founded in 1882 and was the oldest of the Indian reform organizations, had a long tradition of association with missionary groups, followed an avowedly assimilationist and integrationist program, and was chiefly responsible for the philosophy expressed in the General Allotment Act. The missionary, assimilationist temper still prevailed among the Indian Rights Association membership in the late 1920s as evidenced in its monthly publication, *Indian Truth*.[17]

The more recent and aggressive AIDA originated in the Pueblo land controversy of 1922–1924. Its inspirational leader and most influential spokesman was the social engineer and moral reformer, John Collier. In addition, the AIDA attracted university professors like Haven Emerson and others who believed in the use of social science tools and research techniques to solve social problems. Although the AIDA and the Indian Rights Association had clashed periodically since the former was organized in 1923, neither group had much influence with the regime of Commissioner of Indian Affairs Charles Burke. In fact, both organizations regularly attacked Burke and the government's Indian policy during the late 1920s; the cooperation and mutual support between these two groups carried through the first year of the Hoover administration.[18] Furthermore, Hoover's initial moves gave the reformers cause for hope.

The appointment of Hoover's long-time friend, Ray Lyman Wilbur, as Secretary of the Interior pleased the Indian Rights Association and most Indian reformers. As an educator, president of Stanford University, and with an active interest in Indian affairs, Wilbur brought impressive credentials to the office. *Indian Truth* praised the beginning of the new administration: "Wherever the Indian question is discussed by well-informed students of the subject, there is a pronounced feeling of optimism that under the leadership of Herbert Hoover and Secretary Wilbur, a new and better day is dawning for the American Indian."[19] In quick succession the new administration fired Charles Burke and Edgar Meritt and appointed two Quakers—Charles J. Rhoads, a wealthy Philadelphia banker, as commissioner, and J. Henry Scattergood, an equally successful businessman, as assistant commissioner. Both men had worked on relief and reconstruction activities in France at the close of World War I and were active members of the Indian Rights Association. At the time of his appointment to the Indian bureau, Rhoads was president of the association.[20]

The appointment of Wilbur, Rhoads, and Scattergood as the administration's principal Indian policymakers was fraught with trouble for the future. All three represented the assimilationist approach of the Indian Rights Association, and they also worked in close harmony with the quasi-private, missionary-oriented Board of Indian Commissioners. Indeed, the most aggressive aspect of the administration's Indian program was Wilbur's zeal in pressing for an early version of the infamous "termination" policy of the early 1950s. In an earlier letter to his predecessor, Wilbur had listed six steps to an equitable Indian policy: (1) the use of intelligence tests to determine which children should advance beyond the sixth grade; (2) a requirement that all Indian children attend public school; (3) the withdrawal of the federal government from Indian affairs "as soon as possible" and the speeding up of allotment; (4) the improvement of health and education for Indian youth, but on the basis of Indian responsibility; (5) the acceleration of school integration; and (6) the liquidation of tribal assets and the grant of prorated shares to each enrolled Indian.[21]

Even before Rhoads and Scattergood arrived in Washington, Secretary Wilbur outlined the administration's approach to Indian affairs. In a memo to the president, Wilbur said the objective of the Indian office "shall be to make of the Indian a self-supporting, self-respecting American citizen just as rapidly as this can be brought about." He recommended that education and health programs be placed under the respective jurisdictions of the Bureau of Education and the Public Health Service, or, where feasible, made the responsibility of the various states. He proposed that the activities of the Indian bureau be decentralized, that Indian agents gradually be phased out, that children attend public schools where they are accessible, and that, except for large reservations, there "should be a continued allotment of land." Finally, the interior secretary urged improved facilities for Indian people "with the general plan in mind of eliminating the Indian bureau within a period of say 25 years." President Hoover made few alterations in Wilbur's proposals but did suggest that Wilbur consult with the commissioners on Indian affairs "which I think is called the Board of Indian Commissioners . . . They are all sane people."[22] In this instance, the president displayed a lack of familiarity with the workings of the Indian office and a surprising ignorance of his own Quaker heritage. The Quakers, it should be noted, were chiefly responsible for the creation of the original Board of Indian Commissioners in 1869. But, more importantly, Wilbur and Hoover indicated from the beginning that, like previous administrations, they were inclined to favor the missionary-oriented board.[23]

One of the most influential congressional figures the Hoover administration had to confront to obtain funding for its Indian programs was the Republican chairman of the House Appropriations Committee, Representative Louis Crampton of Michigan. Although Crampton was anathema to reformers, he had to be reckoned with if the administration hoped to get legislation through that committee. Moreover, Crampton had forewarned the administration to be on guard. In a letter to the president on April 17, 1929, he expressed alarm about the secretary of the interior's Indian policies. Crampton objected to dropping Indians as "wards of the Nation" (Wilbur's language) and opposed the transfer of Indian health and education policies to the states or to other executive departments. Crampton directed his strongest criticism at Wilbur's proposal that the allotment policy should be continued. Allotment, he argued, "has been more permanently disastrous to the welfare of the Indians" than any other policy advocated "by idealistic but ill-informed Indian administrators." Indians everywhere, he said, were "suffering from a too rapid application of the policy of allotment of land." Crampton warned the president that the interior secretary should "avail himself to the views of men in Congress" who had years of experience on the subject. Hoover's response must have irritated further the Michigan congressman's already negative impression of the administration: "I suggest that you reserve judgment in the matter until you have had an opportunity to take matters up with him."[24]

Toward the end of Hoover's first year in office, his administration became embroiled in a controversy regarding adequate appropriations to provide food and clothing for children attending Indian boarding schools. The issue centered on Crampton's efforts to cut appropriations designated to upgrade boarding school food and clothing allocations (referred to as the Deficiency Bill). The intervention of the AIDA and the subsequent restoration of funds in the Senate effected a compromise and partial victory for the administration. Senate progressives and the forceful arguments of the AIDA, however, probably deserve most of the credit. *The Nation* accused Commissioners Rhoads and Scattergood of being submissive and of defending Crampton's recommendations. It also criticized the president for his inability and unwillingness to discipline members of his own party and for his failure to aggressively support Indian legislation.[25]

The controversy over the Deficiency Bill marked the beginning of the alienation of the AIDA and Hoover's Indian policymakers. Yet what other reformers characterized as failure, the Indian Rights Association described as "the dawn of a new era in Federal administration of Indian affairs." At last the Indian "is getting a new deal," the association emphasized, and it praised Rhoads and Scattergood as the architects of a new plan of action who "have disarmed believers in the old order, harmonized discordant elements, and gained adequate financial support." In its annual report for 1929–1930, the Board of Indian Commissioners also applauded Rhoads and Scattergood for their cautious approach and for avoiding "sensational upheavals" and "dramatized reforms." The criticisms of "captious critics" who berated the hard-working commissioners, the board noted, was an unpleasantness inseparable from the office. It commended the commissioners for making progress "step by step" and not by "sensational leaps and bounds."[26]

While the Indian Rights Association and the Board of Indian Commissioners praised the Indian administrators for ushering in a new era of progress, the AIDA accused Wilbur, Rhoads, and Scattergood of promising the millennium, raising the "highest hopes," and accomplishing "practically nothing." Haven Emerson, the AIDA's president, chastised Wilbur and his subordinates for failure to "fight to a finish for such elementary things as the prevention of starvation of the Indian children." The Indian bureau, Emerson charged, "is, if anything, in worse plight now than under their predecessors, Burke and Meritt."[27] Attacks such as this soon became an obsession with the Interior Department.

Because of Wilbur's excessive sensitivity to even the mildest criticism, he must share some of the responsibility for the increasing alienation of his department from critics in Congress and groups like the AIDA. This sensitivity turned to outright rancor as the months passed and the charges mounted. As early as May 1930, Wilbur complained that AIDA attacks "have required a great deal of the time of the Commissioners" and that the attacks were not based on reality. It was easy for the association to criticize, Wilbur contended, because it "has no responsibility." Moreover, such "outrageous and unworthy" attacks hurt "the opportunities of the government officials to obtain and retain the confidence of the Indian population." He hoped that the association would act more responsibly in the future and discontinue its widespread, intemperate, and illy digested emotional attacks."[28] In his memoirs Wilbur refers to "confusion . . . created by the constant agitations of certain zealots" who "consumed a good deal of the time of government officials which might have been better used for the benefit of the Indians."[29]

These charges were misleading, because Wilbur, the Department of Interior, and the Indian office had become involved in a number of issues that were of great concern to Indian people. One of the most troublesome for the interior secretary and the Indian commissioners was the disposition of the Flathead Indian power issue, a controversy that had been simmering long before the election of Herbert Hoover. The turmoil centered around the application of the Rocky Mountain Power Company, a subsidiary of the Montana Power Company (and with close ties to Anaconda Copper), to develop a hydroelectric site on the Flathead reservation in Montana.[30] Wilbur was deeply involved in the Flathead power case because he was titular head of Indian affairs and chairman of the three-member Federal Power Commission, the agency charged with licensing federal power sites.

The Federal Power Commission rendered its controversial decision to lease the site to the Rocky Mountain Power Company in May 1930. By this time the Hoover administration's Indian policy was already under attack. Assistant Commissioner Scattergood, who negotiated the terms of the lease with the Rocky Mountain Power Company, involved the Flathead Indians only peripherally in the discussions. This process, however, was not unusual, since the government seldom consulted Indian people in such matters. The decision was made more controversial because the case was the first of its kind.[31]

The Flathead decision set Wilbur and the Indian office against progressive forces who viewed the Flathead power issue as a cause célèbre. These included public power advocates such as Judson King, the National Popular Government League, and a coalition of Western progressives in the Senate who favored public power and criticized the administration of Indian policy.[32] To add fuel to the progressive's charges, the president's office failed to intervene in the dispute despite numerous requests to do so. The disposition of the Flathead case certainly worsened Hoover's problems with Congress and discredited his Indian policy administrators. The nation's rapidly contracting economy made matters even more difficult.

There are further indications that the Flathead decision embarrassed the Hoover administration. In a news release hailing the Indian bureau's achievements during his first year in office, the president made no mention of the Flathead power issue. Yet, in his original, six-page memorandum to the president, Commissioner Rhoads included a full-page discussion of the Flathead decision. Hoover released the commissioner's full memorandum to the press with the exception of the information under "Flathead Power Site."[33]

The administration was not without supporters. These attacks on the government's Indian administrators prompted Joseph W. Latimer, a New York attorney, to come to the defense of the administration in mid-1930. Although he "utterly opposed . . . many policies which are apparently those of the present Commissioners," Latimer said they should be commended for asking Congress to assist in "abolishing the Bureau." He praised the new commissioners for being "open-minded" and "honest men, free . . . from any political entanglements," and he attacked John Collier and the Senate Committee on Indian Affairs. The committee, he argued, allowed too much of its testimony from one source—its "star and perpetual witness" who dramatized his opinions "so that they appear in the record as facts." Latimer referred disparagingly to Collier as the "Professional Benevolent" and defended Rhoads, "the mild-mannered, patient Commissioner," who pleaded "for a broader view of Indian affairs" in his testimony to the "inquisitorial Committee."[34]

The mounting congressional attacks and the persistent criticism by the AIDA jeopardized the administration's Indian legislative program. In a candid letter to the president on November 17, 1930, Wilbur outlined some of the administration's difficulties with Congress: "It is becoming clearer that we are not likely to receive substantial constructive help from the Senate Committee on Indian Affairs. They are primarily interested in investigations of alleged abuses or deficiencies. We have found it difficult to obtain a constructive interest on the part of the House Committee."[35] Thus, after dismissing the possibility of getting legislation through Congress, Wilbur proposed a typically Hooverian solution: a commission with legislative authority "to study the tangled treaties, laws, rights and other pressing problems, and to make recommendations for a fresh start." Wilbur got the president's formal approval and had a bill embodying the commission approach introduced in Congress. But this effort to deal with Indian affairs through an elitist commission failed because of the growing crisis of the depression. The Bureau of the Budget informed Wilbur in January 1931 that the expenditure was not in accord with the president's financial program. When the interior secretary appealed to the president, he was informed that "we would be entirely in favor of a moderate appropriation for it if no expenditures were to be undertaken until after the fiscal year 1933."[36] Wilbur's unsuccessful attempt to circumvent a recalcitrant Congress and deal with Indian affairs through the establishment of a commission strongly suggests that the successes and failures of the federal Indian program still depended on legislative appropriations from Congress.

There were other persons involved in shaping the Hoover administration's Indian policy, although some of the administration's early supporters later turned up as some of its most strident critics. One of these was John Collier. The liberal historiography of the New Deal has tended to exaggerate the influence and successes of Collier as commissioner of Indian affairs (1933–1945) under FDR.[37] Because Collier was more intimately associated with reformist activities, it has also been easy to exaggerate the ideological differences between him and Rhoads. Although both men had previously worked with different white-dominated Indian reform organizations—the Indian Rights Association and the AIDA—there was considerable collaboration between the two groups and both had cooperated to push specific Indian legislation in Congress. Collier and the AIDA assisted Rhoads during his first years as commissioner in drafting much of his legislative program and subsequently lobbied for passage of that program through Congress.[38] Rhoads, moreover, was not so unrepentant an assimilationist as Wilbur,[39] and some of his views anticipate the rhetoric and policy of Collier's tour in the Indian office. In his annual report for 1930, Rhoads argued that the federal government should preserve what is best in Indian "traditions, arts, crafts, and associations" and "encourage their development and survival."[40] If anything Rhoads offered a less forceful and less arbitrary administration of Indian policy than his successor.

The major restraint to some of the more progressive proposals coming out of the Indian office was undoubtedly Secretary Wilbur. Although he had formulated his own program and had endorsed the earlier Collier-Rhoads legislation, he was unable to get the measures through Congress. Wilbur's belief that the allotment policy should be continued made it unlikely that he would vigorously pursue Rhoads's recommendation that Congress reverse the direction of the General Allotment Act. Indeed, Wilbur reiterated his opinion in the department's annual report for 1930: "The Government must be divorced more and more from supervision over the Indian's person, through the gradual breakup of the old reservation system."[41]

To make matters more difficult, Wilbur and Hoover gave little support to Rhoads and Scattergood, who repeatedly testified in front of congressional committees on issues related to government Indian policy. There is a note of pessimism in Wilbur's November 17, 1930, letter to the president that Congress would likely oppose any administration-sponsored Indian legislative program.[42] The fact that Rhoads and Scattergood were not forceful personalities confounded even further the administration's problems. Collier recalled in later years that the administration introduced good legislation, but "no amount of persuasion could . . . bring the Secretary and the Commissioner to press in Congress for enactment of the necessary legislation. They furnished, in other words, what could have become an 'ad interim' change of spirit within the Indian Service."[43]

The Hoover administration was also developing a sense of paranoia. Even in those instances when someone praised its Indian policies, the administration seems to have had a wary eye on its chief critic, the AIDA. When Hoover signed the bill authorizing payment of over one million dollars to the Ute Indians for land taken from them through an executive order of President Theodore Roosevelt, he did so "with certain reluctance," because the "bill provides that fees and expenses shall be taken from the Indians and allowed to the lobby promoting the bill." Although such procedures were common practice in most Indian claims' appropriation bills, in this case the "lobby" was the AIDA. Hoover fumed that the "whole background of lobbies in Washington pushing and profiting on behalf of helpless people is most repugnant." He contended that the "Government ought to be able to do justice by its wards without feeding these professional lobbies." Hoover vetoed other appropriations for claims, arguing that the government should not "undertake the revision of treaties"; furthermore, "the increased values have been the result of the efforts of our citizens in building this nation."[44] With the worsening of the depression, such legislation usually fell victim to the administration's economy drive.

Hoover's propensity for administrative reform is clearly illustrated in the experiences of the Indian bureau.[45] He selected Rhoads as commissioner because he "has some understanding of the problems and at the same time has the large business experience necessary to thoroughly reorganize this Bureau." In his first two years as commissioner, Rhoads did just that; he divided the bureau into five field divisions—health, education, agricultural extension and industry, forestry, and irrigation—with a director at the head of each division. The new system replaced a 50-year-old organizational structure and was designed to simplify management and make the Indian office more responsive to "the needs of the field."[46] Only the future could tell whether the more efficient operations of the Indian office would effect change at the grass-roots level.

Most government bureaucrats normally oppose the reorganizing and shifting about of personnel in administrative agencies. This is particularly true of the Indian bureau, which has historically resisted change, administrative or otherwise.[47] In the case of Rhoads's reorganization scheme, bureau employees in the field led the opposition to the plan. Shortly after Rhoads implemented his new administrative structure, complaints filtered into the Indian office regarding the new requirements for appointment to the Indian service. The tradition-bound Board of Indian Commissioners complained "that a considerable number of the older employees are at a disadvantage when promotions are under consideration." The board also contended that graduates of Indian schools were being discriminated against because they lacked the academic requirements:

> The board submits that strict adherence to these academic standards will often work an injustice toward faithful and competent Indian employees and will discourage young and promising Indians from preparing themselves for government service.
>
> The board believes that in closing the door of opportunity to graduates of Indian schools the Indian Office is departing from its declared policy of developing Indian leadership . . . The board further suggests the inconsistency of opening placement offices to secure employment for Indians while, at the same time, denying the opportunity of employment in the Indian service itself.[48]

The board's reasoning was obviously self-serving. It feared that bureau personnel with missionary backgrounds might be replaced in the administrative reshuffling. Its complaints went unanswered and the reports of discharges, promotions, transfers, and demotions continued to cause unrest among field personnel.[49]

Hugh Scott, a respected member of the Board of Indian Commissioners who conducted a survey of conditions in the field service during the summer of 1931, delivered the most damaging critique of all. Although he praised the increases in medical and educational facilities and the improvements in dietary provisions for Indian children, Scott reported that "of the general administration of the Service, this cannot be said." He noted that the "Washington Office has always been noted for a lack of consideration for its field force but I have never seen such a lack since the establishment of the civil service in the Bureau of Indian Affairs." Scott observed that the reorganized Indian bureau was "hostile to the field employees," but he directed his most devastating criticism at the bureau's claim that it had decentralized administration. Because the reorganization plan had delegated authority to division heads, "this decentralization has never gone further than the Washington office." Practical decentralization, Scott reported, had not reached the superintendents who were in closest contact with Indian people. The bulk of the Scott report was a damning indictment of one of the administration's chief claims to achievement in the field of Indian affairs.[50]

As the depression deepened and reports about starvation and demoralized conditions in Indian country became more frequent, one final development made irreversible any rapprochement between the Hoover administration and its Indian policy critics. This concerned the mounting attacks of the Senate Committee on Indian Affairs and the AIDA against Herbert Hagerman, an Albert B. Fall appointee as the

Indian bureau's special commissioner to the Navajos. Hagerman's association with land speculators, railroad interests, and cattle companies and his questionable decisions as an Indian bureau official, made him an ideal target for Senate progressives and Indian reformers.[51] Collier, who led the charge against Hagerman, underscored Hagerman's significance as the "make-or-break component of Rhoads's administration." The Hagerman affair, Collier argued, remained in the spotlight because Wilbur and Rhoads defended Hagerman "with a zeal approaching fanaticism."[52]

With Collier doing most of the initial leg work, the Senate Committee on Indian Affairs compiled documents and evidence that, at the very least, embarrassed the administration and made Hagerman's continuation as special commissioner to the Navajos a real liability. When the Senate committee and Collier's reform associates released information about Hagerman's activities, *Indian Truth* lashed out against the "vicious and unwarranted attack on Herbert J. Hagerman." The magazine accused Senator Lynn J. Frazier, chairman of the Senate committee, of dishonestly using Hagerman in a political attack on the Hoover administration. When the Senate Committee on Indian Affairs published its report in February 1932, it condemned Hagerman's conduct (primarily for his failure to gain fair market value for Pueblo lands when he served on the Pueblo Lands Board) and recommended that he be removed from government service. The House and Senate subsequently removed Hagerman from the government's payroll in midsummer 1932.[53]

Through all of this furor, Secretary of the Interior Wilbur staunchly defended Hagerman. At the time Wilbur thought the Hagerman affair and the Senate committee's activities in the spring of 1932 were part of election-year politics. In his memoirs, however, he recalled that "the attacks on Commissioners Rhoads and Scattergood were so unfair, and at the time so outrageous, that I reached the limit of my patience." Indeed Wilbur was so incensed at Collier's testimony to the Senate committee that he wrote Stella Atwood, a member of the Board of Directors of the AIDA, urging the organization "to get some other leader than Mr. Collier if they want to be of service to the American Indians." Collier, according to Wilbur, had become "a definite handicap to the welfare of the Indians," because he was neither fair nor factual, caused dissension, obstructed legislation, and through his personal attacks pursued "his projected victim with the spirit of the Inquisition."[54]

For his part, Collier thought the Hoover-Wilbur years were tragic because initially the administration "*did* imagine the alternatives; *did* challenge the organic essentials of the inherited system; [and] *did* make detailed and public announcements of an intention to take the lead in changing them." Moreover, he argued that Hoover enjoyed a Senate favorably disposed toward Indian reform and Republicans controlled the House (for two years). However, the administration failed to provide the necessary leadership, Collier claimed, "beyond the initial stage of verbal undertakings." He argued that the Indian office attempted to secure the needed legislation without the assistance of "the Executive or against his passive or active opposition." The president's failure to provide leadership had contributed to an Indian policy that lapsed into "those identical features of the Indian system which the Executive had condemned in 1929." Under the circumstances, with the Congress juxtaposed against an inert and "Executive reactionary," Collier saw little likelihood for change.[55]

The heightened tone of the charges and counterchanges in 1932 indicates the degree to which relations between Hoover and his Indian policy administrators and their critics had deteriorated. The backdrop of political maneuvering in an election year obviously explains part of the furor, but not all. The Hoover administration simply proved itself inept, even in a conventional way, in its handling of Indian policy issues and this exacerbated further its deteriorating relationship with its critics. The Hagerman affair, for instance, should be placed in the context of already strained relations between the president, Congress, and an increasingly critical AIDA. Interior Secretary Wilbur could have dismissed Hagerman, perhaps with some partisan grumbling. Instead, the administration tenaciously defended him against all charges, with the consequence that Hagerman became another of the administration's increasing number of liabilities.

A strong and active sense of direction from the executive branch is usually a prerequisite for conventional reform programs directed at minority groups. This is especially true for colonial and subject people who are relatively powerless and lack the authority and numbers to effectively push ameliorative legislation through Congress. Because such groups generally do not present a threat to the stability of the social system, liberal reformers can usually ignore them. In the instances discussed here, President Hoover never intervened forcefully to push the Indian legislative program through Congress. Moreover, after a series of legislative setbacks in the spring and early summer of 1930 and amidst the mounting criticism of the AIDA, Wilbur became increasingly pessimistic about the prospects of getting any legislation through Congress. The administration's problems with Congress probably date from the spring of 1929, when the president scolded Louis Crampton, chairman of the House Appropriations Committee, for criticizing Wilbur's Indian policy. After Crampton's defeat in the wake of the 1930 congressional election, economic conditions were worsening and a new and more formidable opposition emerged: the Senate progressives. Senators Lynn Frazier, Burton K. Wheeler, and Elmer Thomas supported public power development, the McNary-Haugen farm bills, and public relief programs, and they effectively used their positions on the Senate Committee on Indian Affairs to embarrass Hoover even further.[56]

David Burner and other writers who praise Hoover's Indian policy cite increases in appropriations for Indian programs as one of the administration's most definable accomplishments in the field of Indian affairs. Accordingly, Burner praises the administration for increasing Indian service appropriations from $16 million to $25 million between 1929 and 1932. He fails to mention, however, that of the more than $25 million appropriated in 1932, over $1 million was designated for Alaskan natives (in March 1931, responsibility for the health and education of Alaskan natives was transferred to the Bureau of Indian Affairs). In addition, the Indian service had hired nearly 1,000 new personnel, and salary raises for staff amounted to more than $1 million. There were obvious increments in appropriations for the Indian service; however, Hoover's Indian administrators and some biographers have exaggerated the amount in their effort to enhance the administration's reputation in Indian policy.[57] Moreover, the old liberal argument that increasing appropriations is an indication of doing good for minority people does not fit in this case. From all indications much of the money simply went to inflate the federal bureaucracy.

Even if reform is defined in terms of changing the system to give those at the bottom a better break, the record suggests that the Hoover administration's Indian policy did not work well. Wilbur, Rhoads, and Scattergood were more concerned with visible change at the top— organizational restructuring, shifting school policy, and administrative efficiency—perhaps with the hope that this would ameliorate conditions at the grass-roots level. These changes, which gave the appearance of reform, represented little more than administrative reorganization.

Hugh Scott of the Board of Indian Commissioners said the administrative reforms caused "apprehension," a "demoralization of morale," and a "feeling of distrust of the Bureau." Some of his remarks might represent sympathy for old sinecurists in the field; however, the mere volume of such complaints would indicate otherwise. At the onset of FDR's administration, the respected anthropologist Franz Boas observed that Rhoads and Scattergood made the error of assuming that mere administrative change would better the lot of Indian people.[58]

In addition to the Wilbur-Rhoads propensity for administrative reform, there were real limitations in the ideology and vision of both men. The missionary-assimilationist view of the Indian Rights Association dominated their thinking, and neither man felt comfortable in the presence of Collier and others who advocated engineering approaches to social problems. The ideological strictures of Hoover's Indian administrators limited their field of action to reform measures directed in one way or another to speed assimilation. As criticism of their policies mounted, they became increasingly combative toward social scientists like Collier who were anxious to carry the government's programs much farther (including more interference in the lives of Indian people).[59] When the administration's legislative program for Indian affairs became lodged in a recalcitrant Congress, neither Wilbur nor Rhoads was able to rescue it. To make matters worse, the man at the top was preoccupied with other problems. The record is clear that Indian affairs simply was not in Hoover's repertoire of important interests.

NOTES

1. J. E. Chamberlin, *The Harrowing of Eden: White Attitudes Toward Native Americans* (New York, 1975), p. 93. For a provocative insight into the relationship between colonial governments and indigenous people, see Franz Fanon, *The Wretched of the Earth* (New York, 1968; first published, 1961).

2. For variations on the reform theme, see Kenneth Philp, "Herbert Hoover's New Era: A False Dawn for the American Indian, 1929–1932," *Rocky Mountain Social Science Journal* 9 (April 1972): 53–60; Michael T. Smith, "The Wheeler-Howard Act of 1934: The Indian New Deal," *Journal of the West* 10 (1971): 521–24; Charles J. Weeks, "The Eastern Cherokee and the New Deal," *North Carolina Historical Review* 53 (July 1976): 316–17; B. T. Quinten, "Oklahoma Tribes, the Great Depression and the Indian Bureau," *Mid-America* 49 (January 1967): 29–43; and Randolph C. Downes, "A Crusade for Indian Reform, 1922–1934," *Mississippi Valley Historical Review* 32 (December 1945):

331–45. Articles contemporary to the period include Ray Lyman Wilbur, "The Dawn of a New Era for the American Indian," *The Sunday Star*, May 24, 1931 (copy in Indian Affairs, Ray Lyman Wilbur Papers, Herbert Hoover Presidential Library); John Collier, "The Indian Bureau's Record," *The Nation* 135 (October 5, 1932): 303–5; Editorial, *The Nation* 136 (April 26, 1933): 459; and Oliver La Farge, "The American Indian's Revenge," *Current History* 40 (May 1934): 163–68. The only book-length treatment of Indian reform for the period is Kenneth R. Philp, *John Collier's Crusade for Indian Reform, 1920–1954* (Tucson, 1977). See also Hazel Hertzberg, *The Search for an American Indian Identity: Modern Pan-Indian Movements* (Syracuse, 1971); John Collier, *From Every Zenith: A Memoir and Some Essays on Life and Thought* (Denver, 1963); Arthur M. Schlesinger, Jr., *The Age of Roosevelt*, vol. 2: *The Coming of the New Deal* (Boston, 1958).

3. D'Arcy McNickle, *Native American Tribalism: Indian Survivals and Renewals* (New York, 1973), pp. 85–88; Harold E. Fey and D'Arcy McNickle, *Indians and Other Americans: Two Ways of Life Meet* (New York, 1959), pp. 91–103.

4. David Burner, *Herbert Hoover: A Public Life* (New York, 1979). See especially the chapter, "The Reform Presidency," pp. 212–44.

5. The background to the General Allotment Act is treated in Francis Paul Prucha, *American Indian Policy in Crisis: Christian Reformers and the Indian, 1865–1900* (Norman, Okla., 1976), pp. 227–57; Robert W. Mardock, *The Reformers and the American Indian* (Columbia, Mo., 1971), pp. 192–228; Henry Fritz, *The Movement for Indian Assimilation, 1860–1900* (Philadelphia, 1963), pp. 198–222; Loring Benson Priest, *Uncle Sam's Stepchildren: The Reformation of United States Indian Policy, 1865–1887* (New Brunswick, N.J., 1942), pp. 167–252.

6. For the consequences of the General Allotment Act see Prucha, *American Indian Policy in Crisis*, pp. 257–64; Wilcomb E. Washburn, *The Assault on Indian Tribalism: The General Allotment Law (Dawes Act) of 1887* (Philadelphia, 1975), pp. 28–31; D. S. Otis, *The Dawes Act and the Allotment of Indian Lands* (Norman, Okla., 1973), pp. 124–55.

7. The turmoil of the 1920s is discussed in Downes, "Crusade for Indian Reform," pp. 334–40; and Collier, *From Every Zenith*, pp. 124–55.

8. Downes, "Crusade for Indian Reform," pp. 343–44.

9. *Congressional Record*, 71st Cong., 2d sess., p. 2498.

10. Lewis Meriam, et al., *The Problem of Indian Administration: A Summary of Findings and Recommendations* (Washington, D.C., 1928), pp. 460–88.

11. Stella M. Atwood to Herbert Hoover, September 18, 1928, Pre-Presidential File, 1928–1929, General Correspondence, American Indian Defense Association, Campaign and Transition Papers, Hoover Papers, Hoover Library (hereafter cited as CTHP). Haven Emerson, a Columbia University professor and president of the AIDA, made the original charge according to Atwood's letter.

12. Burner, *Herbert Hoover: A Public Life,* p. 199.

13. Ibid., pp. 224–27. Burner's brief account of Hoover's concern and interest in Indian affairs is exaggerated and poorly documented.

14. P. Narcha to Hoover, July 26, 1928, and George Akerson to Narcha, August 13, 1928, Pre-Presidential File, 1928–1929, General Correspondence, Na–Nas, CTHP.

15. "Our Citizens: Their Crisis," Letter addressed to the presidential candidates by the AIDA, October 6, 1928; Jay B. Nash to Hoover, October 15, 1928; Harry E. Thomas to Alvin Hert, October 18, 1928; and Hoover to AIDA, October 20, 1928—in Pre-Presidential File, 1928–1929, General Correspondence, American Indian Defense Association, CTHP.

16. The administration's unwillingness to press forcefully for measures before Congress exasperated contemporary critics like John Collier. See Collier, "The Indian Bureau's Record," pp. 303–5; and Collier, *From Every Zenith,* p. 152.

17. The early influence of the Indian Rights Association is discussed in Prucha, *American Indian Policy in Crisis,* pp. 138–43. *Indian Truth* was first published in February 1924. See Downes, "Crusade for Indian Reform," p. 337.

18. John Collier, "No Trespassing," *Sunset* 50 (May 1933): 60; Collier, *From Every Zenith,* pp. 134–35; Philp, *John Collier's Crusade for Indian Reform,* pp. 26–54; Philp, "Herbert Hoover's New Era," p. 55.

19. Downes, "Crusade for Indian Reform," p. 344; Philp, "Herbert Hoover's New Era," p. 53; *Indian Truth* 6 (April 1929): 1.

20. Burner, *Herbert Hoover: A Public Life,* p. 224; Downes, "Crusade for Indian Reform," p. 345; Philp, "Herbert Hoover's New Era," p. 53. In his memoirs Ray Lyman Wilbur says Hoover knew Rhoads and Scattergood through their work with the American Red Cross and the YMCA in France at the end of World War I. See Edgar Eugene Robinson and Paul Carroll Edwards, eds., *The Memoirs of Ray Lyman Wilbur* (Stanford, 1960), p. 482n. Elsewhere Wilbur claims Rhoads recommended Scattergood for the position of assistant commissioner. See Wilbur to Hoover, March 16, 1929, Interior—Indian Office, Presidential Papers, Hoover Papers (hereafter cited as PPHP).

21. Wilbur to Hubert Work, December 15, 1924, Box 15, Wilbur Papers, Hoover Library. The Board of Indian Commissioners dates from the administration of Ulysses S. Grant and the inauguration of what was termed as "Grant's Peace Policy." See Prucha, *American Indian Policy in Crisis,* pp. 33–46; and Henry Fritz, "The Making of Grant's Peace Policy," *Chronicles of Oklahoma* 37 (Winter 1959–1960): 411–32. A critical discussion of the termination policy is in Vine Deloria, Jr., *Custer Died for Your Sins: An Indian Manifesto* (New York, 1969), pp. 54–77.

22. Wilbur to Hoover, March 23, 1929, and Hoover to Wilbur, March 25, 1929, Cabinet—Interior—Indian Office, PPHP.

23. Prucha, *American Indian Policy in Crisis,* pp. 47–49.

24. Philp, "Herbert Hoover's New Era," p. 54; Louis Crampton to Hoover,

April 17, 1929, and Hoover to Crampton, April 18, 1929, Interior—Indian Office, PPHP.

25. Ruby A. Black, "A New Deal for the Red Man," *The Nation* 130 (April 2, 1930): 388–90.

26. *Indian Truth* 7 (February 1930): 4. U.S. Dept. of the Interior (USDI), *Annual Report of the Board of Indian Commissioners* (1930), pp. 1–3.

27. Emerson to Wilbur, May 6, 1930, Indian Affairs, Wilbur Papers.

28. Wilbur to Emerson, May 7, 1930, ibid. Copies of the letter were mailed to twelve members of the AIDA's Board of Directors who had signed the May 6 letter to Wilbur.

29. Robinson and Edwards, *Memoirs of Ray Lyman Wilbur*, p. 485.

30. This is only a brief outline of the Flathead controversy as it involved the interior secretary. A subsequent paper will explore in detail the many ramifications of the issue.

31. A summary discussion of the Flathead case is in Philp, *John Collier's Crusade for Indian Reform*, pp. 85–87, 167–69. See also Burner, *Herbert Hoover: A Public Life*, p. 227. It should be noted that the pro-administration monthly publication of the Indian Rights Association, *Indian Truth*, makes no mention of the Flathead controversy. See *Indian Truth* 7 (May and June 1930).

32. Philp, *John Collier's Crusade for Indian Reform*, pp. 167–69.

33. Rhoads to Hoover, August 6, 1930, Indian Office, Wilbur Papers.

34. Joseph W. Latimer, *Let My People Go*, no. 5 (August 1930), copy in Presidential Subject File—Indians, 1929–1930, PPHP. Latimer had served as secretary, confidant, and propagandist for Carlos Montezuma, a leading pan-Indian writer and vitriolic critic of the Bureau of Indian Affairs until his death in 1923. After Montezuma's passing, Latimer continued to spread his message through his newsletter, *The American Indian: Captive or Citizen*. See Laurence M. Hauptman, "Alice Jemison: Seneca Activist, 1901–1964," *The Indian Historian* 12 (Summer 1979): 19.

35. Wilbur to Hoover, November 17, 1930, Interior—Indian Office, PPHP.

36. Wilbur to Hoover, January 13, 1931, and Hoover to Wilbur, January 15, 1931—Interior—Indian Office, PPHP.

37. William E. Leuchtenburg, *Franklin D. Roosevelt and the New Deal, 1932–1940* (New York, 1963), pp. 86, 329; Hauptman, "Alice Jemison," p. 15.

38. Philp, "Herbert Hoover's New Era," p. 54; Burner, *Herbert Hoover: A Public Life*, p. 227.

39. USDI, *Annual Report of the Bureau of Indian Commissioners* (1939), p. 14. Wilbur's entry in his first report shows the breadth of his assimilationist views: "The white man, wanting wholesome food, a comfortable place to live in, [and] opportunities for education and advancement, has a single way of getting them. He works for them. The Indian has often failed to satisfy these same needs because he has not learned the way to competence and happiness through work."

40. USDI, *Annual Report* (1930), pp. 1–2.

41. Philp, "Herbert Hoover's New Era," p. 54; Black, "A New Deal for the Red Man," p. 389; USDI, *Annual Report* (1930), p. 25.

42. Wilbur to Hoover, November 17, 1930, Interior—Indian Office, PPHP.

43. This assumption is based on remarks made by both critics and supporters of the two men. See Collier, *From Every Zenith*, p. 152.

44. Hoover to Wilbur, February 13, 1931, and Wilbur to Hoover, February 13, 1931—Interior, Indian Office, PPHP; Hoover to the Senate, February 18, 1931, Subject File: Indians, PPHP.

45. The emphasis on administrative efficiency and administrative reorganization emerges early in Hoover's career. See Burner, *Herbert Hoover: A Public Life*, pp. 159–89; Ellis Hawley, "Herbert Hoover, the Commerce Secretariat, and the Vision of an 'Associative State,' 1921–1928," *Journal of American History* 61 (June 1974): 116–40.

46. Hoover to Senator David A. Reed, n.d., and Memorandum for the press, March 30, 1931—Interior—Indian Office, PPHP.

47. See the highly amusing chapter on Bureau of Indian Affairs' lethargy in Deloria, *Custer Died for Your Sins*, pp. 125–45.

48. USDI, *Annual Report of the Board of Indian Commissioners* (1931), p. 14.

49. Ibid., p. 17. Indian bureau teachers employed at the elementary level were now required to have three years of education beyond high school (ibid., p. 9).

50. Hugh L. Scott to Samuel A. Eliot, chairman of the Board of Indian Commissioners, October 1, 1931, Interior—Indian Office, PPHP.

51. Philp, "Herbert Hoover's New Era," pp. 56–57. Philp correctly sees the Hagerman affair as the final breaking point between Hoover and his critics on Indian policy.

52. Collier, *From Every Zenith*, pp. 153–54.

53. Philp, "Herbert Hoover's New Era," p. 57; *Indian Truth* 8 (February 1931): 1; Subcommittee of the Senate Committee on Indian Affairs, "Report on the Charges of Misconduct of Mr. Herbert J. Hagerman, Special Commissioner to Negotiate with Indians and a Former Member of the Pueblo Lands Board," February 16, 1932, copy in Interior—Indian Office, PPHP.

54. Robinson and Edwards, *Memoirs of Ray Lyman Wilbur*, pp. 490–91; Wilbur to Stella M. Atwood, March 19, 1932, Indian Affairs, 1932, Wilbur Papers.

55. John Collier, *The Indian Affairs Tragedy Since 1929 and a Suggestion of Political Realism*, pamphlet (April 28, 1932), copy in Indian Affairs, 1932, Wilbur Papers.

56. Hoover to Crampton, April 18, 1929, Interior—Indian Office, PPHP; Philp, "Herbert Hoover's New Era," p. 57.

57. Burner, *Herbert Hoover: A Public Life*, p. 226; USDI, *Annual Report* (1931), p. 85; (1931), p. 26; (1932), p. 21; Charles Rhoads to Senator William H. King, January 18, 1933, Interior—Indian Office, PPHP.

58. Hugh Scott to Samuel A. Eliot, October 1, 1931, Interior—Indian Office,

PPHP. For the many letters of complaint to the Indian office see Interior—Indian Office, PPHP; and Franz Boas to Louis M. Howe, secretary to President Roosevelt, March 18, 1933, Official File, 6c, Department of the Interior, Office of Indian Affairs, Franklin D. Roosevelt Library. Boas, incidentally, did not support John Collier for commissioner of Indian affairs. His choice was Lewis Meriam.

59. This point is illustrated in a letter from George W. Hinman to Wilbur, April 23, 1933, Indian Affairs, 1933, Wilbur Papers. Hinman was secretary to the Service Committee on Indians of the Home Missions Council: "What we shall be able to do in contacts with the Indian Bureau hereafter will depend very much on the character and policy of the new Commissioner. There could have been no finer cooperation than we have had with Commissioners Rhoads and Scattergood. If John Collier should be the appointee of the Roosevelt administration, I would be doubtful about the future."

Index

A

Aid, 112, 117–18. *See also* Relief programs
AIDA, 169–79 *passim*
Alaskan natives, 183
Allotment policy, 168–69, 171, 178
American Construction Council, 137
American Indian Defense Association (AIDA), 169–79 *passim*
American individualism, 36, 39
American Individualism, 36
American Relief Administration (ARA), 27, 34–35, 87
American Relief Committee, 50
Anderson, Clinton P., 97
Antitrust activity, 77
ARA, 27, 34–35, 87
Argentina, 102, 133
Assimilation: of Indians, 171, 172, 187(n39)
Atomic bomb, 14
Australia, 30–31

B

Band of Hope, 57
Barnes, Harry Elmer, 14
Bates, Sanford, 61
Beard, Charles A., 14
Belgium, 33–34; relief programs, 90, 93–94, 95–96

Bewick, Moreing and Company, 59
Birth, 29
Blockade: British, 90, 91–92, 93
Blodgett, John W., Jr., 14
Board of Indian Commissioners, 172–80 *passim*, 184, 189(n59)
Boulder Canyon dam, 152–53
Boy's Club, 38
Bureaucracy, *see* Government
Bureau of Education, 172
Bureau of Indian Affairs, 61, 179–80, 181
Burke, Charles H., 168–69, 171, 172
Business role, 59–60, 74. *See also* Engineering career

C

California, 30, 144, 148, 152–53
Campaigns, 5; presidential, 147–58 *passim*
Canada, 98
Capitalism, 16
Career, 7–8
Challenge of Liberty, The, 37
Childhood, 29, 57
China, 31, 112
Churchill, Winston, 90, 91, 92, 96, 131
Civil liberties, 61–62
Cold War, 14

Collier, John, 169, 177–78, 181, 182, 186(n16)
Combined Food Board, 97–98
Commerce secretary, *see* Secretary of commerce
Commission for Polish Relief, 89
Commission for Relief in Belgium (CRB), 33–34, 50, 87, 90
Commission on the Conservation and Administration of the Public Domain, 48
Communism, 113–22 *passim*
Conservation, 45, 46, 47, 52, 97; human resources, 49–50; natural resources, 48–49, 50–51; secretary of commerce, 47–48, 78
Coolidge, Calvin, 10, 28, 151
Crampton, Louis, 173, 174, 183
CRB, 33–34, 50, 87, 90

D

Davis, Chester, 97
Davis, Norman, 89
Dawes, Charles M., 114, 152, 153
Dawes Act, 168–169, 171, 178
Defense, 116, 121; importance of, 117–19, 120
Deficiency Bill, 174
Dennis, Lawrence, 14
Department of the Interior, 174, 175
Dewey, Thomas, 17
Domestic policy, 16–17; World War II, 15–16
Dulles, John Foster, 119, 135

E

Economy, 76–77, 116
Eisenhower, Dwight D., 12
Emergency banking legislation, 129
Engineering career, 30–32, 47, 57–58, 59, 74–75
England, *see* Great Britain

F

Fall, Albert B., 168
Family Life, 29
Famine: psychological effects, 87–88, 103; relief programs, 98–102, 115
Famine Emergency Committee, 97
Famine Survey Mission, 99–102
Federal Oil Conservation Board, 48
Federal Power Commission, 175
Federal prison system, 61
Finland, 88, 89–90
Finnish Relief Fund, 89
Fisheries conservation, 48–49
FitzGerald, Dennis, 98, 100
Flathead reservation, 175–76
Flood control, 48
Flood relief, 10, 78–79
Flynn, John T., 14
Food, 100, 101; conservation of, 50–51; postwar situation, 97–98; production, 50, 101; relief programs, 87–97 *passim*, 115
Food Administration, 34
Food Administrator, 148
Food Appropriation Act (1919), 147
Foreign policy, 8, 12, 143; European defense, 115–116; Hoover's views, 12–17 *passim*, 112–13; post–World War II, 115–16, 117–19, 120; World War II, 111, 113–14
Frazier, Lynn, 183
Friend's Pacific Academy, 29
Fumimarō, Konoe, 111

G

Galpin, Perrin, 88, 99
General Allotment Act (1887), 168–69, 171, 178
George Fox College, 29
Germany, 115, 134–35; World War II, 90–94 *passim*, 131
Gibson, Hugh, 91, 98–102 *passim*, 115

Government, 129; reorganization, 75, 76–77, 84(n26), 115–16, 128
Grand Coulee Dam, 48
Grazing lands, 48
Great Britain, 32, 112; postwar relief, 97–98; World War II, 90, 91–92, 94–95, 131
Great Depression, 4, 11, 156–57
Great Engineer, 7, 9
Great Humanitarian, 9–10

H

Hagerman, Herbert, 180–81, 182
Halifax, Lord, 94
Hamilton, Alice, 17–18
Harding, Warren G., 28, 143, 149–50, 151
Hartigan, John, 91
Hoover, Hulda, 29, 57
Hoover, Jesse, 29
Hoover, John Y., 57
Hoover, Lou Henry, 5, 31, 87, 156
Hoover, Theodore, 5, 29
Hoover Commission, 115
Hoover Dam, 48
Hoover War Library, 112
Hull, Cordell, 94, 95
Humanitarianism, 10, 12, 34–35, 60, 130; reforms, 61–62
Human resources, 46, 47; conservation, 49–50; Quaker influences, 61–62
Hutchins, Robert, 114

I

Ickes, Harold, 169
Idaho, 48
Ideology, *see* Philosophy
Inauguration, 155
Indian bureau, 61, 179–80, 181
Indian policy, 169–70, 175; administration approach, 172–73, 176–77; funding, 173–74; Hoover's interest, 169–70, 171; reform, 167–68, 171–72, 177–78, 180–81, 182–84, 188(n49)
Indian Rights Association, 168, 174, 184; assimilation, 171, 172, 187(n39)
Inheritance taxes, 38
Interventionism, 113–14
Iowa, 29, 57
Isolationism, 13
Italy, 115

J

Janin, Louis, 30
Japan, 111
Johnson, Hiram, 143–44, 145; campaigning, 148–49; elections, 150–52, 153–54; on Harding, 149–50; Hoover presidency, 155–57; relief, 146–47; Roosevelt candidacy, 158–60
Johnson Act, 145
Jones, Jesse, 14

K

King, Judson, 176
Knowland, William, 17
Korean War, 14, 116, 117

L

Landon, Alfred, 114, 160
Leadership, 5
League of Nations, 111, 143
Lehman, Herbert, 97
Lend-Lease, 112, 133, 134
Lever Act, 146, 147
Lewis, John L., 114
Lindbergh, Charles A., 14
Lippman, Walter, 14
Little Hoover commissions, 12
Lothian, Lord, 93, 104(n20)
Luxembourg, 90

M

McNary-Haugen farm bills, 183
Marriage, 31
Mason, Frank, 99
Mass media, 4, 10–11
Mellon, Andrew, 152
Meriam Report, 169–70
Meritt, Edgar, 168, 169, 172
Michelson, Charles, 4
Mining, *see* Engineering career
Minthorn, Henry John, 29, 57
Mississippi valley, 10
Moore, C. C., 150
Morley, Felix, 114

N

National Committee on Food for the Small Democracies, 93, 95
National Food Administration, 148
NATO, 115–16, 120, 121
Natural resources, 46, 47, 48–49
Neo-institutional history, 69–70, 71–72
Netherlands, the, 90
Newberg (Oregon), 29
New Deal, 12–16 *passim*, 73, 22(n22)
North Atlantic Treaty Organization (NATO), 115–16, 120, 121
Norway, 90
Nye, Gerald P., 14

O

Oil, 48, 49
Oil Pollution Act (1924), 49
Old Guard, 144
Old Right, 12, 15, 22(n22)
Oregon, 29–30
Oregon Land Company, 29–30

P

Pacifism, 56–57, 58

Panama-Pacific International Exposition of 1915, 145–46
Pate, Maurice, 88, 99
Pepper, Claude, 14
Perón, Juan, 102
Pew, Joseph, 14
Philosophy, 28–29, 36, 40, 80–81; equality of opportunity, 36–37; political, 7, 14–15, 16–17; Quakerism, 55–56, 58, 61; social system, 38–39
Poland, 88, 89, 90
Pollution, 49
Popularity, 10–11
Presidency, 35–38, 79, 128; candidacies, 147–58 *passim*; Johnson's views, 155–57; Quaker influence, 61–62; rating, 8–9
Private sector, 75
Progressivism, 8, 9, 10, 15
Public career, 73–74, 128–29; interpreting, 68–69; neo-institutional views, 70–71; postpresidential, 109–10; post-World War II, 109–10; wartime organization, 74–75; World War II, 112–14. *See also* Presidency; Public image
Public Health Service, 172
Public image, 3–12 *passim*, 18(n2)
Public relations, 5, 6

Q

Quakerism, 19(n9), 60, 173; influence of, 55–56, 61; politics, 56–57, 58–59

R

Red Cross, 88, 89
Red Scare, 62
Reform: government, 76–77, 84(n26), 115–16, 128; Indian policy, 167–68, 171, 182, 183–84
Relief programs, 20(n14), 27, 60, 62, 183; famine, 98–102, 115; post-

war, 97–102, 115; World War I, 33, 49–50, 51, 87, 146–47; World War II, 88–97, 131
Remedy for Disappearing Game Fishes, 49
Republican Party, 135, 144; Hoover candidacy, 147–48; 1920 election, 148–50; Old Right, 12, 15
Rhoads, Charles J., 172–79 *passim*, 184, 186(n20)
Rickard, Edgar, 88
Rocky Mountain Power Company, 175
Roosevelt, Franklin D., 12, 13, 133–34, 136–37, 138–39; candidacy, 158–60; World War II, 89, 91, 96
Roosevelt administration, 109–10
Russia, 51. *See also* Soviet Union

S

Sawtelle, Raymond, 88
Scattergood, J. Henry, 172, 174, 178, 186(n20)
Scott, Hugh, 180, 184
Secretary of commerce, 60, 143–44, 150, 152; conservation, 47–48; economy, 76–77
Segregation, 62
Senate Committee on Indian Affairs, 180, 181
Smith, Al, 170
Social doctrine, 60, 73–74. *See also* Humanitarianism; Philosophy
Society: neo-institutional views, 70–72; reorganization, 72–73, 75–76
Soviet Union, 113, 115, 116, 122, 134
Stalin, 134, 135
Stanford University, 7, 8, 30
Stimson, Henry, 14
Stone, I. F., 14
Swing, Phillip, 152
Swing-Johnson Bill, 152–53

T

Taft, Robert A., 14, 113, 119, 120
Tansill, Charles C., 14
Tatum, Lawrie, 57
Taylor, Glen H., 14
Technocracy, 73
Tennessee Valley, 77
Thomas, Elmer, 183
Totalitarianism, 113, 115
Trade, 78
Treaty of Versailles, 35, 111
Trueblood, Daisy, 5–6
Truman, Harry S., 12, 14, 96–97, 115–16, 119, 131–32, 136
Truman administration, 13–14, 61
Tuck, William Hallam, 88, 99
Turner, Frederick Jackson, 37

U

United Nations, 116
United Nations Relief and Rehabilitation Administration (UNRRA), 97
Ute Indians, 178–79

V

Veblen, Thorstein, 61
Villard, Oswald Garrison, 14

W

Wallace, Henry A., 14, 97
War, 15, 112, 113–14, 115
Warburg, James Paul, 14
War corporatism, 75–76
Warren, Earl, 17
Water projects, 48, 152–53
Welfare, 78
Welles, Sumner, 94
Wheeler, Burton K., 183
White House Conference on Child Health and Protection, 87
Wilbur, Ray Lyman, 48, 171–72, 174, 175, 181–84 *passim*, 187(n39)

Williams, William Appleman, 8
Wilson, Woodrow, 10
Work, Hubert, 152, 169, 170
World War I, 33–34, 87, 146. *See also* Relief programs
World War II, 14, 111, 112, 133–35; domestic impact, 15–16; relief efforts, 88–97; U.S. involvement, 112–15

Y

Yōsuke, Matsuoka, 111